THE BUSINESS OF EDUCATION

The Business of Education—a comprehensive view of how education policy is made in the US and, in some cases, globally—analyzes and critiques the influence of educational policy networks in a wide range of contexts and from a variety of perspectives, including testing, college preparation, juvenile detention centers, special education, the arts, teacher evaluation systems, education of undocumented immigrants, college faculty preparation, and financial aid. A network chart in most chapters illustrates how the major political actors, mainly private philanthropic foundations, for-profit companies, government officials, and politicians involved in the network, are linked. Joel Spring, internationally renowned scholar and analyst of educational policy, situates and frames the network studies in an introduction discussing general theories of education policy networks.

Joel Spring is Professor at Queens College/City University of New York and the Graduate Center of the City University of New York, USA.

John Eric Frankson is Assistant Program Officer in the Office of Educational Opportunity and Diversity at the Graduate Center of the City University of New York, USA.

Corie A. McCallum is Student Life Specialist/Student Conduct Advisor at New York City College of Technology/City University of New York, USA.

Diane Price Banks is an Instructor in the Biological Sciences Department at Bronx Community College/City University of New York, USA.

Sociocultural, Political, and Historical Studies in Education
Joel Spring, Editor

Reagan • *Non-Western Educational Traditions: Local Approaches to Educational Thought and Practice, 4th Edition*
Spring/Frankson/McCallum/Banks, Eds. • *The Business of Education: Networks of Power and Wealth in America*
Bowers • *A Critical Examination of STEM: Issues and Challenges*
Spring • *Deculturalization and the Struggle for Equality: A Brief History of the Education of Dominated Cultures in the United States, 8th Edition*
Spring • *American Education, 17th Edition*
Spring • *Economization of Education: Schools, Corporations, World Markets*
Martusewicz/Edmundson/Lupinacci • *EcoJustice Education: Toward Diverse, Democratic, and Sustainable Communities, 2nd Edition*
Spring • *Globalization and Education, 2nd Edition*
Portes/Salas/Baquedano-López/Mellom, Eds. • *U.S. Latinos and Education Policy: Research-based Directions for Change*
Wolfmeyer • *Math Education for America?: Policy Networks, Educational Business, and Pedagogy Wars*
Spring • *Political Agendas for Education: From Race to the Top to Saving the Planet, 5th Edition*
Picciano/Spring • *The Great American Education-Industrial Complex: Ideology, Technology, and Profit*
Spring • *Education Networks: Power, Wealth, Cyberspace and the Digital Mind*
Hemmings • *Urban High Schools: Foundations and Possibilities*
Spring • *The Politics of American Education*
Smith/Sobel • *Place- and Community-based Education in Schools*
Sandlin/McLaren, Eds. • *Critical Pedagogies of Consumption: Living and Learning in the Shadow of the "Shopocalypse"*
Shapiro, Ed. • *Education and Hope in Troubled Times: Visions of Change for Our Children's World*

For additional information on titles in the Sociocultural, Political, and Historical Studies in Education series visit **www.routledge.com/education**

THE BUSINESS OF EDUCATION

Networks of Power and Wealth in America

Edited by Joel Spring, John Eric Frankson, Corie A. McCallum, and Diane Price Banks

NEW YORK AND LONDON

First published 2018
by Routledge
711 Third Avenue, New York, NY 10017

and by Routledge
2 Park Square, Milton Park, Abingdon, Oxon, OX14 4RN

Routledge is an imprint of the Taylor & Francis Group, an informa business

© 2018 Taylor & Francis

The right of Joel Spring, John Eric Frankson, Corie A. McCallum, and Diane Price Banks to be identified as the authors of the editorial material, and of the authors for their individual chapters, has been asserted in accordance with sections 77 and 78 of the Copyright, Designs and Patents Act 1988.

All rights reserved. No part of this book may be reprinted or reproduced or utilised in any form or by any electronic, mechanical, or other means, now known or hereafter invented, including photocopying and recording, or in any information storage or retrieval system, without permission in writing from the publishers.

Trademark notice: Product or corporate names may be trademarks or registered trademarks, and are used only for identification and explanation without intent to infringe.

Library of Congress Cataloging-in-Publication Data
Names: Spring, Joel H., editor.
Title: The business of education : networks of power and wealth in America / edited by Joel Spring, John Eric Frankson, Corie A. McCallum, Diane Price Banks.
Description: New York : Routledge, 2017. | Series: Sociocultural, political, and historical studies in education | Includes bibliographical references and index.
Identifiers: LCCN 2016059087 | ISBN 9781138206267 (hardback) | ISBN 9781138206274 (pbk) | ISBN 9781315465418 (ebk)
Subjects: LCSH: Education and state--United States. | Education--Political aspects--United States.
Classification: LCC LC89 .B876 2017 | DDC 379.0973--dc23
LC record available at https://lccn.loc.gov/2016059087

ISBN: 978-1-138-20626-7 (hbk)
ISBN: 978-1-138-20627-4 (pbk)
ISBN: 978-1-315-46541-8 (ebk)

Typeset in Bembo
by Saxon Graphics Ltd, Derby

We dedicate this book to all those who walk the halls of academia fighting the good fight and never resting on their laurels. Honoring the authentic voices of each of our chapter contributors, we hope that this work will illuminate and inspire, question, and invite critical thought on the controversial issues plaguing education today.

CONTENTS

Preface   ix

1 The New Politics of American Education   1
  Joel Spring

2 Admitting Privilege   16
  John Eric Frankson

3 AVID about College: A Look into AVID's Governing Structure   32
  Robert P. Robinson

4 A Not So Individualized Education Plan: Examining NYC DOE Contract with Maximus that Brought Us SESIS   45
  Amy Goods

5 Turning Against (Public) Arts Education: An Arts Perspective of the Business of Education   58
  Robert Randazzo

6 Policy Networks and Political Decisions Influencing the Dream Act: The Power of the Dreamers   69
  Aminata Diop

7 The Call for Faculty Preparation   83
   Diane Price Banks

8 Exploring Federal Financial Aid Networks: Who Cares
   and Why?   105
   Corie A. McCallum

9 A Political Economy of Incarceration:
   Race, Schooling, and the Criminal Justice System   118
   Sakina Laksimi-Morrow

10 A Shared Path to Success: The Promise and Challenge
   of Special Education in New York City   137
   Melanie Waller

List of Contributors   *155*
Index   *157*

PREFACE

This book is distinctive in illustrating and analyzing how education policy is made and how it works in a variety of contexts and from a range of perspectives. Each chapter focuses on a different network. At the end of most chapters a chart illustrates how the major political actors, mainly private philanthropic foundations, for-profit companies, government officials, and politicians involved in the network are linked.

In Chapter 1, Joel Spring discusses general theories of education policy networks. In Chapter 2, John Eric Frankson uses the Graduate Record Examination to exemplify the networks of power and influence inherent in the highly monopolistic ecosystem of high-stakes testing. Robert Robinson, in Chapter 3, uses the AVID (Advancement Via Individual Determination) program to highlight network relations. Currently, AVID is operating in 5,000 schools, impacting more than 800,000 students in 44 states and 16 countries. Amy Goods, in Chapter 4, studies the outsourcing of some special education functions to Maximus, a for-profit company whose slogan is "Helping Government Serve the People." In Chapter 5, Robert Randazzo explores the funding and purposes of art education with a focus on the American culture capital New York City. In Chapter 6, Aminata Diop explores the policy networks and political decisions influencing the Dream Act Bill for undocumented immigrant students. Similarly there is the problem of faculty preparation to teach immigrant and low-income college students. Diane Price Banks explores this issue in Chapter 7 against the background of policy networks. Banks proposes a model for preparing college faculty for instructing low-income students. There is also the issue of financial support for low-income college students. As Corie McCallum describes in Chapter 8, there is a crisis in federal student funding and McCallum wants to know why. In Chapter 9,

Sakina Laksimi-Morrow discusses the policy networks and for-profit prison industry influencing the school to prison pipeline. Chapter 10 by Melanie Waller examines the financial influences on special education policies in New York City. Together the chapters provide a comprehensive view of a range of diverse educational policy networks.

1
THE NEW POLITICS OF AMERICAN EDUCATION

Joel Spring

The chapters in this book illuminate the complex web of venture philanthropists, politicians, and for-profit businesses influencing today's educational politics. It is difficult to place a value judgement on this educational power structure because of differences in values and goals of the various actors. One thing that can be said is that the new politics of education has decreased public control of schools and that it tends to favor the power of wealth and for-profit education companies. On the other hand, many act not for personal profit, but because of an altruistic desire to improve schools. However, these altruistic efforts may result in ideological conflict. Some people might, as I will discuss later, believe that choice, market forces, and charter schools are key to school improvement, while others think government intervention and control are necessary to ensure equality of educational opportunity.

This complex web of economic and political relationships influences the knowledge schools disseminate and how public education will be funded. What is taught in schools is not neutral. There are continuous struggles about teaching economic and political ideas. There are concerns about how ethnic groups and religions will be presented in the curricula and books. Some see schools as a source of profit. Book publishers, computer and software companies, tutoring and testing organizations, and makers of classroom apparatuses compete for public school funds. The result is an educational system that is constantly changing and creating problems of policy implementation, where the general public is often clueless about what's happening in schools.[1]

To exemplify the new politics of education and the web of relationships, I will discuss the educational career of James H. Shelton. Then I will examine the evolution of political control from nineteenth-century school boards to the present complex set of influences by venture philanthropists, for-profit companies, education networks, and federal, state, and local politicians. This will be followed by a short theoretical discussion of the new shadow elite and the new nation state.

James Shelton: A Case Study of the New Shadow Elite

Janine R. Wedel would consider James Shelton's career as exemplifying the shadow elite currently determining government policies.[2] Wedel would call Shelton a flexian, who makes career moves between government, for-profit companies, universities and philanthropic organizations.[3] For example, it was announced in the May 11, 2016, *Education Week* that Shelton would step down as president and chief impact officer for the for-profit 2U technology firm to head the education efforts of a new educational philanthropic organization created by Facebook founder Mark Zuckerberg. Prior to the presidency of 2U, Sheldon was U.S. deputy secretary of education. He was recruited to this position from being a program director at the Bill & Melinda Gates Foundation and partner at the NewSchools Venture Fund.[4] The NewSchools Venture Fund describes itself: "As a nonprofit venture philanthropy firm, we use the charitable donations we receive to support education entrepreneurs who are transforming public education to create great results for all students."[5]

Prior to the NewSchools Venture Fund, the Gates Foundation, and the U.S. Department of Education, as described on the U.S. Department of Education's website:

> Shelton … co-founded LearnNow, a school management company that later was acquired by Edison Schools. He spent over four years as a senior management consultant with McKinsey & Company in Atlanta, Ga., where he advised CEOs and other executives on issues related to corporate strategy, business development, organizational design, and operational effectiveness. Upon leaving McKinsey, he joined Knowledge Universe, Inc., where he launched, acquired and operated education-related businesses.[6]

Shelton's career illustrates policy networks linking private philanthropy, government, and for-profit businesses. Others have also emphasized these policy networks.[7]

This new form of governance involving shadow elites is discussed in a global context by British sociologist Stephen Ball. He calls it "Global Education Inc." and links global philanthropy and for-profit companies to the development of education policies within different nation-states. His network models span the globe. He writes, "So, I contend that policy networks do constitute a new form of governance, albeit not in a single and coherent form, and bring into play in the policy process new sources of authority and indeed a 'market of authorities'."[8] Ball's concern is with groups advocating free markets and the reduction of national governments' role in education and the support and spread of these ideas by global philanthropies and educational businesses. Others have also noted the work of these new global policy networks and their effects on schooling.[9]

Can U.S. Education Be Democratic: From School Boards to the Corporate State

The policy networks described above raise issues about democratic control of U.S. schools. What does democratic control of schools mean? Does it include democratic control of the content of the public school curriculum and selection of teachers—the two most important aspects of schooling? Of course, the overarching question is whether or not public schools should be democratically controlled, or should they be controlled by educational experts or the policy networks described in this volume.

Elected representative governance was the earliest form of U.S. public school control. Locally elected school boards selected curricula, teachers, and administrators, and allocated local property tax for buildings, maintenance, and salaries. There were complaints about local wealth and power dominating school board elections and political favoritism in hiring teachers and administrators. In the early twentieth century, several studies focused on the wealth of school board members.[10]

In the late nineteenth and early twentieth century, increasing involvement of state governments and the growth of bureaucratic school administration eroded the power of school boards. State governments played a greater role in credentialing teachers and school administrators and defining general goals for schools.[11] These changes reduced democratic control of what is taught in schools and increased the controlling role of the business community.[12]

The federal role expanded in the middle of the twentieth century as national legislation was passed to use the schools in the military race with the Soviet Union. The federal government exerted power primarily by offering money to local and state governments to carry out federal policies. These efforts led to the federal government influencing local curricula, particularly in science and math. During the same period, the civil rights movement demanded schools be desegregated and that schools help in ending poverty. The resulting legislation, the 1958 Educational Defense Act, 1964 Civil Rights Act, and the 1965 Elementary and Secondary Education, put local schools in service to national politicians and policy objectives.[13]

The argument in the 1960s that education could end poverty came from economists, who also promoted free markets and competition for schools.[14] Key to this effort was passage of the 1965 Elementary and Secondary Education Act.[15] During the same period, economists argued for increasing family control over education by giving families the power to choose schools for their children. The first choice plan was made by Milton Friedman, who portrayed public schools as monopolies that could be improved by competition between public, private, and for-profit schools.[16] As a result, since the 1960s there have been ongoing debates about school vouchers, tax credits, and creating and expanding charter school networks. Some suggested schools would function better if they were operated for profit.

In addition to increased federal involvement, in the 1970s there was rapid growth of venture philanthropy designed to influence school policy. James Smith, in his 1991 book *The Idea Brokers*, wrote, "In the early 1970s, executives in a handful of traditionally conservative foundations redefined their programs with the aim of shaping the public policy agenda and constructing a network of conservative institutions and scholars."[17] A leader and articulate spokesperson for the movement was William Simon, who left his job in 1976 as Secretary of the Treasury in the Nixon and Ford administrations to become head of the John Olin Foundation. The goal, in Simon's words was, "to support those individuals and institutions who are working to strengthen the free enterprise system."[18]

Reflecting Simon's economic beliefs, the preface and foreword for his book *A Time for Truth* were written, respectively, by Milton Friedman and free market advocate F. A. Hayek. In the preface, Friedman sounded the warning that intellectual life in the United States was under the control of "socialists and interventionists, who have wrongfully appropriated in this country the noble label 'liberal' and who have been the intellectual architects of our suicidal course."[19] Applying marketplace concepts to intellectual life, Friedman argued that the payoff for these "liberals" was support by an entrenched government bureaucracy. In his mind, the liberal elite and the government bureaucracy fed off each other. Using a phrase that would be repeated by conservatives throughout the rest of the twentieth and into the twenty-first centuries, Friedman contended that "the view that government is the problem, not the cure," is hard for the public to understand.[20] According to Friedman's plea, saving the country required a group of intellectuals to promote a general understanding of the importance of the free market.

To counter the supposed rule of a liberal intelligentsia, Simon urged the business community to support intellectuals who advocated the importance of the free market. Simon called on businesspeople to stop supporting colleges and universities that produced "young collectivists by the thousands" and media "which serve as megaphones for anticapitalist opinion." In both cases, Simon insisted, business people should focus their support on university programs and media that stress procapitalist ideas.[21] He insisted, "Foundations imbued with the philosophy of freedom ... must take pains to funnel desperately needed funds to scholars, social scientists, writers, and journalists who understand the relationship between political and economic liberty."[22]

In light of Simon's leadership of the John Olin Foundation in the 1970s, it is interesting that two of the leading writers for the conservative cause in education, Chester Finn, Jr. and Dinesh D'Souza, are, respectively, John Olin Fellow at the Manhattan Institute and the American Enterprise Institute. Besides supporting scholars at the conservative Manhattan Institute and the American Enterprise Institute, the John Olin Foundation backed many right-wing causes and, according to one writer, "its pattern of giving became [in the 1970s] more sophisticated and more closely attuned to the potential of grantees for influencing debates on national politics."[23]

Although conservatives talk about the invisible hand of the free market, the trickle-down distribution of ideas has been very well planned using the following methods:

1. Creating foundations and institutes that fund research and policy statements supportive of school choice, privatization of public schools and, more recently, charter schools.
2. Identifying scholars to conduct research, write policy statements, and lecture at public forums that are favorable to school choice, privatization of public schools, and charter schools.
3. Financing conferences to bring like-minded scholars together to share ideas and publish reports, articles, and books.
4. Paying scholars to write newspaper opinion pieces that are then distributed to hundreds of newspapers across the country.

This fourth point is an important element in the trickle-down theory of ideas. It is a big leap from writing a research report to being featured on the opinion-editorial page of the *New York Times* or other leading newspapers. It requires connections and a public relations staff to gain quick access to media. Providing media access is an important strategy for spreading the conservative agenda. With public relations help from libertarians, I appeared in the 1970s as an "academic expert" on radio and television shows across the country. On one occasion, after the physical exercise portion of an early morning television show, I fielded call-in questions ranging from "Why can't my daughter read?" to "Why are all college professors socialists?" There was never any hint that my appearance on the program resulted from the work of conservative organizations.

In *The Transformation of American Politics: The New Washington and the Rise of Think Tanks*, David Ricci described attempts to mobilize and control public opinion. "Those who talked about developing conservative ideas," Ricci stated, "were committed not just to producing them but to the commercial concept of a product, in the sense of something that, once created, must be placed before the public as effectively as possible."[24]

Examples of foundations and think tanks influencing education policy, include the work of the Broad Foundation, the Heritage Foundation, the Fordham Institute, the Bill & Melinda Gates Foundation, and many others. These became important actors in shaping educational policy. For instance, during the Obama administration there was movement of personnel between the Bill & Melinda Gates Foundation, the U.S. Department of Education, and universities.[25]

By the end of the twentieth century, technology companies targeted schools as consumer markets for computers, tablets, data systems, and learning software. This expanded the number of private businesses seeking profits from public school coffers. These companies, particularly technology companies, want to influence public school budgets to ensure that money is spent on their products. I satirized this competition in my novel, *Common Core: A Story of School Terrorism*.[26]

The politics and economics of information and communication technologies (ICT) exemplify the continued growth of corporatism in education. ICT politics, as I use the concept, refers to power struggles to sell hardware and software to schools and promote online instruction. These are all interrelated particularly when new curricula are rolled out and there is increased pressure for educational institutions to collect an analysis of data. There are many reasons for the expansion of ICT in schools, including the desire by education companies, comprising publishers, software producers, and other producers of learning materials, to sell their products.[27]

Another boom for for-profit companies came in 2009, when the federal government promoted state adoption of the *Common Core State Standards*. These standards were adopted so rapidly that school systems often had to rely on purchased curricula, lessons, software, and tablets to translate the standards into classroom practice. The for-profit education sector had already expanded with the 2001 passage of the *No Child Left Behind Act (NCLB)*, which emphasized testing and required failing schools in their fourth year to provide tutorial services.[28]

No Child Left Behind (NCLB), *Race to the Top*, and *Every Student Succeeds Act (ESSA)* support expansion of charter schools.[29] Operating independently of local school districts and by private boards, they contribute to reduction of democratic control of publically financed schools. They have also developed charter school management organizations, such as Kipp and Success. This has created a new set of actors interested in state and federal legislation that supports charter schools.

Shadow Elite and Swiss Cheese Government

In summary, from the simple days of school districts managing their own affairs evolved a complex political system with many actors trying to influence state and federal education legislation. The previously mentioned work by Janine Wedel provides one framework for understanding this new political system.[30] I will use her conceptual framework to analyze the networks between governments and the education industry. She uses the term "performance state" to describe modern states that act like businesses and depend on data to analyze their successes.

Wedel argues that one global trend is for governments to outsource traditional government functions to private firms. She calls the bureaucracies of these governments "Swiss-cheese" to symbolize the holes left in government as services are turned over to private companies. In some cases, governments hire for-profit companies to implement new programs. Thus there are two categories of "Swiss-cheese" governments. The first involves governments turning over services, which they provided in the past, to for-profit industries. The second involves governments implementing new legislation by hiring outside agencies.

The holes in Swiss-cheese government bureaucracies cause a reduction in government staffs, making it difficult to regulate government services. Wedel writes:

Because the number of government contracts and contractors has risen, while the number of civil servants available to supervise them has proportionately fallen, thus decreasing the government's capacity to oversee the process, even when government officials sign on the dotted line, they are sometimes merely rubber stamping the work of contractors.[31]

The concept of a Swiss-cheese bureaucracy relates directly to education with more and more school services being privatized. *No Child Left Behind* specifically provides for the hiring of for-profit companies. For instance, the section of the legislation dealing with failing schools provides for technical assistance which "shall include assistance in analyzing data ... [which] may be provided ... by ... a private not-for-profit organization or *for-profit organization*, an educational service agency, or another entity with experience in helping schools improve academic achievement" [author's emphasis].[32] For schools requiring improvement, the legislation specifies hiring outside instructional help for students including for-profit services:

> a *for-profit entity*, or a local educational agency that—(i) has a demonstrated record of effectiveness in increasing student academic achievement; (ii) is capable of providing supplemental educational services ... the term "supplemental educational services" means tutoring and other supplemental academic enrichment services that are—(i) in addition to instruction provided during the school day; and (ii) are of high quality, research-based, and specifically designed to increase the academic achievement of eligible children [author's emphasis].[33]

In summary, NCLB opens the door for schools to hire at government expense for-profit companies to analyze data and test scores and provide tutoring and enrichment programs.

Accountability: The Decline of Public Control of Schools

As I suggested earlier, it would be hard to defend an argument that American education is democratically controlled. In fact, some argued that public schools should not be democratically controlled, but that education experts should be in charge. This was a central tenet of the accountability movement, which advocated that experts report school conditions to the public and in turn the public could complain. In some ways, the accountability movement can be seen as a reaction to the demands during the 1970s for community control of the schools by civil rights organizations that complained about racist teachers, curriculum, and administrators. The goal was to turn decision making about hiring and the curriculum over to community representatives.[34] It could be argued that this was the dying gasp of efforts to democratize school control.

The reaction to community control was a call for an accountability movement based on expert control. This argument was made by Leon Lessinger, future U.S. Associate Commissioner for Elementary and Secondary Education, in his 1970 book, *Every Kid A Winner: Accountability in Education*.[35] Lessinger uses a hospital example to criticize the concept of democratic control. He argues that in a hospital, patients and the general community do not, and should not, participate directly in decisions regarding medical treatment or surgery because these areas of decision making require expert knowledge and training. For Lessinger, the idea of democratic control in surgery is ludicrous and dangerous to the patient. In his opinion, users of medical services have the right to complain, but decisions about their complaints should remain in the hands of medical experts.

Lessinger felt the hospital example was applicable to education. Modern schooling, he maintained, is based on professional knowledge gained through research and study. Most community members do not have the training necessary to make correct educational decisions. Like the hospital clientele, the community has the right to complain, but does not have the right or the knowledge to make decisions regarding the resolution of complaints. Only the educational expert should be entrusted with decision-making power.

While giving power to education experts, Lessinger recognized that in a democratic society the schools should be responsive to the public. He felt this responsiveness could be achieved by schools reporting their accomplishments and failures to the public. This public accounting of the results of schooling was the heart of the accountability movement. Lessinger envisioned the creation of a national educational accounting firm operated by educational engineers who would measure educational results by the use of achievement tests and report the results to the public. He assumed that these results would provide the public with expert data that could be used to express approval or criticism of the accomplishments of the school system.

As the accountability movement spread in the early 1970s, states and local communities began to require schools to annually publish standardized test scores. The use of test scores to measure the schools' success kept power in the hands of educational experts. In the schools, students found themselves taking an increasing number of achievement tests in order to satisfy the requirements of accountability. One result was that testing, or measurement, became central to school operations.[36]

Accountability ideas permeated twenty-first-century federal legislation and were included in the *No Child Left Behind*, *Race to the Top*, and *Every Student Succeeds* acts.[37] Accountability through testing reported the school performance to the public and was used for state evaluation of individual schools. Combined with charter schools, the accountability and testing movement precluded any ideas about democratic control of public schools. It also opened the door for the growth of for-profit test makers and their efforts to maintain a steady flow income from the public school coffers.

Will Free Markets Democratize Schools?

A major complaint about turning schools over to experts is that it has continued school segregation and racist practices. As mentioned in the previous section, community control of schools was proposed as one answer to this problem. In line with previously free market ideas of economist Milton Friedman, John E. Chubb and Terry Moe in *Politics, Markets & America's Schools* propose a similar solution for educational bureaucracy and school racism.[38] In addition, they believe there is a link between political control and student achievement.

Chubb and Moe argued that control by an educational bureaucracy and experts promotes segregative practices in schools and denies certain groups equality of educational opportunity. Their central argument is that racist practices could be reduced with representatives from affected groups, such as Hispanics and African Americans, being present on boards of education. Since school boards have lost power to experts, bureaucracy, and state and federal governments, it is difficult for low-income and minority cultures to influence school policies. Chubb and Moe argue that political power has been transferred to business, the middle classes, and the educational professionals in charge of the bureaucratic system. The losers in this political scheme are "the lower classes, ethnic and religious minorities, and citizens of rural communities."[39] They argue that most reform movements after this period take this structure for granted. Even when civil rights groups in the 1960s and 1970s attacked the bureaucracy as racist, it maintained its power over public schools and resisted community control of the schools.

Chubb and Moe link federal, state, and local education bureaucracies to racism and segregation and low student achievement. Consequently, they argue (a) that a major hindrance to student achievement is the existence of large bureaucratic structures, and (b) that the best organizational condition for improving student achievement is the ability of schools to operate free of bureaucratic control. According to Chubb and Moe, in addition to bureaucracies continuing educational racism, they do not allow principals and teachers to exercise their professional expertise and judgment; rather, they deny them the flexibility needed to work effectively together to assure student achievement.

The current political structure of schools, Chubb and Moe contend, promotes bureaucracy and therefore hinders student achievement. By making policies part of the bureaucratic process, elected officials and experts try to protect their favored policies against changes from opponents who might be elected in the future.

In contrast, Chubb and Moe argue, schools controlled by competition in a free market are not bureaucratic and, consequently, promote student achievement and reduce racism. They envisioned public schools, free of bureaucracy, allowing principals and teachers to work together to ensure policies and practices promoting student learning. Pressure from competition between schools would force educators to attend to community desires. The resulting combination of autonomy and pressures from competition would result, according to the authors, in higher student achievement and reduced racism in schools.

This line of reasoning leads to the conclusion that public schools under the control of bureaucratic experts are inherently flawed regarding their ability to improve student achievement and reflect the wishes of their constituents. The major hope for basic reform of public schools, Chubb and Moe concluded, is a basic change in the method of political control.

The system of governance proposed by Chubb and Moe is based on the ability of parents to choose between schools. In their proposal, students would be free to attend any school in their state, and every effort would be made to provide transportation for students to schools outside their immediate area. A parent information center would distribute information on schools, which would also collect applications for schools. While conforming to nondiscrimination requirements, each school would decide on admissions. Chubb and Moe argue that schools cannot define their own mission and establish programs if a student population is forced on them.

In Chubb and Moe's plan, schools would be funded through a system of state scholarships that would go directly to the schools chosen by parents or students. A choice office would determine the amount of the scholarship to be awarded to each student according to the student's needs. For instance, children with disabilities, learning problems, economic problems, and those identified as at risk would receive higher scholarships to cover their more costly educational programs. The higher amount of these scholarships for these students would provide an incentive for schools to provide programs that would attract them.

Each public school in this choice plan would be free to decide its own governing structure. For instance, a school could be run by a committee of teachers, a principal, or a combination of educators and members of the community. The state would not tell schools how to do their work. It would continue to certify teachers but would have only minimum requirements. This would allow schools greater flexibility in the selection of teachers. In summary, Chubb and Moe believe that their choice plan would contribute to the improvement of student achievement in public schools and reduce racism.

The claim that free markets will reduce racism is similar to the arguments for community control. It is believed that through choice, parents can directly influence the content of instruction and eradicate racism among teachers. However, free markets for public schools never occurred, but its justifications are reflected in charters schools supported by NCLB and ESSA.[40]

The New Politics of Education

The chapters in this volume will illuminate many aspects of the complex nature of current education politics. First, there is a shadow elite that moves between government, venture philanthropy, and for-profit companies. Besides self-promotion, these shadow elites are interested in school funding that benefits their particular companies, such as book publishers, computer and software companies, tutoring and testing organizations, and makers of classroom apparatuses. Then there is a shadow elite associated with nonprofit groups trying to influence schools. They often receive money from venture philanthropists. There are also interests groups, such as teachers' unions and charter school networks, wanting policies that benefit them. And, of course, there are elected representatives on school boards, in state legislatures and the federal government. But with the expansion of state and federal control of schools, school board members are left primarily with fulfilling dictates from above and not the demands of local school parents. State and federal elected officials do influence educational legislation. However, their influence is deluded in the implementation of laws by federal and state education bureaucracies.

Where is the "public" in public schools? Does this new school governance discussed in the following chapters reflect public desires for schools? Or, should we reject the notion of democratic control of public schools?

Notes

1 (Spring, *Political Agendas for Education: From Race to the Top to Saving the Planet 5th Edition* 2013). (Spring, *Conflict of Interests: The Politics of American Education 5th Edition* 2004).
2 (Wedel, *Shadow Elite: How the World's New Power Brokers Undermine Democracy, Government and the Free Market* 2009).
3 (Wedel 2009), 5–12.
4 (*Education Week* 2016).
5 (NewSchools Venture Fund 2016).
6 (U.S. Department of Education 2011).
7 (Reckhow, *How Foundation Dollars Change Public School Politics* 2013). (Saltman, *The Gift of Education: Public Education and Venture Philanthropy* 2010). (Saltman, *The Failure of Corporate School Reform* 2013). (Saltman, *Collateral Damage: Corporatizing Public Schools, A Threat to Democracy* 2000). (Spring, *Education Networks: Power, Wealth, Cyberspace, and the Digital Mind* 2012). (Picciano, *The Great American Education-Industrial Complex: Ideology, Technology, and Profit* 2012). (Spring, *Political Agendas for Education: From Race to the Top to Saving the Planet, 5th Edition* 2013). (Epstein, *Who's in Charge Here?: The Tangled Web of School Governance and Policy* 2006). (Apple, *Education and Power 2nd Edition* 1995). (Hursh, *The End of Public Schools: The Corporate Reform Agenda to Privatize Education* 2015). (Russakoff, *The Prize: Who's in Charge of America's Schools?* 2015). (Bracey, *The War Against America's Public Schools: Privatizing Schools, Commercializing Education* 2001). (Au, *Mapping Corporate Education Reform: Power and Policy Networks in the Neoliberal State* 2015).
8 (Ball, *Global Education Inc.: New Policy Networks and the Neo-Liberal Imaginary* 2012), 9.
9 (Spring, *Globalization of Education: An Introduction 2nd Edition* 2014). (Baker, *The Schooled Society: The Educational Transformation of Global Culture* 2014). (Tooley, *The*

Global Education Industry: Lessons from Private Education in Developing Countries 1999). (Adamson, *Global Education Reform: How Privatization and Public Investment Influence Education Outcomes* 2016).
10. (Spring, *The American School: A Global Context from the Puritans to the Obama Era 8th Edition* 2011, 270–295). (Nearing, "Who's Who in Our Boards of Education" 1917). (Counts, *The Social Composition of Boards of Education: A Study in Social Control of Education* 1927). (Cohen, *Progressives and Urban School Reform* 1964).
11. (Tyack, *The One Best System: A History of Urban Education* 1983) (Callahan, *Education and the Cult of Efficiency* 1962). (Berman, "Business Efficiency, American Schooling and the Public School Superintendent" 1983).
12. (Spring, *Education and the Rise of the Corporate State* 1973). (Cronin, *The Control of Urban Schools: Perspectives on the Power of Educational Reformers* 1973). (Nearing 1917).
13. (Spring, *The Sorting Machine Revisited: National Education Policy Since 1945* 1988). (Eisenhower, "Message from the President of the United States Transmitting Recommendations Relative to Our School System" 1958).
14. (Spring, *Economization of Education: Human Capital, Global Corporations, Skills-Based Schooling* 2015).
15. (Spring 2011), 371–383. (Council of Economic Advisors 1964).
16. (Friedman, *Capitalism and Freedom* 1962).
17. (Smith, *The Idea Brokers and the Rise of the New Policy Elite* 1991), 181.
18. (Simon, *A Time for Truth* 1978), 233.
19. (Simon 1978), xii.
20. (Simon 1978), xii.
21. (Simon 1978), 232–233.
22. (Simon 1978), 230. (Smith 1991), 182.
23. (Smith 1991), 182.
24. (Ricci, *The Transformation of American Politics: The New Washington and the Rise of Think Tanks* 1993), 166.
25. (Spring 2012).
26. (Spring, *Common Core: A Story of School Terrorism* 2013).
27. (Spring 2012). (Picciano 2012).
28. (U.S. Department of Education 2002). (The Common Core State Standards 2015).
29. (U.S. Department of Education 2015). (U.S. Department of Education 2002). (U.S. Department of Education 2009).
30. (Wedel 2009).
31. (Wedel 2009), 86.
32. (U.S. Department of Education 2002), 58.
33. (U.S. Department of Education 2002), 70.
34. (Schiff, "The Educational Failure of Community Control in Inner-City New York" 1976).
35. (Lessinger, *Every Kid a Winner: Accountabiltiy in Education* 1970).
36. (Spring 2011), 432–433.
37. (U.S. Department of Education 2002). (U.S. Department of Education 2015). (The White House: Office of the Press Secretary 2009).
38. (Chubb and Moe, *Politics, Markets & America's Schools* 1990).
39. (Chubb and Moe 1990), 4.
40. (U.S. Department of Education 2002). (U.S. Department of Education 2015).

References

Adamson, Frank (Editor), Bjorn Astrand (Editor), and Linda Darling-Hammond (Editor). *Global Education Reform: How Privatization and Public Investment Influence Education Outcomes.* New York: Routledge, 2016.
Apple, Michael. *Education and Power 2nd Edition.* New York: Routledge, 1995.
Au, Wayne. *Mapping Corporate Education Reform: Power and Policy Networks in the Neoliberal State.* New York: Routledge, 2015.
Baker, David. *The Schooled Society: The Educational Transformation of Global Culture.* Palo Alto: Stanford University Press, 2014.
Ball, Stephen J. *Global Education Inc.: New Policy Networks and the Neo-Liberal Imaginary.* New York: Routledge, 2012.
Berman, Barbara. "Business Efficiency, American Schooling and the Public School Superintendent." *History of Education Quarterly,* 1983: 297–319.
Bracey, Gerald W. *The War Against America's Public Schools: Privatizing Schools, Commercializing Education.* New York: Pearson, 2001.
Callahan, Raymond. *Education and the Cult of Efficiency.* Chicago: University of Chicago Press, 1962.
Chubb, John and Terry Moe. *Politics, Markets & America's Schools.* Washington, D.C.: Brookings Institution, 1990.
Cohen, Sol. *Progressives and Urban School Reform.* New York: Teachers College Press, 1964.
Council of Economic Advisors. "The Problem of Poverty in America." *The Annual Report of the Council of Economic Advisors.* Washington, D.C.: U.S. Government Printing Office, 1964.
Counts, George S. *The Social Composition of Boards of Education: A Study in Social Control of Education.* Chicago: University of Chicago Press, 1927.
Cronin, Joseph M. *The Control of Urban Schools: Perspectives on the Power of Educational Reformers.* New York: Free Press, 1973.
Education Week. "Transitions," May 11, 2016: 5.
Eisenhower, Dwight. "Message from the President of the United States Transmitting Recommendations Relative to Our School System." *U.S. Congress, Senate Committee on Labor and Public Welfare: Science and Education for National Defense: Hearings Before the Committee on Labor and Public Welfare.* Washington, D.C.: U.S. Government Printing Office, 1958.
Epstein, Noel. *Who's in Charge Here?: The Tangled Web of School Governance and Policy.* Washington, D.C.: Brookings Institution Press, 2006.
Friedman, Milton. *Capitalism and Freedom.* Chicago: University of Chicago Press, 1962.
Hursh, David W. *The End of Public Schools: The Corporate Reform Agenda to Privatize Education.* New York: Routledge, 2015.
Lessinger, Leon. *Every Kid a Winner: Accountabiltiy in Education.* Chicago: Science Research Associates College Division, 1970.
Nearing, Scott. "Who's Who in Our Boards of Education." *School and Society,* 1917: 89–90.
NewSchools Venture Fund. "Our Model". May 16, 2016. www.newschools.org/about-us/our-model/ (accessed May 16, 2016).
Picciano, Anthony, and Joel Spring. *The Great American Education-Industrial Complex: Ideology, Technology, and Profit.* New York: Routledge, 2012.
Reckhow, Sarah. *How Foundation Dollars Change Public School Politics.* New York: Oxford University Press, 2013.
Ricci, David M. *The Transformation of American Politics: The New Washington and the Rise of Think Tanks.* New Haven, CT: Yale University Press, 1993.

Russakoff, Dale. *The Prize: Who's in Charge of America's Schools?* Boston: Houghton Mifflin Harcourt, 2015.

Saltman, Kenneth. *Collateral Damage:Corporatizing Public Schools, A Threat to Democracy.* New York: Rowman & Littlefield Publishers, 2000.

Saltman, Kenneth. *The Gift of Education: Public Education and Venture Philanthropy.* New York: Palgrave Macmillan, 2010.

Saltman, Kenneth. *The Failure of Corporate School Reform.* New York: Paradigm Publishers, 2013.

Schiff, Martin. "The Educational Failure of Community Control in Inner-City New York." *The Phi Delta Kappan*, 1976: 375–378.

Simon, William. *A Time for Truth.* New York: Reader's Digest Press, 1978.

Smith, James. *The Idea Brokers and the Rise of the New Policy Elite.* New York: Free Press, 1991.

Spring, Joel. *Education and the Rise of the Corporate State.* Boston: Beacon Press, 1973.

Spring, Joel. *The Sorting Machine Revisited: National Education Policy Since 1945.* New York: Longman, 1988.

Spring, Joel. *Conflict of Interests: The Politics of American Education 5th Edition.* New York: McGraw-Hill, 2004.

Spring, Joel. *The American School: A Global Context from the Puritans to the Obama Era 8th Edition.* McGraw-Hill: New York, 2011.

Spring, Joel. *Education Networks: Power, Wealth, Cyberspace, and the Digital Mind.* New York: Routledge, 2012.

Spring, Joel. *Common Core: A Story of School Terrorism.* New York: Phoenix Books, 2013.

Spring, Joel. *Political Agendas for Education: From Race to the Top to Saving the Planet 5th Edition.* New York: Routledge, 2013.

Spring, Joel. *Globalization of Education: An Introduction 2nd Edition.* New York: Routledge, 2014.

Spring, Joel. *Economization of Education: Human Capital, Global Corporations, Skills-Based Schooling.* New York: Routledge, 2015.

The Common Core State Standards. *The Common Core State Standards.* 2015. www.corestandards.org/ (accessed May 28, 2016).

The White House: Office of the Press Secretary. *Fact Sheet: The Race to the Top.* November 4, 2009. https://www.whitehouse.gov/the-press-office/fact-sheet-race-top (accessed June 1, 2016).

Tooley, James. *The Global Education Industry: Lessons from Private Education in Developing Countries.* London: Institute of Economic Affairs, 1999.

Tyack, David. *The One Best System: A History of Urban Education.* Cambridge: Harvard University Press, 1983.

U.S. Department of Education. *Public Law 107-110-Jan, 8, 2002, No Child Left Behind Act of 2001.* 2002. www.ed.gov/policy/elsec/leg/esea02/107-110.pdf (accessed February 1, 2009).

U.S. Department of Education. *Every Student Succeeds Act.* 2015. www.ed.gov/essa?src=rn (accessed May 26, 2016).

U.S. Department of Education. "States Open to Charters Start Fast in 'Race to Top'." June 8, 2009. www2.ed.gov/news/pressreleases/2009/06/06082009a.html (accessed May 30, 2016).

U.S. Department of Education. "James H. Shelton III, Assistant Deputy Secretary for Innovation and Improvement, Biography." May 2, 2011. www2.ed.gov/news/staff/bios/shelton.html (accessed July 24, 2011).

Verger, Antoni (Editor), Christopher Lubienski (Editor), and Gita Steiner-Khamsi (Editor). *World Yearbook of Education 2016: The Global Education Industry*. New York: Routledge, 2016.

Wedel, Janine R. *Shadow Elite: How the World's New Power Brokers Undermine Democracy, Government and the Free Market*. New York: Basic Books, 2009.

2

ADMITTING PRIVILEGE

John Eric Frankson

"I am not going to grad school."
"I know it."

That's the text I received from a student recently. Just those two lines. Its finality was alarming considering this is a student with a perfect grade point average. A student who, when not in class, or doing homework, or making the 2-hour commute to school, or helping her working-class family stay afloat, interns in a research lab at an Ivy League institution. This is a student whose depth of disciplinary knowledge is as demonstrably evident as her passion for scholarship that makes a positive impact on the lives of marginalized groups in education. Then I remembered that she was scheduled to take the GRE that morning and my alarm turned to dismay. When I spoke with her on the phone later that day her tone of utter defeat was pronounced and words like "failure" repeatedly punctuated her acceptance of the fact that the GRE had destroyed the likelihood of her getting into a graduate program.

Sadly, this scenario plays out for far too many students desirous of a graduate degree, as most graduate programs (outside of the professional fields of law, medicine, or business) require an applicant to provide GRE scores.[1] Recent legislation in New York State takes specific aim at graduate-level teacher preparation programs by requiring applicants to provide GRE scores with their admissions portfolio. This is no random or surprising manifestation of this statute as a policy, though. It has wended its way through policy channels with guidance from key individuals and organizations. It has been buoyed by "lean times" in higher education that necessitate rationing of access to public resources, namely a quality public education. It has become the default convenient choice for decision makers, despite credible evidence of discriminatory aspects of the test itself and growing dissatisfaction with undemocratic educational reform policies that relentlessly feature standardized tests as the de facto measure of quality.

This chapter presents a glimpse of the various sources of support for the GRE in graduate admissions aimed less at leaving the reader a breadcrumb trail through the policy and more at reminding us to look up and "mind the forest." Our academic spaces continue to bear the mark of a positivistic legacy that provides little pressure to think about issues holistically. Instead, we are compelled and conditioned to focus in ways that obscure the role of our increasingly interconnected socioeconomic reality and the growing size and constitution of policy networks and actors that mediate that reality. Considering the New York State GRE requirement, support for such a policy naturally comes from Educational Testing Service (ETS) and test prep companies like Kaplan. They may not directly influence legislation or policy that we know of, but given the business position of ETS as producer and owner of the company that administers the test, and Kaplan (and its nearest competitors in the test-prep market), it would seem unlikely they would offer resistance to such a policy. Other sources of support are more diffuse amongst the noise inherent in contemporary education practice and policy. Nevertheless, by conceptualizing these sources as a network of reinforcing elements we can understand them in their complexity, identify who is present, who is connected to whom, and what each is saying or doing to legitimize GRE usage in graduate admissions.

These networks of power and money are unbelievably expansive and loosely connected in some cases, which obscures our ability to actually see how everything functions as a system all at once. It makes it easy to point the finger at specific targets but very difficult to assign accountability, much less sustain a culture of educational justice and fairness. The "snapshot" we are ultimately able to achieve of such a fluid construct has an extremely short half-life; everything and everyone framed are always in motion, which makes it hard to separate "what was" from "what is." My hope is that this chapter helps reframe the present consideration of neoliberal education policies away from exclusively naming actors and organizations as neoliberal entities and instead highlights how they—and we— behave neoliberally and inevitably preserve inequalities in graduate education and our nation's educational spaces.

Endangered Spaces

Adding a Gordian Knot-like quality to the present case is one very important aspect of teacher education—its inherent generative capacity. The results of teacher education programs ripple through time and place as graduates disperse out in every imaginable corner of the education world and in turn educate successive generations of would-be scholars. Research conducted within these institutions makes its way into new scholarship and best practices that generate new lines of inquiry. This cyclical characteristic, a feedback loop of sorts that keeps the system alive and vibrant, becomes an Achilles heel when things go awry and the effects of bad policy ricochet through the education system. Graduate-level teacher preparation programs are formative spaces—part of an ecosystem—that demand a renewed public debate on this hotly contested space where primary, secondary, and tertiary systems overlap and engage each other.

The list of challenges facing education generally, and public education more specifically, is immense and complicated. Teacher shortages are a common concern of late, as are high turnover, demoralization of the teaching force, draconian assessment regimes implemented in an ad hoc fashion, deteriorating infrastructure, fiscal crises, and undeniable acts of violence and bigotry that create toxic environments, to name a few. Racial, ethnic, gender, and economic minorities—whose marginalization outside of school is mirrored by marginalization inside of them—are particularly hard hit, despite our "best efforts" to close achievement gaps. Lost completely in the conversations amongst education power brokers is the growing body of research by critical scholars that appreciate these challenges for the systemic, cyclical, and multivariate issues they are. We know poverty, hunger, segregation, tax policy, and wealth inequality affect learning in dramatic ways. We also know that students, especially students who are struggling, benefit from having demographically similar teachers. We know students who are allowed to use their native language in class can learn English (and other languages) much more effectively. We know this in large part because of the work of countless scholars—many with their own stories of marginalization in American public education—who used these experiences to ground critical work that challenged the hegemonic power structures within education that perpetuate educational injustice. Such scholarship has shown the power of culturally sustaining pedagogies, restorative justice programs, and critical theories in education research and practice. This work connects the disciplines of psychology, sociology, history, economics, and political science in formulating policy and practice that eschew the one-size-fits-all approach to more democratically address our common challenges.

We also know the GRE's ability to broadly predict how well a student will do in their chosen graduate program is unimpressive and its potential to underpredict for students of color and women is troubling. Why would we include GRE scores in an admissions file when they are so questionable? And why would we further starve the research pipeline of the kind of powerful and just scholarship informed by the unique positionality and perspectives of students whose talents are deemed inadmissible when they include something as problematic as GRE scores?

Neoliberal Notions of Accountability

As Stephen Ball cautions, the term neoliberalism has a tendency to be used "so widely and so loosely that it is in danger of becoming meaningless."[2] While I wholeheartedly agree that this does complicate shared understandings of meaning, this challenge instead compels us to empirically appreciate neoliberalism's presence in even the most mundane corners of our daily lives as well as how it pervades the hegemonic discourses of our political and educational arenas.

In a nutshell, neoliberalism is an economic philosophy that favors deregulation of markets and businesses, the reduction of taxes, and the privatization of government functions. It privileges the individual. This set of ideas generates a host of ideological narratives than can be generally, and incompletely, summarized as: 1.) the economy is a self-regulating entity that always balances out and is the only legitimate arbiter of resource allocation; 2.) individual interests (and responsibilities) trump those of other individuals and society at large; 3.) government gets in the way of the individual or private enterprise and their self-interested pursuit of profit and resource accumulation; 4.) wealth and profits trickle down from those at the top to those at the bottom.

Neoliberalism's privileging of individual (or private) self-interest, unfettered markets, and cost-cutting to increase profitability—essentially subjecting education to a constant cost/benefit analysis—has turned our educational spaces into increasingly hyper-competitive environments that perpetuate the neoliberal position that education is both a private benefit and a private responsibility.[3] To facilitate the distribution of what limited resources are available (remember, neoliberalism seeks efficiency), assessment regimes prominently feature standardized measures as the primary means of determining which schools and students need support. While nothing new, this obsession with outcomes-based reform took center stage in 2002 with the passing of the No Child Left Behind (NCLB) Act. It marked a turn to "test-and-punish" models that threatened punitive action for sub-par performance. The withholding of funding, probationary periods, and shuttering of schools engendered justifiable paranoia; thousands of schools were closed and hundreds of thousands of teachers lost their jobs as a result. Passage of the Every Student Succeeds Act (ESSA) in 2015 by the Obama Administration attempted to address the issue by suggesting the federal government would return some power to the states, but critics have realized very little will change. Despite mollifying rhetoric from education leaders that acknowledge growing frustration amongst students and parents, the federal government did not necessarily lose its teeth. The Feds issued warnings very early in 2015 that states could face sanctions if participation in ESSA testing dropped below the 95 percent required by the law in response to a burgeoning nationwide Opt-Out movement.[4]

Ham-fisted attempts at accountability were not just relegated to primary and secondary classrooms. In early 2010 the National Council on Accreditation for Teacher Education (NCATE) established a Blue Ribbon Panel to study and make recommendations to improve clinical teacher training programs.[5] It was co-chaired by Nancy Zimpher, Chancellor of the State University of New York from 2009 to present, and Dwight D. Jones, then Commissioner of Education for the State of Colorado.[6] The panel's final report called for a bevy of changes needed to turn teacher prep "upside down."[7] While the report was silent on graduate-level teaching programs, a key recommendation of the report was more rigorous admission standards in teacher training programs overall. In 2013, NCATE and the Teacher Accreditation Council (TEAC) officially merged to form The Council for the Accreditation of Educator Preparation (CAEP).[8] Having consolidated the two accrediting bodies' authority, CAEP laid out a set of standards in August of 2013 that were more concise than the NCATE report and certainly reflected a move to a more formidable set of minimum requirements for admission to graduate-level teacher prep programs, namely a minimum average GRE score.[9] A month later, Zimpher submitted a proposal to the SUNY Board of Regents requesting the policy be adopted system-wide based on a controversial report from Governor Cuomo's NY Education Reform Commission as well as the CAEP standards.[10] Then the policy formally appeared as part of Cuomo's executive budget proposal in 2015, which was passed by the state legislature and signed into law.[11]

Clearly neoliberal notions of accountability and excellence are best articulated as genuine barriers to entry, not thoughtful stewardship of our public resources and rights. Accountability, as it functions in our society, is almost exclusively directed downward. It is one-way accountability. Surely many school administrators and policy makers are casualties of political battles, but those at the top rarely seem to pay any price. Zimpher has been, and continues to be, a subject of criticism for her tendency to leave important stakeholders out of the decision-making processes.[12] John King, widely considered to have bungled the Common Core implementation as New York Commissioner of Education, now serves as U.S. Secretary of Education.[13] Even his replacement, Mary Ellen Elia, who took over as commissioner in 2015, left her previous post as superintendent of one of the largest school districts in the nation under less than ideal circumstances.[14] Cuomo's NY Education Reform Commission was chaired by Richard D. Parsons, former chairman of Citigroup and former CEO of Time Warner. Parsons also has extensive ties to Republican elites and was tapped by George W. Bush to co-chair a commission tasked with privatizing Social Security to save it from collapse. What of Governor Cuomo himself, who relies a great deal on hyperbolic rhetoric and political brinksmanship to stack committees with neoliberal-minded reformers and make policy decisions by fiat?

Does this sound like excellence? Frances Maher and Mary Kay Thompson Tetreault answer in the affirmative in *Privilege and Diversity in the Academy*,[15] but only based on the masking of privilege with the veneer of excellence:

> Excellence [has become] a code word for commonly agreed-on high standards of academic performance—in other words, rigorous scholarship with universal applicability—and a deservedly high stature for those who meet these standards ... [however] the use of the term excellence is

employed not so much as a mark of quality [than] as a mark of privilege ... the operations of privilege, embedded in the structures, processes, and standards of the academy, are the barriers against and through which the newcomers must negotiate their way.

(pp. 3–4)

In the case of education policy at the federal and state levels, accountability is centered on a definition of educational excellence that it is only concerned with reducing costs to appease those already in power. What do we expect? Aside from the occasional educator, parent, or union representative, the committees, task forces, and rulemaking bodies charged with fixing what ails our education system are stacked with privileged experts. Zimpher's single voice in particular registers in so many policy spaces, as well as with the general public. She serves as an education advisor to the Obama White House, has the ear of the governor and state politicians, and serves on boards of professional associations and accrediting bodies.[16] Her comments and thoughts appear regularly in various media outlets and consistently single out the need for "quality" teachers. I, of course, do not disagree. However, failing to use your authority to advocate for "quality" teacher training programs—and that necessitates leading the moral charge against the neoliberal idea that education can and should operate like a business—is a dispiriting display of privilege. In neoliberal thinking, success or failure is completely dependent on the choices and talents of the individual student with no regard to the limitation imposed upon them by our economized and compromised education and political system.

It's All About the Money

Funding for public education at all levels is a prickly topic. Americans have watched state and local funding for elementary and secondary schools dwindle as increased spending on prisons and the military, tax cuts, and other discretionary budget items have been prioritized at the expense of public K-12 education.[17] At the other end of the educational continuum, successive Republican and Democratic administrations have also effectively enabled a decades-long shift in responsibility for funding higher education to the student (the individual), reducing state contributions to the operating budgets of colleges and universities and adding to astronomical levels of student debt and financial insecurity. Cuts to public education and the narratives that support them also mirror cuts to America's social safety net. Combined with the generational drag of wealth and income inequality, students and their families are struggling to make ends meet. Before the 2008 recession hit, there were about 16 million schoolchildren living in high-poverty school districts; by 2013 that number would skyrocket to almost 24 million. The number of Free or Reduced-Price Lunches (FRPL) has also seen a post-recession spike. Nearly 75 percent of all lunches served in our schools now qualify as FRPL.[18] It had hovered between 56 percent and 60 percent in the decade prior.[18]

Common complaints on many college campuses range from larger class sizes, increased reliance on part-time labor, shoddy academic facilities, narrowing of curriculum, fewer counselors and advisers and more self-service options, less support for those with disabilities, and diminished capacity for maintenance of the very basic operation of an educational institution. These are but a few of the ways that disinvestment in education mediates the level of preparedness undergraduates actually possess at the point of entry to graduate school. Students can, of course, avail themselves of any number of market-based solutions such as tutoring and test preparation, but herein lies the reality of equal opportunity in education: some are more equal than others. For poorly resourced schools, doing more with less—you will often hear this couched as "value"—can rob students of the types of meaningful educational experiences they rightfully deserve. They experience "value" as a loss. If they choose to pursue a graduate degree, every dollar they spend and every hour dedicated to test-prep just to compete with more privileged applicants only add insult to injury.[19] Money is a great educational equalizer when it is used to level the playing field. It is a source of inequity when it is used to gild the lily.

With regard to the preponderance of GRE scores' use in admissions decisions, one does not have to stretch the imagination too far to see how such lean financial times can also attenuate the amount of attention faculty are able to devote to the admissions process. There is not enough time to be as thorough as one would like and for those who are not concerned with thoroughness, the lack of time can be a convenient pressure to simply use "cutoff scores" to winnow down the number of applications to be reviewed.[20] Limited discretionary funds also constrain recruiting efforts that could at the very least add depth to students' admissions files.

How can a system, sapped of its ability to perform the most basic functions, divert adequate resources to provide the kind of incidental support our students require? How can we expect excellence in graduate school applicants when their primary, secondary, and undergraduate careers are subject to such precarious conditions? You would be hard pressed to find the slightest mention from educational leaders, legislators, and pundits—especially those with the type of celebrity status mentioned earlier—that challenges the decades-long denial of stable funding to public education and social services. Instead they kowtow to the wishes of a wealthy and powerful elite that are happy to swap contributions to the public purse for self-interested philanthropy; relying on charity rather than civic duty.

Distracted, Selfish, and Ignorant

Naomi Klein's *Shock Doctrine* brilliantly lays out how neoliberal and neoconservative policies exploit public crises for private financial and sociopolitical gain, referring to it appropriately as "disaster capitalism."[21] From the violent imposition of Chicago

School economic regimes in South and Latin America in the mid-twentieth century to the 2003 invasion of Iraq by the George W. Bush administration, a massive amount of wealth has been (and continues to be) siphoned out of public coffers to pay those in private enterprise that offer "solutions" to our most intractable problems. Natural disasters are ripe for exploitation as well, not just war or political unrest. In the immediate aftermath of Hurricane Katrina, neoliberal actors with the support of, again, the Bush Administration, shuttered over 100 public schools to make way for the charter school takeover of K-12 education in New Orleans.[22] The neoliberal American Enterprise Institute infamously stated, "Katrina accomplished in a day ... what Louisiana school reformers couldn't do after years of trying."[23] Chaos is good for business.

The contentious battles over education issues in the State of New York fostered a massively congested space for debate, which allowed undemocratic policies to gain traction. Dominating much of the discourse were issues like the aftermath of NCLB, Race to the Top, and ESSA, bungled Common Core and teacher assessment standards, squabbles over mayoral control of New York City schools, a budget showdown between the governor of New York and mayor of New York City over funding for the City University of New York, and an impending labor strike at the City University of New York (the result of 7 years without a contract). The invocation of crisis brought things to a fever pitch, replete with the business community, "edupreneurs," think tanks, and politicians and citizens from both sides of the aisle bemoaning the impending calamity if schools did not better prepare students for the workforce.

Direct attacks on teachers did not help matters. Educators and the unions that represent them, already threatened by anti-union "right to work" legislation in state after state, faced an onslaught of criticism for the terrible state of affairs. They were both the "source" of our nation's terrible education outcomes and the "hostile" element when they challenged neoliberal efforts at reform. Consider too the confusion caused by the shifting involvement of multiple accrediting agencies and the presence of alternative certification programs that have different admissions requirements. What effect did the rash of school shootings or racist trends in school discipline have on the context in which hundreds of policy decisions were made? How could anything coherent come out of this mess? Perhaps a better question is, does anyone care?

Certainly there are many individuals who care, but as Paul Roberts argues in his 2014 book, *The Impulse Society*, many do not. Roberts lays out a compelling argument that the shift from a production-driven economy to an overwhelmingly consumer-driven one has fostered a socioeconomic calculus that is decidedly impulsive, self-serving, and unfortunately quite apathetic.[24] Delving into the psychology and neuroscience behind what he calls the merging of the "self and the market," he explores the myriad ways our everyday consumerist behavior manifests itself in, and concomitantly reinforces, our everyday consumerist identity.[25] His thoughts are worth quoting in their entirety:

> In the aftermath of [the financial meltdown of 2008], we should all be working, collectively and individually, to change the financial system—and the corrupt political system that enables it. Instead, we've mostly done just the opposite: we've retreated deeper into our own lives and lifestyles and selves. Here is the trap created by a society that insists on delivering more life-shaping power to its citizens yet has largely stopped talking about how those powers might best be put to use. Indeed, we blithely defer to the wisdom of the market and assume that if some new increment of capability is being offered that allows us to disengage even further from the broader society and its irksome problems—it is, by definition, entirely acceptable and even desirable. It's the Impulse Society's signature move: every man, woman, and hipster for themselves.
>
> (p. 119)

We are no longer concerned with what we need. Our lives are more and more about what we want and how soon we can get it and the market is all too happy to respond accordingly. We also discount, and often flat-out ignore, the effects of our consumer decisions on others and society at large as businesses and institutions constantly churn out newer, better, and faster products and services. In addition to material goods, our self-centeredness and impulsivity also drive the uncritical consumption of knowledge and information, affecting our ability to adequately conceive of our most pernicious issues as the interconnected reality they are. To be sure, there is a buffet of information served up—ready and waiting. In addition to the major television networks and national newspapers and magazines, we have access to a digital repository of news, data, research (and more frequently self-serving opinion, grandstanding, and punditry) that is virtually "available" 24 hours a day.

That has, however, done little to counter the stereotype of the "stupid American"—while anecdotal, one need only do a quick Internet search to feel the pang of contrition. With his second term nearing an end, you'll find Americans that do not believe that President Obama was born in the U.S. and plenty that still believe Saddam Hussein was responsible for the 9/11 attacks on the World Trade Center. Our political discourse itself is choking on "zombie lies"—those rumors that never die despite all evidence to the contrary—and misinformation that have sadly (and dare we hope finally) reached the high water mark in the 2016 U.S. election. Studies and scientific polling confirm our general lack of content knowledge and awareness of current events, history, geography, science, and social studies.

Rick Shenkman in his recent book, *Political Animals*, puts it bluntly: we are ignorant.[26] Our brains, built for living in small hunter-gatherer groups, simply have not evolved to deal with the expanding social ties and resulting nuanced social knowledge with which we are now confronted.[27] Even if we were able to pay attention, education topics rarely get much airtime anyway as a 2009 Brookings Institution report makes clear:[28]

> [T]here is virtually no national coverage of education. During the first nine months of 2009, only 1.4 percent of national news coverage from television, newspapers, news Web sites, and radio dealt with education. ... Of the education news that is reported across any education level, little relates to school policies and ways to improve the curriculum or learning processes. ... Instead, most stories this year dealt with budget problems, school crime, and the H1N1 flu outbreak.
>
> (p. 1)

Education is so tightly woven into the lore of the American Dream. While not explicitly stated in our founding documents, our country and its inhabitants on the whole have long acknowledged the integral role of an educated citizenry in furthering our democracy. So what happens when we reduce the amount of time spent in our schools and universities teaching the subjects we seem to be so terrible at knowing? Analysis of data from the National Assessment of Educational Progress is not encouraging. Only 18 percent, 27 percent, and 23 percent of our nation's eighth-graders demonstrate proficiency in U.S. History, Geography, and Civics, respectively.[29] That is our fault. The narrowing of curricula throughout the entire education continuum, pushing out certain disciplines or subjects in favor of more "popular" ones, is well documented and nothing new. The Right's Culture Warriors have spent the last half-century removing anything that questions America's pale, pious, and patriarchal "creation myth." Now standardized tests, overwhelmingly focused on math and ELA, perform the same function. We should take stock of how the past decade or so of "reform" has undercut our collective capacity to deal with twenty-first century democracy and remain steadfast in our support for public education.

Consider this: we have the GRE because it works for those in power. It works for the testing and test-prep businesses that rake in millions of dollars in revenue. It works for those in higher positions inside academia and politics who can blithely latch on to pseudo-egalitarian notions of meritocracy in the face of shrinking budgets and reduced access to public graduate education. It works because as a body politic we have unwittingly internalized the cold logic of the market as a legitimate arbiter of who gets what. When that "what" sits in your Amazon Shopping Cart, or your driveway, or your pocket we might be forgiven for the occasional lapse in empathy. When that "what" consists of life, liberty, and the pursuit of happiness—constitutionally guaranteed inalienable rights that include equal protection under the law—it should jolt us out of our complacency.

No Child Left Behind was in place for 13 suffocating years. Distraction, the new opiate of the masses, kept it in place. The recent groundswell of grassroots activism steeped in ideals of social justice and a critique of the neoliberal imaginary has broken through some of the din. As educators we would be wise to keep up the fight. Our institutions are broken and relying on them as if they are some sort of impartial entity capable of effecting meaningful change is misguided at best. In all of this chaos we are still told education is the key to success; the requisite for lifting one up by one's bootstraps. It is this notion of individual responsibility, divorced from any responsibility of society toward the individual that prompted my student's text of abject defeat by the GRE.

I assert it is socioeconomic progress that enables quality education, not the other way around, which makes this a people problem. When it comes to empathy, "We the People" average out to mediocrity, not excellence—with the privileged few pulling themselves up at the expense of those left waiting outside on the doorstep. These bodies—especially these black and brown bodies—are pushed out of their communities, out of the education system, out of the American dream, and out of existence. The presidential election of 2016 has emboldened an utterly disgusting element of our populace. Now we must direct our collective energies, not at dismantling institutional racism and sexism, but to pushing back against bald-faced racist and misogynistic rhetoric on display that for so long we have been patronizingly told was a figment of our imagination; the ravings of an overly sensitive lot. This disturbing reality throws into stark relief both what is at stake and how effective neoliberalism is at deflecting even the most obvious moral critique.

In New York State, the new GRE requirements for graduate-level teacher prep programs is set to take effect in January 2017. Proponents of the policy breathlessly decry the lack of teacher quality and, to be sure, lament the lack of diversity in our teaching force. It is abundantly clear, however, where their priorities lie when measures of quality and accountability—deeming who is worthy of being educated to be an educator—begin to sound an awful lot like the literacy tests of our supposed past and further erode the democratic ideals of education for all and *by* all.

Notes

1 Geoff Decker, "After Rancorous Debate, Lawmakers Pass Big Changes to Evaluations," Chalkbeat, April 1, 2015, www.chalkbeat.org/posts/ny/2015/04/01/after-rancorous-debate-lawmakers-begrudgingly-pass-big-changes-to-evaluations/
2 Stephen J. Ball, *Global Education Inc.: New Policy Networks and the Neoliberal Imaginary* (London: Routledge, 2012), 3.
3 Joel H. Spring, *Economization of Education: Human Capital, Global Corporations, Skills-based Schooling* (New York: Routledge, 2015), 2.
4 Valerie Strauss, "U.S. Education Department Threatens to Sanction States over Test Opt-outs," *Washington Post*, January 28, 2016, https://www.washingtonpost.com/news/answer-sheet/wp/2016/01/28/u-s-education-department-threatens-to-sanction-states-over-test-opt-outs/?tid=a_inl
5 "Blue Ribbon Panel on Clinical Preparation and Partnerships for Improved Student Learning," National Council for Accreditation of Teacher Education, November 2010, www.ncate.org/Public/ResearchReports/NCATEInitiatives/BlueRibbonPanel/tabid/715/Default.aspx

6 Ibid.
7 Ibid.
8 Stephen Sawchuk, "Teacher-Prep Accreditation Group Seeks to Regain Traction," *Education Week*, September 24, 2016, www.edweek.org/ew/articles/2016/08/24/teacher-prep-accreditation-group-seeks-to-regain-traction.html
9 CAEP Commission Recommendations to the CAEP Board of Directors, Report, February 13, 2015, www.caepnet.org/~/media/Files/caep/standards/final-board-amended-20150612.pdf
10 "SUNY Educator Preparation Programs and the New NY Education Reform Commission," Nancy L. Zimpher to Members of the Board of Trustees, September 18, 2013.
11 Governor Andrew M. Cuomo, "Governor Cuomo Announces Highlights from the Passage of the 2015–16 State Budget," News release, April 1, 2015, https://www.governor.ny.gov/news/governor-cuomo-announces-highlights-passage-2015-16-state-budget
12 United University Professions, "UUP Rips SUNY over TeachNY Report," News release, May 18, 2016, http://uupinfo.org/communications/uupdate/1516/160518A.php
13 Alyson Klein, "Arne Duncan to Step Down as Ed. Sec., John King to Head Up Department," *Education Week*, October 2, 2015, http://blogs.edweek.org/edweek/campaign-k-12/2015/10/arne_duncan_to_step_down_in_de.html
14 Marlene Sokol, "Sticker Shock: How Hillsborough County's Gates Grant Became a Budget Buster," *Tampa Bay Times*, October 23, 2015, www.tampabay.com/news/education/k12/sticker-shock-how-hillsborough-countys-gates-grant-became-a-budget-buster/2250988
15 Frances A. Maher and Mary Kay Thompson Tetreault, *Privilege and Diversity in the Academy* (New York and London: Routledge, 2006).
16 Libby A. Nelson, "Meet Obama's Favorite College Leader," *Politico PRO*, January 17, 2014, www.politico.com/story/2014/01/barack-obama-nancy-l-zimpher-102326
17 Stephanie Stullich, Ivy Morgan, and Oliver Schak, *State and Local Expenditures on Corrections and Education*, Report, July 2016, https://www2.ed.gov/rschstat/eval/other/expenditures-corrections-education/brief.pdf
18 *National School Lunch Program: Participation and Lunches Served*, Report, October 7, 2016, www.fns.usda.gov/sites/default/files/pd/slsummar.pdf
19 Ibid.
20 Eduardo Porter, "Education Gap between Rich and Poor Is Growing Wider," *The New York Times*, September 22, 2015, www.nytimes.com/2015/09/23/business/economy/education-gap-between-rich-and-poor-is-growing-wider.html?_r=0
21 Naomi Klein, *The Shock Doctrine: The Rise of Disaster Capitalism* (New York: Metropolitan Books/Henry Holt, 2007), 5.
22 Ibid.
23 Ibid.
24 Paul Roberts, *The Impulse Society: America in the Age of Instant Gratification* (New York: Bloomsbury, 2015), 6.
25 Ibid.
26 Richard Shenkman, *Political Animals: How Our Stone Age Brain Gets in the Way of Smart Politics* (New York: Basic Books, 2016), 17.
27 Ibid, xxvii.

28 Darrell M. West, Grover J. "Russ" Whitehurst, and E. J. Dionne, "Invisible: 1.4 Percent Coverage for Education Is Not Enough," *Brookings*, December 2, 2009, https://www.brookings.edu/research/invisible-1-4-percent-coverage-for-education-is-not-enough/

29 "The Nation's Report Card: 2014 U.S. History, Geography, and Civics at Grade 8," National Center for Education Statistics, April 25, 2015, http://nces.ed.gov/pubsearch/pubsinfo.asp?pubid=2015112

References and Further Reading

Ball, Stephen J. *Global Education Inc.: New Policy Networks and the Neoliberal Imaginary.* London: Routledge, 2012.

"Blue Ribbon Panel on Clinical Preparation and Partnerships for Improved Student Learning." National Council for Accreditation of Teacher Education. November 2010. http://www.ncate.org/Public/ResearchReports/NCATEInitiatives/BlueRibbonPanel/tabid/715/Default.aspx

Brown, Emma. "Map: How Student Poverty Has Increased Since the Great Recession." *Washington Post.* August 24, 2015. https://www.washingtonpost.com/news/education/wp/2015/08/24/map-how-student-poverty-has-increased-since-the-great-recession/

Burnette, Daarel, II. "ESSA Poses Capacity Challenges for State Education Agencies." *Education Week.* January 19, 2016. www.edweek.org/ew/articles/2016/01/20/essa-poses-capacity-challenges-for-state-education.html

CAEP Commission Recommendations to the CAEP Board of Directors. Report. February 13, 2015. www.caepnet.org/~/media/Files/caep/standards/final-board-amended-20150612.pdf

Clayton, Victoria. "The Problem With the GRE." *The Atlantic.* March 1, 2015. www.theatlantic.com/education/archive/2016/03/the-problem-with-the-gre/471633/

Clukey, Keisha. "As Shortage Looms, State Rethinks How It Recruits and Treats Its Teachers." *Politico PRO.* March 7, 2016. www.politico.com/states/new-york/albany/story/2016/03/as-shortage-looms-state-rethinks-how-it-recruits-and-treats-its-teachers-032004

Clukey, Keshia. "Education Task Force Members Express Concern over New Federal Law." *Politico PRO.* July 15, 2016. www.politico.com/states/new-york/albany/story/2016/07/education-task-force-members-express-concern-over-lack-of-flexibility-in-new-federal-law-103860

Clukey, Keshia. "Regents Panel to Revisit Tough Teacher Certification System." *Politico PRO.* April 20, 2016. http://www.politico.com/states/new-york/albany/story/2017/01/regents-panel-to-revisit-tough-teacher-certification-system-108597

Cochran-Smith, Marilyn, Rebecca Stern, Juan Gabriel Sánchez, Elizabeth Stringer Keefe, M. Beatriz Fernández, Wen-Chia Chang, Molly Cummings Carney, and Megina Baker. "Holding Teacher Preparation Accountable: A Review of Claims and Evidence." National Education Policy Center. March 2016. http://nepc.colorado.edu/publication/holding-teacher-preparation-accountable-a-review-of-claims-and-evidence

Debot, Brandon, and David Reich. "House Budget Committee Plan Cuts Pell Grants Deeply, Reducing Access to Higher Education." Center on Budget and Policy Priorities. October 21, 2015. www.cbpp.org/research/house-budget-committee-plan-cuts-pell-grants-deeply-reducing-access-to-higher-education

Decker, Geoff. "After Rancorous Debate, Lawmakers Pass Big Changes to Evaluations." *Chalkbeat.* April 1, 2015. www.chalkbeat.org/posts/ny/2015/04/01/after-rancorous-debate-lawmakers-begrudgingly-pass-big-changes-to-evaluations/

Egalite, Anna J., Brian Kisida, and Marcus A. Winters. "Representation in the Classroom: The Effect of Own-race Teachers on Student Achievement." *Economics of Education Review* 45 (January 31, 2015): 44–52. doi:10.1016/j.econedurev.2015.01.007

Fang, Marina. "Poverty Among College Students Increases The Overall Rate." ThinkProgress. July 30, 2013. https://thinkprogress.org/poverty-among-college-students-increases-the-overall-rate-ae283dcd3c47#.lktw4bvvc

Governor Andrew M. Cuomo. "Governor Cuomo Announces Highlights from the Passage of the 2015–16 State Budget." News release. April 1, 2015. https://www.governor.ny.gov/news/governor-cuomo-announces-highlights-passage-2015-16-state-budget

Klein, Alyson. "Arne Duncan to Step Down as Ed. Sec., John King to Head Up Department." *Education Week.* October 2, 2015. http://blogs.edweek.org/edweek/campaign-k-12/2015/10/arne_duncan_to_step_down_in_de.html

Klein, Naomi. *The Shock Doctrine: The Rise of Disaster Capitalism.* New York: Metropolitan Books/Henry Holt, 2007.

Leachman, Michael, Nick Albares, Kathleen Masterson, and Marlana Wallace. "Most States Have Cut School Funding, and Some Continue Cutting." Center on Budget and Policy Priorities. January 25, 2015. www.cbpp.org/research/state-budget-and-tax/most-states-have-cut-school-funding-and-some-continue-cutting

"TeachNY Letter March 29." Karen E. Magee and Frederick E. Kowal to Chancellor Nancy L. Zimpher. March 29, 2016. http://uupinfo.org/committees/pdf/teached/NYSUTLettersTestimony/TeachNYletterMarch29.pdf

Maher, Frances A. and Mary Kay Thompson Tetreault. *Privilege and Diversity in the Academy.* New York and London: Routledge, 2006.

McGrath, Darryl. "NYSUT, UUP Blast Teacher Ed Report." NYSUT UUP Blast Teacher Ed Report. June 2, 2016. www.nysut.org/news/nysut-united/issues/2016/june-2016/nysut-uup-blast-teacher-ed-report

Miller, Casey, and Keivan Stassun. "A Test That Fails." Nature.com. June 11, 2014. http://www.nature.com/naturejobs/science/articles/10.1038/nj7504-303a

Murphy, Justin, and Jon Campbell. "Cuomo: Common Core Implementation 'Not Working'." *Rochester Democrat and Chronicle.* September 3, 2015. www.democratandchronicle.com/story/news/education/2015/09/03/cuomo-common-core-implementation-not-working/71644568/

Nelson, Libby A. "Meet Obama's Favorite College Leader." *Politico PRO.* January 17, 2014. http://www.politico.com/story/2014/01/barack-obama-nancy-l-zimpher-102326

"The Nation's Report Card: 2014 U.S. History, Geography, and Civics at Grade 8." National Center for Education Statistics. April 25, 2015. http://nces.ed.gov/pubsearch/pubsinfo.asp?pubid=2015112

National School Lunch Program: Participation and Lunches Served. Report. October 7, 2016. www.fns.usda.gov/sites/default/files/pd/slsummar.pdf

"New York No 'State of Opportunity' for SUNY Students." News release. January 22, 2015. United University Professions. http://uupinfo.org/communications/2015releases/150122.php

Newfield, Christopher. *Unmaking the Public University: The Forty-year Assault on the Middle Class.* Cambridge, MA: Harvard University Press, 2011.

O'Neil, Moira. "Overarching Patterns in Media Coverage of Education Issues." Frameworks Institute. November 2012. www.nmefoundation.org/getmedia/61d7bf15-9c3f-4268-b3da-fa89c5228830/ecs-mca-overarching-final

Porter, Eduardo. "Education Gap Between Rich and Poor Is Growing Wider." *The New York Times*. September 22, 2015. www.nytimes.com/2015/09/23/business/economy/education-gap-between-rich-and-poor-is-growing-wider.html?_r=0

"Putting Students First—Final Action Plan." New NY Education Reform Commission. January 6, 2014. www.governor.ny.gov/sites/governor.ny.gov/files/archive/assets/documents/NewNYEducationReformCommissionFinalActionPlan.pdf

Rich, Motoko. "Where Are the Teachers of Color?" *The New York Times*. April 11, 2015. www.nytimes.com/2015/04/12/sunday-review/where-are-the-teachers-of-color.html

Richmond, Emily. "What Do the Contentious New Teacher Rankings Really Mean?" *The Atlantic*. June 20, 2014. www.theatlantic.com/education/archive/2014/06/teacher-prep-ratings-leave-mixed-messages/373140/

Richmond, Emily. "How Ineffective Government Funding Can Hurt Poor Students." *The Atlantic*. June 8, 2015. www.theatlantic.com/education/archive/2015/06/how-funding-inequalities-push-poor-students-further-behind/395348/

Roberts, Paul. *The Impulse Society: America in the Age of Instant Gratification*. New York: Bloomsbury, 2015.

Sawchuk, Stephen. "Steep Drops Seen in Teacher-Prep Enrollment Numbers." *Education Week*. October 21, 2014. www.edweek.org/ew/articles/2014/10/22/09enroll.h34.html?tkn=YWSFbbgnoCJPXXnAgpHLjViLrKdzrvacqAt+

Sawchuk, Stephen. "Scholars Lament Decline of Ed. History Courses in Teacher Prep." *Education Week*. September 15, 2015. www.edweek.org/ew/articles/2015/09/16/scholars-lament-decline-of-ed-history-courses.html

Sawchuk, Stephen. "Teacher Education Group Airs Criticism of New Accreditor." *Education Week*. March 17, 2015. www.edweek.org/ew/articles/2015/03/18/teacher-education-group-airs-criticism-of-new.html

Sawchuk, Stephen. "Teacher-Prep Accreditation Group Seeks to Regain Traction." *Education Week*. September 24, 2016. www.edweek.org/ew/articles/2016/08/24/teacher-prep-accreditation-group-seeks-to-regain-traction.html

Shenkman, Richard. *Political Animals: How Our Stone Age Brain Gets in the Way of Smart Politics*. New York: Basic Books, 2016.

Sparks, Sarah D. "Achievement Gaps and Racial Segregation: Research Finds an Insidious Cycle." *Education Week*. April 29, 2016. http://blogs.edweek.org/edweek/inside-school-research/2016/04/achievement_gaps_school_segregation_reardon.html

Spring, Joel H. *Economization of Education: Human Capital, Global Corporations, Skills-based Schooling*. New York: Routledge, 2015.

Sokol, Marlene. "Sticker Shock: How Hillsborough County's Gates Grant Became a Budget Buster." *Tampa Bay Times*. October 23, 2015. www.tampabay.com/news/education/k12/sticker-shock-how-hillsborough-countys-gates-grant-became-a-budgetbuster/2250988

Stratford, Michael. "House Republicans Again Propose 10-year Freeze on Pell Grant Maximum Award." March 18, 2015. https://www.insidehighered.com/news/2015/03/18/house-republicans-again-propose-10-year-freeze-pell-grant-maximum-award

Strauss, Valerie. "Illinois Gov. Rauner Once Said Half of Chicago's Teachers Are 'Virtually Illiterate'." *Washington Post*. July 26, 2016. https://www.washingtonpost.com/news/answer-sheet/wp/2016/07/26/illinois-gov-rauner-once-said-half-of-chicagos-teachers-are-virtually-illiterate/

Strauss, Valerie. "U.S. Education Department Threatens to Sanction States over Test Opt-outs." *Washington Post*. January 28, 2016. https://www.washingtonpost.com/news/

answer-sheet/wp/2016/01/28/u-s-education-department-threatens-to-sanction-states-over-test-opt-outs/?tid=a_inl

Stullich, Stephanie, Ivy Morgan, and Oliver Schak. *State and Local Expenditures on Corrections and Education*. Report. July 2016. https://www2.ed.gov/rschstat/eval/other/expenditures-corrections-education/brief.pdf

"SUNY Educator Preparation Programs and the New NY Education Reform Commission." Nancy L. Zimpher to Members of the Board of Trustees. September 18, 2013.

"The Disappearance of Black and Latino Teachers in New York City." *Teachers Unite*. October 17, 2014. http://www.teachersunite.net/content/new-publication-disappearance-black-and-latino-teachers-new-york-city

Turner, Cory, Reema Khrais, Tim Lloyd, Alexandra Olgin, Laura Isensee, Becky Vevea, and Dan Carsen. "Why America's Schools Have a Money Problem." *NPR*. April 18, 2016. http://www.npr.org/2016/04/18/474256366/why-americas-schools-have-a-money-problem.

Ujifusa, Andrew. "Congress Weighs Federal Footprint as ESSA Rolls Out." *Education Week*. March 8, 2016. www.edweek.org/ew/articles/2016/03/09/congress-weighs-federal-footprint-as-essa-rolls.html

United University Professions. "UUP Rips SUNY over TeachNY Report." News release, May 18, 2016. http://uupinfo.org/communications/uupdate/1516/160518A.php

Walker, Tim. "Testing Obsession and the Disappearing Curriculum …" *NeaToday*. September 2, 2014. http://neatoday.org/2014/09/02/the-testing-obsession-and-the-disappearing-curriculum-2/

West, Darrell M., Grover J. Russ Whitehurst, and E. J. Dionne. "Invisible: 1.4 Percent Coverage for Education Is Not Enough." *Brookings*. December 2, 2009. https://www.brookings.edu/research/invisible-1-4-percent-coverage-for-education-is-not-enough/

Westervelt, Eric. "Where Have All The Teachers Gone?" *NPR*. March 3, 2015. http://www.npr.org/sections/ed/2015/03/03/389282733/where-have-all-the-teachers-gone

Zinshteyn, Mikhail, and Emily Richmond. "What Do Americans Really Think About Education Policy?" *The Atlantic*. August 25, 2015. www.theatlantic.com/education/archive/2015/08/two-polls-conflict-on-americans-views-of-education/402244/

3

AVID ABOUT COLLEGE

A Look into AVID's Governing Structure

Robert P. Robinson

AVID, Advancement Via Individual Determination, is a non-profit organization whose main purpose is to assist underrepresented students in their pursuit of higher education.[1] Founded in 1980 by Mary Catherine Swanson, a high school English teacher in San Diego, California, AVID seeks to provide this access by nurturing study skills, critical thinking skills, collaboration, writing development, careful reading, inquiry, and organizational skills.[2] While the program initially began in this one teacher's classroom, it has expanded across the United States and several countries, priding itself on using "research based" methods that increase its endorsements from policy makers and school districts. Schools create AVID elective courses and sections structured on these methods in hopes of using in-school time to inform the habits of mind that will increase students' chances of college entrance and persistence.[3] AVID's structure encourages schools to support the mission of a college-going culture and reinforces these practices through an implementation and coaching model based on 11 essentials.[4] Schools must meet all of these essentials as evidenced through self-assessment and observations from district directors. When schools meet these annual assessment measures, they are certified by the AVID Center as a legitimate AVID site.[5] If a school fails to meet any essential by the end of the year, it can lose certification and endorsements, thus reducing the site to "affiliate status," which lowers its recognition by the organization and universities.[6]

AVID's Funding Structure

AVID receives a large part of its funding from school districts and individual schools. In order to be an AVID site, a school or its district has to pay AVID an annual fee. In addition to these fees, districts must send at least ten faculty members to the AVID summer institute their first year. Schools maintain their certification based on the number of members who use the latest AVID strategies and suggested governing/school protocol measures taught at these summer institutes. The average cost of AVID Institute is $600 for 1 week. Maintaining a sense of style, AVID reserves hotels for all of its institutes and holds them in a number of locations in the United States, two in San Diego, its birthplace. In addition to these, there are a number of training sessions held throughout the school year for AVID coordinators, content and elective teachers, and district directors. To advance towards a "Highly Certified Site," schools must have a high percentage of their site AVID trained. They are also required to maintain an extensive "AVID Library," composed of the most recently published AVID materials. The principal must attend the AVID Institute at least once every 2 to 3 years. In short, schools and districts can pay thousands of dollars annually to maintain certification. AVID does not fund teachers' salaries or district directors' stipends, but schools and districts use Title I funds and discretionary funds to account for these positions. AVID *does* waive the training fee and institute fees for district directors as compensation for their furtherance of the AVID mission. It also provides district directors with free materials, including a complete AVID library.[7]

While this is the current funding approach, this has not always been the case. The state of California specifically allocated dollars to Mary Catherine Swanson's expansion of AVID with a 3-year grant of $195,000 through the San Diego County Office of Education beginning in 1986. With the program's rapid success and widespread growth, the state increased its AVID funding significantly. By the 1995–1996 school year, the state explicitly outlined funds to improve college-going success that had direct implications of $1 million for AVID's growth. The numbers continued to increase to a state-funded high of $12.3 million in the 2000–2001 academic year but fluctuated over subsequent years.[8] The California Department of Education funded between 100,000 and 1.2 million annually until Governor Jerry Brown's 2012 budget veto shifted all of AVID's funding to individual districts. The current iteration of district and site-based AVID implementation and certification maintenance has been in place since. Under this system, each site coordinator and site team decide the direction of AVID at the school, but those programs are certified through AVID Center's district directors.[9]

Board of Directors

AVID Center in San Diego is the organization's headquarters. Its board of directors is composed of 13 members, which includes the founder, Mary Catherine Swanson. All 13 members come from a variety of backgrounds; most of which are education related. These board members help to further AVID's mission. The CEO, Sandy Husk, is the only board member who is full-time employed by the AVID Center. The following pages will explore the board members' affiliations with other governmental, for-profit, and non-profit entities. Hopefully, these relationships will elucidate the intricate cross-educational connections within its governing body that are also reflected in the lower tiers of the organization.

Mary Catherine Swanson: Founder. Mary Catherine Swanson began the program in 1980, three years after she identified the basis for the program in her Master's thesis. The following year, she created the first site team at her school in order to supervise the successful implementation of the program.[10] This team served as the model for future sites as it included interdisciplinary teacher support, administrator presence, student representation, tutors, and university support. Twelve years later, with AVID present at more than 340 sites, Swanson established the AVID Center. She is no longer a school teacher, and she retired as CEO in 2006,[11] but she has organized a system that is now present at 5,000 schools, impacting more than 800,000 students in 44 states and 16 countries. As the long-standing face of the organization, Swanson designates the scholarship criteria for AVID center scholarships in San Diego and still speaks at AVID Institutes and conferences.

Dr. Monte Moses: Chairman of the Board. Dr. Moses was a superintendent in Colorado. Prior to this appointment, he was an administrator in the state, and before then he was administrator in Texas and Wyoming.[12] He has published two books and simultaneously served in commissions, including the Colorado iteration of the Race to the Top policies and a benchmark assessment implementation organization on the west.[13] The overlap of his standardization involvement is not coincidental, considering Race to the Top's advancing of uniform standardization. His brother has also been a Texas Commissioner of Education and Superintendent with more than one district in Texas.[14]

Dr. Sandy Husk: CEO. Dr. Sandy Husk became AVID's CEO in 2014. She implemented AVID for more than 17 years.[15] Her previous experience includes leading as a superintendent and director of schools in Oregon, Colorado, and Tennessee. Her primary focus as AVID CEO is to maintain AVID's focus on closing the achievement gap and increasing overall student achievement.[16]

Dr. Matt Gianneschi: Member. Like Husk, Matt Gianneschi has a link to Colorado. He is the CEO and Chief of Staff of a multi-school community college—Colorado Mountain College.[17] In addition, he has served as an adjunct in two Colorado institutions of higher learning as well as a university administrator at two sites. His advisory roles also extend to the regional council of governments. His background in policy and advisory across the three tiers of college education, along with his experience with College Board[18]—close partner with AVID—and ACT,[19] make him a sustainable member of the AVID Board of Directors.

Dave Gordon: Member. Dave Gordon has also served on a "number of boards and commissions, including the California Commission on Teacher Credentialing and the California Curriculum Development Commission."[20] Gordon also served on the National Assessment Governing Board during both the Bush and Obama administrations[21]—a period of time when states across the nation were instituting exit exams in their high schools. He is currently a County Superintendent of Education in Sacramento.[22]

Dr. Lionel "Skip" Meno: Member. Dr. Meno, too, shares a state governance position as a former Commissioner of Education for Texas. He currently works at San Diego State University as a "Special Assistant to the President for P-12 Education."[23] He was actively involved as the Dean of the College of Ed at the university from 1999–2007. During this time, SDSU was actively involved in the City Heights Educational Collaborative, a joint effort of Price Philanthropies[24] (formerly Price Charities), San Diego Unified School District, and San Diego State University. It seeks to improve academic achievement for the economically disadvantaged community through improved instruction and educative experiences from pre-K through higher education.

Dr. Stephen Weber: Treasurer. Continuing with San Diego State and the City Heights Educational Collaborative,[25] Dr. Stephen Weber was one of its founding members. He was instrumental in increasing the City Heights educational movement from pre-school to graduate school, even while he expanded the research reputation of San Diego State University in his presidential tenure from 1996–2011.[26] Prior to his SDSU presidency, he was the interim provost of the State University of New York and 7-year president of the Oswego campus of the system.[27] His career as a university administrator stretches more than 30 years.[28]

Dr. Eric J. Smith: Member. Another Commissioner of Education, Smith was instrumental in the evaluation criteria for teachers in Florida as he instituted "grading formulas" and specific graduation criteria.[29] Like Dr. Montes, he has a past affiliation with the College Board, assisting with their "College Readiness" initiative. He is also a Colorado alum—Colorado State University. He is now advisor to the George W. Bush Institute's Advancing Accountability program.[30]

Melendy Lovett: Member. Melendy Lovett's trajectory is an intriguing one. She worked with Texas Instruments for a number of years as both their Senior Vice President and President of their Ed Tech Business.[31] She worked in both this capacity and in her role on the advisory board simultaneously.[32] I do not believe this is coincidental, since Texas Instruments is the premier calculator with high SAT approval.[33] Lovett is a certified accountant and major proponent for female inclusion in STEM.[34] Last year, she left Texas Instruments and accepted a role as Senior Vice President with Trinity Industries, a company that raked in $1.68 billion last quarter across its divisions, $220 million of which was net income.[35]

Lower-Profile, Big Income: Clarence Fields, Nori Juba, Sue Levin, and Todd Gutschow. Clarence Fields was in Mary Catherine Swanson's inaugural AVID class. He is Secretary of the AVID Board of Directors. He has worked for Xerox for 20 years. Nori Juba is "co-chair of the Bend La Pine School District in Bend, OR."[36] Juba was also a private investor and business consultant. This private investment is connected to LF Investments, which shares a connection with Swader Pace Capital and Prudential Capital.[37] Sue Levin is "Chief Marketing Officer at Bolt Threads, Inc." She also serves on a non-profit advisory board where she was once the Executive Director. Her focus is on movement and play in education. She created her own women's active wear company for which she presides as CEO.[38] Todd Gutschow is retired from Fair Isaac & Company, which acquired HNC Software Incorporated. He founded the latter in the 1980s, and developed software for large retail companies and financial organizations/ institutions.[39] He was also a former school board member in Poway and now serves on a variety of advisory boards.

From the Board to Executive Leadership

In addition to Dr. Sandy Husk, five other members operate in the "executive" domain. These members collaborate to carry out the missions established by Swanson, Husk, and the advisory board, and each is active in the AVID Center based in San Diego, California. The following subsection will only discuss the roles of two members: the Chief Financial Officer (CFO), Robert Markee, and the Executive Vice President of Curriculum and Learning, Michelle Mullen. The remaining Executive Vice Presidents are Dr. Edward Lee Vargas, Robert Gira (research communication and quality teams), and Steve Silberman (business operations). The combined narratives of the executive team will be discussed with more detail in the "Implications for AVID's Focus" section.

Robert Markee: Chief Financial Officer. Markee joined AVID in 2008. As CFO, he oversees "accounting contracts, events, human resources procurement, and travel teams."[40] Besides 30 years in finance, human resources, accounting, and similar fields, Markee was responsible for Starwood Hotels and Resorts' processing system, which garnered over $400 million annually. Some of the programs he previously oversaw included, but were not limited to, public relations, global sales, and marketing.[41]

Michelle Mullen: Executive Vice President, Curriculum and Learning. With a considerable teaching career and 10-year National Board Certification tenure, Mullen serves as a long-standing practitioner. She has also served as director and adjunct professor of the Single Subject Credential Program[42] at California State University San Marcos.[43] In her earlier time with AVID, Mullen was the national director of curriculum and initiatives and lead of AVID's English Learner College Readiness initiatives. She currently oversees "professional learning, leadership, IDEA (Instructional Design & Learning Arts) curriculum, EL, and publication teams." Mullen has some of the most significant responsibilities in curriculum development for the organization, as she coordinates the AVID national Conference and the AVID Summer Institute.[44]

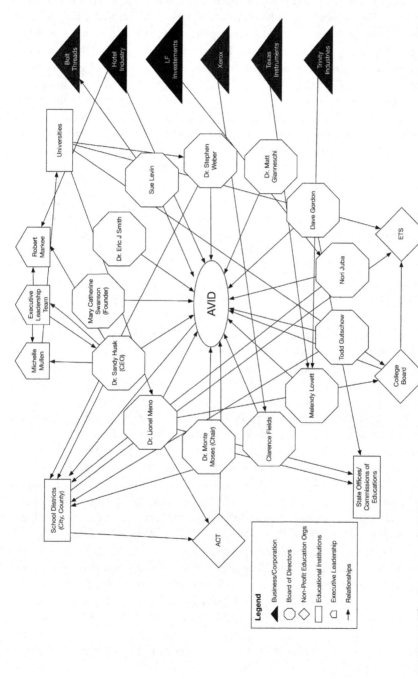

FIGURE 3.1 The Structure of AVID

Implications for AVID's Focus

After examining this web, one can notice a number of connections. Obviously, many of the members of the board have a history of district leadership, university administration experience, and/or state policy governance. This is a logical line-up, considering how AVID is a college preparatory program that emphasizes persistence beyond the post-secondary years. At the same time, given its growth over the past 35+ years, AVID has morphed significantly since its inception.[45] What was initially more of a culturally relevant[46] organization built on deep holistic growth between teacher, student, tutor, and family, has become a large-scale organization[47] that has spread beyond the local context and into small international footprints.[48] The background of the board members might speak to the more bureaucratized look of AVID. Let us take a closer look.

Looking at the work of Dave Gordon, the reader can recall that he has spent a significant amount of time with the national body responsible for assessment. Call it coincidence, but his tenure extended through both terms of the Bush administration, a period of time when state Title I measures[49] became attached to schools' respective high school education exit requirements. Also during this time, prior to the Common Core, the federal government instituted uniform assessment at specific grade levels that would determine ways schools were funded. These "No Child Left Behind" (NCLB) compliant assessments have implications for all schools' and districts' federal funding. If schools do not demonstrate adequate progress on these standardized measures for the target populations, the federal government can restructure or close the school.[50] Along these same premises of bureaucratic federal funding, we can apply a similar lens to Dr. Monte Moses' Race to the Top background in Colorado. As chairman of the board, he sets the framework for the vision. Race to the Top offered a nearly 10 percent additional incentive to states that agreed to be early adoptees of the Common Core State Standards by offering federal funds.[51] This national symbol of bureaucracy through state policy mirrors AVID's hierarchical structure from the board to the students through use of the 11 essentials framework. At the AVID 2012 National Conference, entire sessions focused on AVID and the Common Core. AVID's attempt to remain relevant in a Common Core-driven curricular and pedagogical moment is logical as these uniform visions of skills-based education also impact higher education. The other members' histories can speak to this attempt at relevance.

Continuing the discussion of testing and standardization, we cannot overlook AVID's relationship with the College Board. AVID partners with the organization annually for its national conference. More important, under the 11 essentials, AVID requires each site to provide SAT or ACT scores for a majority of its juniors and all of its seniors.[52] Keep in mind that College Board has one of the largest connections to higher education institutions via the SAT and a number of their preparation efforts.[53] With 4-year institutions as their main focus, both non-profits work in concert. AVID's connection to the ACT (American College

Test/Testing) Program is not as strong, but as an entrance exam organization, they are also listed in the certification criteria. Dr. Gianneschi's earlier work with the ACT organization demonstrates yet another bridge, a place where AVID again connects to the world of testing. The ACT is also a sponsor of the AVID National Conference.[54] Because AVID is so heavily dependent upon these tests and sustains multiple connections to their supervising organizations, one must question their impact on AVID as an organization.

Along with testing, curricular transitions are also an important point of analysis. As previously stated, AVID requires all of its school sites to implement the AVID curriculum, and these materials are made available through their annual fees as well as purchases of AVID libraries,[55] *AVID Weekly*,[56] and trainings at the AVID Institute. All of these curricula and resources require district funding and additional educator time. They align with current trends in education, which is important for any college preparatory program's status in the field of education. Furthermore, it is no coincidence that the executive vice president who heads the curricular leadership position holds a National Board Certification or that the CEO is a former superintendent. For these reasons, and the aforementioned funding change in California that moved away from regional AVID programs, we see the shift to a district director model in leadership wherein each district pays an existing employee a sub-modest stipend to supervise any number of AVID sites. This certification process is akin to the current administrators' protocol at school sites, which favor data-driven analysis. With the number of superintendents who advise in the AVID program, and the additional leadership presence of accountability expert, Eric J. Smith—who works for the George W. Bush Institute—one could understand how AVID strictly adheres to the 11 essentials. The organization is merely a reflection of its core leadership.

The executive leadership team members also reveal much about the changes in the organization's trajectory. With the exception of the CFO and the VP of business operations, all of the members have strong educational backgrounds, which include two former superintendents, one administrator, and one National Board Certified educator. The CFO also served at the height of his particular field prior to his AVID tenure; $400 million in annual sales for a hotel company that hosts some of the largest names in luxury hotels is more than noteworthy. Equally impressive is the Human Resources lead, Steve Silberman's Fortune 500 background. AVID's mission for *excellence* is embedded into all tiers of the leadership, and no more evident is the list of credentials than with the board of directors and the executive leadership team.

Money in education is a complicated but necessary conversation. Remembering the executive leadership team, let us explore AVID's role with money, beginning with the CFO. Markee previously developed finance accounting and reporting tools for the Starwood Hotel and Resorts company. AVID holds every national conference at a major hotel. The last four alone have been held at Hilton locations,[57] and every AVID Summer Institute is held at a hotel, so one must consider how the chief financial officer would have a background in hotel finance. Granted, Markee's former employer was not connected to Hilton, but the close industry experience cannot be overlooked.

As previously noted, AVID receives funding from the ACT and College Board for their national conference. Texas Instruments, former home of board member Melendi Lovett, has also donated to the AVID national conference. In return, the organization promotes other college-going organizations and receives indirect funding from them via schools and districts. Remember this: districts and schools fund the AVID program at sites. Schools will often pay for AVID through funds available in other spaces. GEAR UP (Gaining Early Awareness and Readiness for Undergraduate Programs), a federally funded college preparation grant that assists cohorts of low-income students from middle school to high school, funds multiple sites that have AVID programs.[58] On AVID's site, they list GEAR UP as a potential source for funding its measures. In turn, GEAR UP—through its annual capacity building workshops—lists AVID as a form of college-going sustainability for schools who are thinking about life after the GEAR UP grant. GEAR UP is not alone in its AVID support network; Trio, SIG, and i3[59] are also listed among other government-funded organizations, in addition to the more than 50 "friends of AVID" non-profit, government, and for-profit contributors.[60] AVID's network is composed of people who move fluidly between two or more high-powered non-profits organizations; Stephen J. Ball would refer to them as flexians.[61] Some of AVID's flexians include Melendy Lovett, Matt Gianneschi, Stephen Weber, and Dave Gordon, respectively connected to STEM education/Texas Instruments (formerly), ACT, Price Philanthropies, and the College Board. Such flexians speak to an organization of cross-pollination wherein businesses, philanthropic organizations, and government interests carry considerable voice in the direction of an education-based organization. How consistent are these interests with the original educational mission of the organization, and what are the direct implications on AVID site teams and the students they serve?

In order to maintain its reputation, AVID requires each site to monitor and report its own data. Data include demographics of the programs at each site and their relationship to the greater school demographics, including population of free/reduced lunch, attendance, and graduation rates. AVID Center uses this data to provide incentive for other sites to adopt AVID, and for other non-profits or local businesses to fund AVID endeavors at each site. Consequently, sites, organizations, and AVID are caught in this cycle, wherein each feeds the other. Sadly, while AVID and the non-profit organizations receive positive recognition from the schools' data and positive PR, schools rarely receive enough to fund tutors necessary to meet student needs or certification requirements. In short, AVID requirements place undue strains on those most closely connected to the population it professes to serve by placing the onus for program sustainability on the coordinators and instructors.

Still, even after this analysis, there are no major financially salacious findings. AVID does not maintain a private jet or high-powered investments on the stock market. Nevertheless, they charge enormous amounts to financially strapped schools and districts to maintain their programs with no additional compensation for the teachers and coordinators who put in the necessary teaching effort and extensive amounts of data entry. They provide scant subsidized opportunities for their institutes and materials, and their meager compensation for student speakers/presenters include meals and a T-shirt. While they are a college-focused organization, they provide few direct scholarship opportunities. Perhaps the scandal lies in the grandeur and expensiveness of their conferences and Institutes, as they stand in stark contrast to thousands of exploited, under-compensated teachers and underfunded lower socioeconomic students.

Conclusion

College entrance and success is still at AVID's core, but the focus on the essentials leaves a rigid adherence to its uniform implementation. Less of a rich explication of the AVID teacher's role[62] as counselor, teacher, and advisor, the program has been—according to a teacher I once spoke with—more "checklist focused." Teachers see their work with AVID Center as unnecessarily bureaucratic and tedious—a data-driven force that does more to impede their creative development of pedagogy and strategies for student success. Consequently, the teachers and coordinators have an increasingly adversarial relationship with district directors or AVID Center leads. But this rigidity makes sense in light of the number of people who have worked with initiatives based on large-scale standardization. Of the nine board members who are not business people, over half worked with some major standardized initiative. Of the six executive leads, half were administrators and two of those three are former superintendents. These realities speak to an increasingly corporatized version of AVID that looks much different from the class of 32 students in the initial years.[63] Furthermore, even after being accepted to more prestigious institutions, the economically disadvantaged students who make up the plurality of the target group are forced to scour for college funding in order to reduce student loan debt.[64] Only those with the most elite scores of the group receive scholarship money from AVID Center or scholarship organizations. Worse yet, in cities like Chicago that face some of the harshest socioeconomic and educational hurdles, educators wonder whether or not AVID is truly impacting student success.[65] Being mindful of these complicated educational and socioeconomic dynamics, important questions remain. What is the purpose of a high-profile leadership team with connections to business, testing agencies, and major educational entities if the teachers remain over-worked and underpaid and only the most elite AVID students receive college funding support? How do these key players within systems of governance[66] shape or reshape the mission of the organization? Finally, in its attempt to maintain relevance in an ever-economized education system, has AVID fallen subject to practices that further reveal, or sometimes perpetuate, the marginalization of already marginalized groups?

Notes

1 "What Is AVID?," accessed June 28, 2016, www.avid.org/what-is-avid.ashx
2 "AVID's History," accessed June 28, 2016, www.avid.org/history.ashx
3 "AVID Secondary Student' College Enrollment and Persistence: What Equity Gaps?," accessed August 1, 2016, www.avid.org/_documents/NSC.pdf. Note: persistence here refers to students' continued enrollment in 4-year/4-year+ educational institutions.
4 "What Is AVID?"
5 Charlotte S. Ford, "Impact of the Advancement via Individual Determination (AVID) Program on Closing the Academic Achievement Gap" (Ph.D., The University of Texas at Arlington, 2010).
6 "Fall Certification Packet With Guidelines," accessed June 28, 2016, https://my.avid.org/files/4115.pdf
7 "Event Registration: My Registration List," accessed June 28, 2016, https://my.avid.org/event_registration/registration_list.aspx. Note this cited information is connected to a password-protected login that shows the author's training as an AVID elective teacher, AVID Coordinator, and AVID District Director.
8 Joseph Robert Radding, "From Invention to Reform: The Evolution of AVID in California's Public Schools" (Ed.D., University of California, Davis, 2010), http://search.proquest.com.ezproxy.gc.cuny.edu/education/docview/757340624/abstract/2655A78104FA4AC5PQ/18
9 John Fensterwald, July 10 and 2012, 8 Comments, "Brown's Veto Throws Wrench in AVID College Prep Program," EdSource, accessed June 28, 2016, https://edsource.org/2012/browns-veto-throws-wrench-in-avid-college-prep-program/17521
10 Radding, "From Invention to Reform."
11 "Board of Directors," accessed June 28, 2016, www.avid.org/board-of-directors.ashx
12 "Board of Directors."
13 "Monte Moses, Ph.D., Rose Community Foundation," accessed June 24, 2016, www.rcfdenver.org/content/monte-moses-phd
14 "Board of Directors."
15 "Sandy Husk, Ph.D.," U.S. News STEM Solutions, accessed June 24, 2016, http://usnewsstemsolutions.com/speakers/sandy-husk-ph-d/
16 "Board of Directors."
17 "Dr. Matt Gianneschi of Colorado Department of Higher Ed to Deliver Commencement Address," accessed June 24, 2016, https://www.ccaurora.edu/news-events/news-releases/gianneschi-to-give-commencement-address
18 "Board of Directors."
19 "2015 National Conference," accessed June 28, 2016, www.avid.org/2015-national-conference.ashx
20 "Board of Directors."
21 "Overview/NAGB," accessed June 24, 2016, https://www.nagb.org/who-we-are/overview.html. Board responsible for the Nation's Report Card—reveals standardized progress across the country.
22 "David Gordon," Alliance for Excellent Education, accessed June 24, 2016, http://all4ed.org/people/david-gordon/
23 "Board of Directors."

24 "Background, Price Philanthropies," accessed June 24, 2016, http://pricephilanthropies.org/about-us/price-philanthropies/
25 "Board of Directors."
26 "NewsCenter, SDSU, SDSU President Stephen Weber to Retire in 2011," accessed June 28, 2016, http://newscenter.sdsu.edu/sdsu_newscenter/news_story.aspx?sid=72325
27 "Board of Directors."
28 "San Diego State University Oral Histories, SDSU Library and Information Access," accessed June 28, 2016, http://library.sdsu.edu/scua/sdsu-oral-histories/weber
29 "Board of Directors."
30 "Eric J. Smith," accessed June 24, 2016, www.bushcenter.org/people/eric-j-smith.html
31 P. R. Newswire, "TI's Peter Balyta to Head Education Technology Division; Melendy Lovett To Retire," TheStreet, February 7, 2014, https://www.thestreet.com/story/12317320/2/tis-peter-balyta-to-head-education-technology-division-melendy-lovett-to-retire.html
32 "Trinity Industries, Inc. Announces Executive Appointment by Texas Instruments—US and Canada," accessed June 24, 2016, https://education.ti.com/en/us/about/press-center/press-listing-content-module/02-17-2014-melendy-trinity
33 "Calculator Policy," SAT Suite of Assessments, January 13, 2016, https://collegereadiness.collegeboard.org/sat/taking-the-test/calculator-policy
34 "WITI—Women in Technology Hall of Fame—Melendy Lovett, President, Texas Instruments Education Technology," accessed June 24, 2016, www.witi.com/center/witimuseum/halloffame/128735/Melendy-Lovett-President-Texas-Instruments-Education-Technology/
35 "Trinity Industries Announces Strong Second Quarter 2015 Results—Windtech International," accessed June 28, 2016, www.windtech-international.com/company-news/trinity-industries-announces-strong-second-quarter-2015-results
36 "Board of Directors."
37 Carver Scientific Inc. et al., "Nori Juba, LinkedIn," accessed June 28, 2016, https://www.linkedin.com/in/norijuba
38 "Board of Directors."
39 Self Employed et al., "Todd Gutschow, LinkedIn," accessed June 28, 2016, https://www.linkedin.com/in/todd-gutschow-9047243
40 "Executive Leadership," accessed June 29, 2016, www.avid.org/executive-leadership.ashx
41 "Starwood Hotels & Resorts," accessed June 24, 2016, www.starwoodhotels.com/corporate/about/index.html.
42 "Distinguished Teachers in Residence Program, Outreach/Partnerships, School of Education, CSUSM," accessed June 29, 2016, https://www.csusm.edu/soe/collaborationandoutreach/dtir.html
43 Michelle Mullen "EDSS 511 – Teaching and Learning in Secondary Schools" syllabus, accessed June 29, 2016, https://lynx.csusm.edu/coe/ArchiveSyllabi/Summer2005/EDSS.511-Stall.Mullen.pdf
44 "Executive Leadership."
45 Radding, "From Invention to Reform."
46 Michael R. McKenna, "Examining the Advancement Via Individual Determination (AVID) Program Using the Framework of Social Capital Theory: A Case Study of the AVID Program in a High-Achieving, Suburban High School" (Ed.D., Temple University,

2011), http://search.proquest.com.ezproxy.gc.cuny.edu/education/docview/874271479/abstract/98F06D9073D842CEPQ/1

47 Ford, "Impact of the Advancement via Individual Determination (AVID) Program on Closing the Academic Achievement Gap."
48 "What Is AVID?"
49 "Title I, Part A Program," Program Home Page, October 5, 2015, www2.ed.gov/programs/titleiparta/index.html. Title I is the federal program created under the Elementary and Secondary Education Act (ESEA) of 1965 that provided funds to schools with high concentrations of economically disadvantaged students.
50 Diane Ravitch, *The Death and Life of the Great American School System How Testing and Choice Are Undermining Education* (New York: Basic Books, 2010).
51 "Innovation in America's School under Race to the Top" accessed June 24, 2016, http://www2.ed.gov/programs/racetothetop/rttfinalrptfull.pdf
52 "AVID Implementation Essentials," accessed June 28, 2016, https://my.avid.org/files/9493.pdf
53 "About Us," The College Board, October 10, 2013, https://www.collegeboard.org/about
54 "2015 National Conference."
55 The more AVID libraries, the higher the school's certification score.
56 "AVID Implementation Essentials." AVID Weekly is AVID's student-friendly close reading of reprinted texts from reputable news sources, which also includes lesson plans.
57 "Previous Conferences," accessed June 29, 2016, www.avid.org/Previous-Conferences.ashx
58 "Gaining Early Awareness and Readiness for Undergraduate Programs (GEAR UP)," accessed June 28, 2016, http://www2.ed.gov/programs/gearup/index.html
59 "Higher Education Public Funding Resources," accessed June 29, 2016, http://www.avid.org/higher-ed.ashx
60 "Friends of AVID," accessed June 29, 2016, www.avid.org/friends-of-avid.ashx
61 Stephen J. Ball, *Global Education, Inc.: New Policy Networks and the Neoliberal Imaginary* (London; New York: Routledge, 2012).
62 Radding, "From Invention to Reform."
63 "AVID's History."
64 McKenna, "Examining the Advancement Via Individual Determination (AVID) Program Using the Framework of Social Capital Theory a Case Study of the AVID Program in a High-Achieving, Suburban High School."
65 Sarah D. Sparks, "Chicago Study Finds Mixed Results for AVID Program—Education Week," *Education Week*, May 11, 2011, www.edweek.org/ew/articles/2011/05/06/30avid_ep.h30.html
66 Ball, *Global Education, Inc.: New Policy Networks and the Neoliberal Imaginary*.

4

A NOT SO INDIVIDUALIZED EDUCATION PLAN

Examining NYC DOE Contract with Maximus that Brought Us SESIS

Amy Goods

Freddie Boyce: A Child Lost in the System

Born in 1941, Freddie Boyce was the second son of Mina Boyce. At age 20, Mina Boyce was made a widow when her husband committed suicide months before Freddie was born. One day Mina Boyce left her two sons, the eldest 2 years and the youngest 6 months, alone at home as she went out. A neighbor heard the boys alone in their tenement apartment and called the police. Social services intervened, separating the family and sending the boys to live in different foster care homes. And so, at age 6 months, Freddie entered the foster care system. He would spend the next 7 years of his life being sent from one loveless foster home to the next until being ultimately institutionalized at age 7. The reason for the institutionalization? Freddie would be deemed "feeble minded," labeled "mentally retarded" by a court psychiatrist.

Freddie Boyce had tested poorly on the Intelligence Quotient (IQ) Test administered by the court psychiatrist. At the age of 7, Freddie could neither read nor write. How could he? Only one of his foster parents had attempted to send him to school. At age 6, that school had deemed Freddie too far behind his peers to warrant an education, saying that they would have to hire a special teacher to catch Freddie up. The school claimed that since Freddie was not really a member of the community, but rather a ward of the state, the local school should not be burdened by the cost.

And so, as Freddie Boyce sat to take the IQ test he was puzzled by the crayons that he was asked to draw with, as he had never before used crayons. He could not answer the arithmetic questions. Shapes and colors eluded him. Therefore, Freddie Boyce, a child, was sent to the infamous Fernald School. Freddie would spend his formative years locked away from the rest of the world. At the Fernald

School, Freddie received a rudimentary education. He was tortured, made to sit silently for hours on a wooden bench unmoving. He bore witness to children being hit and humiliated, with no advocates to protect them. He was experimented on—joining a "science club" where researched boys were fed radioactive oatmeal in order to study the effects.[1]

In 1993, Freddie Boyce had his day in court, speaking eloquently and "from the heart"[2] about his experiences at Fernald. Freddie was awarded a small settlement for the atrocities committed against him. However, the money could not cure the growing cancer within him from the horrific experiments conducted on him as a child.

Freddie was lost in a system. He never had an advocate. As a child, he never received the education that he deserved. Freddie's story is just one of many stories of children who needed special services and were cast aside by society. What happened to Freddie is unconscionable. We need a system that ensures all children, regardless of upbringing, receive a fair and equitable education. We need a system that holds schools and institutions accountable for providing appropriate services to our children. We need to make sure that our most vulnerable children have an advocate and a chance at the best possible life.

What is an IEP?

Individualized Education Plans (IEPs) emerged from the Education for All Handicapped Children Act (EHA) passed by the United States Congress in 1975.[3] EHA made it mandatory for schools to provide special education services to students with special needs, requiring that all students, regardless of special education status, have the right to receive an education. Over time, EHA was amended to include specific rules and guidelines for schools to ensure that all students would have access to equitable services. As part of this amendment process, EHA was renamed[4] in 1990 and is now referred to as the Individuals with Disability in Education Act (IDEA). IEP documentation emerged as a result of IDEA.

Individualized Education Plans (IEPs) are documents written specifically for students who require special "individualized services" in order to fully participate in the school day. A student is eligible for an IEP and its services if the student meets one or more of the following criteria: Autism, Deafness, Deaf-Blindness, Emotional Disturbance, Hearing Impairment, Learning Disability, Intellectual Disability, Multiple Disability, Orthopedic Impairment, Other Health Impairment (for example illness, Tourette's, or ADHD), Speech or Language Impairment, Traumatic Brain Injury, or Visual Impairment. If a student is deemed to meet one or more of the above criteria, then a unique team composed of the student's teachers, parents, administrators, and, if appropriate, the student is convened to develop an IEP.

Currently, the IEP of each student with special needs in the NYC DOE fits into a uniform template. The uniformity of this template makes thousands of individualized education plans look nearly identical. To begin, the IEP includes a cover page that states the student name, date of birth, date of annual review of IEP, and the disability category in which the student fits. Following the cover page is the Present Level of Performance, or PLOP. The PLOP includes evaluation results from state tests, Wechsler test, Woodcock Johnson test, and/or other IQ evaluation exams that outline a student's performance. The PLOP also contains a section on academic achievement, social development, physical development, and management needs.

Following the PLOP are sections of the IEP that contain a behavioral plan (if needed) and individualized goals used to measure student progress. These goals should align with the rationale for designing an IEP. The goals can be academic in nature, but also include goals outside the realm of academics such as social goals, organizational goals, and/or physical goals. If a student requires external goals beyond the academic goal structure then the student will often also receive additional services. These services may include occupational therapy, counseling, speech, and/or physical therapy. Some schools offer such services within the school day, others do not. If it is determined that a student needs physical therapy, for example, and there is no physical therapist on staff at the school, the school must then work with the family to provide services. This may mean bringing in a physical therapist to the school or arranging for the student to receive services outside the school day. To ensure that goals are being met and services are provided, there is a section of the IEP entitled "reporting to parents." This section outlines how often parents will receive updates on student progress.

Following "reporting to parents" there is a section on "testing accommodations," which outline how students with an IEP will participate in mandated state testing. Accommodations may include extra time, use of a scribe or computer, large print tests, directions or questions read aloud, a separate location with fewer students taking an exam, frequent breaks or snacks, or an alternative test format.

Following the section on "testing accommodations" the remaining sections include transportation needs of the student (i.e. bussing), transitional needs of the student (i.e. job training/housing after the student leaves the school) and need for alternative placement (i.e. a private school or year-round services). Finally, there is a summary page. On this page, the previous documentation is displayed in a concise form. Additionally, the summary page includes any modifications to the IEP. Modifications are ways in which the curriculum is altered for students with an IEP. In New York State, students are required to master certain standards in math and English Language Arts (ELA) in order to pass to the next grade. Up until the 2015–16 academic year, students had to score proficiently on state math and ELA tests in order to pass to the next grade. If a student with an IEP had modifications, this meant that they would only be required to master a certain percentage of the standards in order to advance to the next grade. The school must provide evidence that the student met the modified criteria indicated on the IEP in order for that student to advance to the next grade. Modifications, however, only apply to students who are grades K-8. High school students with an IEP must master all standards set forth by the New York State Board of Regents in order to graduate with a Regents diploma.

What is SESIS?

The Special Education Student Information System (SESIS) provides a centralized system for educators to access IEPs within New York City schools. As shown above, there are many essential components in putting together an IEP. Before SESIS, IEPs were largely handwritten and stored in filing cabinets in school offices. Schools had their own approaches to writing IEPs. When writing IEPs there was little oversight and implementation was spotty. Under the previous system, in order to investigate service implementation, Department of Education (DOE) representatives had to visit each school, pore over the paper IEPs located in filing cabinets, and observe classrooms to see if special education services were in compliance with IEPs. With the adaptation of SESIS, oversight committees are now able to log onto SESIS and view IEP documents electronically. Furthermore, there is peace of mind from the teachers and administration that all required parts of an IEP are filled out. The program does not let the school finalize an IEP until all required components of the IEP are complete. Furthermore, if the IEP is not finalized by the annual review date, a notice is sent to the DOE oversight office and the school is considered "out of compliance."

SESIS not only made oversight easier, it also made implementation easier. Through SESIS, educators and school service providers (such as occupational therapists, speech therapists, physical therapists, counselors, and social workers) can view, create, and edit the IEPs. Instead of having to go down to the central office to read about students and review documents, a service provider or teacher can log onto SESIS on their computer and review IEPs, making it easier to learn about students and provide services as IEPs are amended, changed, and implemented.

Individualized Education Plans emerged from the Education for All Handicapped Children Act (EHA) passed by the United States Congress in 1975. EHA made it mandatory for schools to provide special education services to students with special needs, requiring that all students, regardless of special education status, are required to receive an education. Over time, EHA was amended to include specific rules and guidelines for schools to ensure that all students would have access to equitable services.

In New York City public schools nearly 200,000 students receive special education services. The New York City Department of Education saw a need to streamline the IEP process. The DOE was looking for a computerized system that allowed data on student services to be shared easily between service providers and teachers, as well as from school to school. The DOE also hoped that a system could be developed that insured that all IEPs were written to a certain quality standard, and hoped that the data tracking system could put into place central monitoring capabilities to ensure that all schools were in compliance with federal IDEA.[5]

SESIS acts as a centralized database where student information can be stored and monitored for compliance with special education laws and policies. There is no doubt that a centralized database makes writing and implementing IEPs easier for teachers and service providers. However, the SESIS system is not without its faults. SESIS loses student data, crashes, and is not compatible with other student data tracking systems within the DOE. With a $79 million price tag, all the issues with SESIS makes one ask the question, is SESIS the *best* system for NYC DOE?

Maximus and the Contracting of SESIS in New York City

Special Education Student Information System (SESIS) was born out of concerns from DOE officials in an effort to stream special education services across the district. In 2009, Maximus, a Virginia-based consulting company, won the DOE contract and signed the $79 million agreement offering computer software services as a solution to the lack in continuity in IEP development and implementation in NYC.[6] The program offered by Maximus was not entirely new. Admittedly, the special education software was simply a repackaging of the software TIENENT, a special education reporting tool first designed for the Chicago Public Schools. Initially, some officials had concerns with the repurposed system. The Chicago Public Schools System pupil population is around one-third as large as New York City Schools. Officials in the DOE were worried that the SESIS system could not sustain the additional student numbers in New York. However, Maximus officials quelled the fears, stating, "Naturally, we'll have to interface it with the systems of New York City, and we'll have to train the users in New York City on how to use it. But it should not be viewed as a custom-build situation."[7] Ultimately, the fact that the system had been used in the Chicago School System with relative success gave officials in the DOE peace of mind, and Maximus won the contract, not only for the software itself, but also for the professional development of teachers that went with the implementation of the software.

New York City's Deputy Superintendent of Office of Special Education Initiative, Linda Wernikoff, was a strong supporter of Maximus's proposal.[8] In 2009, after contract negotiations with Maximus were complete, Ms. Wernikoff left the DOE and was hired at the Fund for Public Schools as a DOE consultant on SESIS. Though Ms. Wernikoff had not yet been out of the DOE long enough to qualify for this job transition (the consultant job with Fund for Public Schools was a conflict of interest), the DOE signed a waiver allowing for Ms. Wernikoff to collect a $1,000-a day consulting contract from the Fund for Public Schools on top of her DOE pension.[9] It is also an interesting coincidence that 3 years after Ms. Wernikoff's departure from the DOE and subsequent job with Fund for Public Schools, a Fund for Public Schools 2013 Annual Report revealed that Maximus donated $50,000–$99,000 to the Fund.[10]

Problems with the Roll Out of SESIS

The roll out of SESIS in the New York City DOE was bumpy. A 2013 audit completed by the Office of City Comptroller found that SESIS had failed to uphold its end of the contract in that it had failed to "meet its overall goal to provide users with accurate and reliable data."[11] The report found that data of special education students in SESIS included multiple errors, causing information to be lost and data to be duplicated. As a result, many IEPs had to be manually edited, negating the purpose of the SESIS program in the first place. Not only was the program not working as advertised, 4 years in, but it had not yet been integrated with Automate the Schools (ATS), the existing data system used by NYC DOE schools. ATS allows NYC DOE schools to hold biographical information, student enrollment and transfers, grade level, attendance, student immunizations, as well as state test scores. Instead of integrating with existing systems, information from SESIS had to be manually entered from SESIS into ATS. Furthermore, Maximus had failed to make timely corrections with "bugs" in the software systems, leading to website crashes and 100,000 errors in data entry per month.

The Office of City Comptroller outlined 17 suggestions for the DOE to follow through with in order to meet the requirements of the 2009 agreed-upon contract with Maximus. One such suggestion was to "immediately perform an on-site review of Maximus's operations in order to ensure that Maximus's policies and procedure comply with DOE directives and contract agreements."[12] In response to the 17 suggestions, Andrew Buher,[13] Chief Operating Officer of the DOE, went on record as defending Maximus, stating that the office of Comptroller's investigation was premature as Maximus had not yet had ample time to work out the kinks of the new operation (Comptroller Report Appendix).[14]

The audit also found users of SESIS were unhappy with the program as they were frustrated with the constant crashing of the system and viewed SESIS as adding little value to their teaching practice.[15] While the investigation of The Office of the Comptroller on SESIS was underway, the United Federation of Teachers was also conducting its own investigation. Because of SESIS's glitches and poor training of employees during its roll out, many teachers and service providers were forced to log on to SESIS to complete their work after contracted hours. In April of 2013, the UFT was awarded a settlement of $41 million in back pay to nearly 30,000 teachers and service providers who had logged onto SESIS to complete mandatory work after contracted hours.[16]

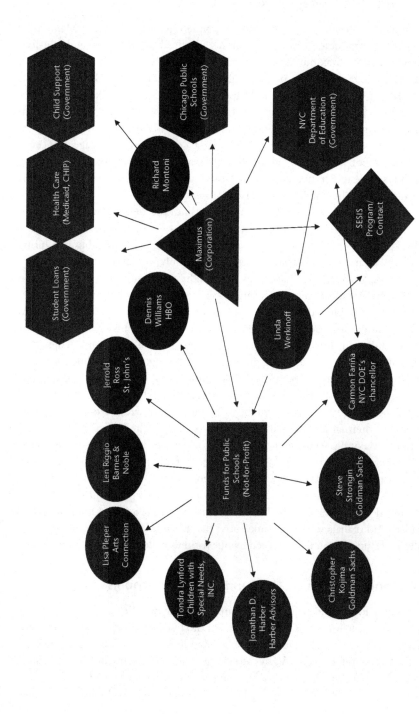

FIGURE 4.1 Structure of The Fund for Public Schools

Following the Money: Maximus

Maximus Inc's motto is "helping the government to help people."[17] Maximus is a for-profit corporation that does business with mostly government and non-for-profit agencies.[18] Maximus is publicly traded and is currently valued at nearly $4.5 billion. It has gained profits by securing contracts in the United States, Australia, Canada, the United Kingdom, and Saudi Arabia.[19] The Chief Executive Officer of Maximus is Richard Montoni. Between the years of 2008 and 2012, Montoni received compensation packages totaling $16,194,847, making him the "highest paid social worker in the country."[20] This large compensation package came after a $30.5 million settlement in a 2007 criminal case whereupon Montoni and Maximus came under investigation for falsifying Medicaid claims with the District of Columbia's Child and Family Services Agency.[21]

On Maximus's website[22] the company outlines the fields in which Maximus provides services. The reach of services includes areas such as health, managing federal programs, child support, education, workforce, consulting, business hiring compliance, and tax credit incentives. Most notably, Maximus corporation also services such government accounts as Children's Health Insurance Program (CHIP), Medicaid, Medicare, welfare-to-work, and child support services.

In 2010, the United States Congress passed the Affordable Care Act (ACA) and Maximus positioned themselves to make great profits from ACA. The company did this by offering DecisionPoint™, a set of "solutions designed to help states manage their growing public insurance programs, including Medicaid, CHIP and state-based marketplaces."[23] Maximus competed with companies such as FTI Consulting, Korn/Ferry International, and ICF International for state and federal healthcare exchange contracts. Maximus ultimately won the contract because of their familiarity with the inner workings of the health care system.[24]

Since Maximus went public in 1997, stock prices have risen steadily. Since 2010, after the passage of the ACA, Maximus's stock prices rose from just under $20 a share to over $60 a share, and have been consistently rising ever since.[25] The most recent bump in stock prices came from a 2014 announcement that Maximus was awarded a contract by the U.S. Department of Education's Office of Federal Student Aid management. Maximus now has its hand in managing the nearly $1 trillion of student loan debt accrued by our nation's college educated individuals.[26]

Following the Money: The Fund for Public Schools

The Fund for Public Schools was started by Mayor Michael Bloomberg and Schools Chancellor Joel Klein in 2002. On the Fund for Public Schools website, their mission states "The Fund for Public Schools is dedicated to improving New York City's public schools by attracting private investment in the school system."[27] The board members include Carmon Fariña, NYC DOE's current chancellor, as well as Jonathan D. Harber (Harber Advisors, LLC), Christopher

Kojima (Goldman Sachs), Tondra Lynford (Resources for Children with Special Needs, Inc.), Lisa Plepler (ArtsConnection), Len Riggio (Barnes & Noble), Jerrold Ross (The School of Education at St. John's University), Steve Strongin (Goldman Sachs), Dennis Williams (HBO), and Kathy Wylde (The Partnership for New York City).[28] It is estimated that the Fund for Public Schools raises over $48.5 million annually to provide "innovative system-wide change to NYC public schools."[29] An examination into the board of the Fund for Public Schools raises these questions: Why would corporations and private entities be interested in investing in an organization that invests in public schools? If the corporation wanted to donate money to our schools, why not give directly? What is the need for an organization such as the Fund for Public Schools?

In May of 2015 the *New York Times* reported that the Fund for Public Schools was having difficulty raising money under Mayor Bill de Blasio.[30] In the Bloomberg administration, the Fund for Public Schools had raised an average of $29 million dollars per year. Under Mayor Bill de Blasio the figure was closer to $18 million, leaving many New York City school programs underfunded.[31] Why would corporations and private entities give less under the De Blasio administration? It was no secret that the Bloomberg administration merged many private and public educational ventures during De Blasio's tenure as mayor of New York City. Did donating parties hope for a "quid pro quo"?

In 2013, Maximus donated between $50,000 and $99,000 to the Fund for Public Schools. The donation occurred around the same time as the scathing New York City Comptroller report. This leads to questioning the motives of Maximus. What do they gain from a partnership of this nature? Given the connection Maximus has as a contractor for the NYC DOE and their history of work with the Chicago Public Schools, this leads to inquiring whether their donation is ethical. Would such a donation provide extra influence or incentive to continue the partnership?

The Expansion of Maximus Special Education Systems

As of 2007, Maximus's TIENET education software could be found in Chicago Public Schools in Illinois; Tucson Unified School District in Arizona; Baltimore County Schools District in Maryland; Richland Schools in California; Martin and Taylor Counties Schools in Florida; Passaic School District in New Jersey; and Eden School District in New York.[32] Since this time, Maximus has expanded to over 700 school districts though the United States.[33] The scope of the TIENET special education products has also expanded. Maximus's TIENET products now include: TIENET 504 (a system for the data tracking of student with 504s—a legal document entitling student to accommodations in schools as per Section 504 of the Rehabilitation Act), TIENET service capture (a system that lets schools bill Medicaid directly), TIENET Response to Intervention (RtI) Management System (a system that identifies "underperforming" students and recommends and documents "research based support strategies" customized to each student), and TIENET Instructional Management System (a "one stop" system to help teachers and administrators develop curricula, instruction, and assessment that aligns to No Child Left Behind).[34]

In April of 2014, Maximus announced that they would be joining with Pearson to add TIENET student data to Powerschool. Powerschool is a Student Information System (SIS) that tracks data on student and staff demographics, standards-based grading and reporting, discipline management and reporting, attendance management and tracking, school course information, and student family management.[35] The merger between TIENET and Powerschool expanded Maximus's role in student data tracking beyond special education and into that of general education student tracking.

The merger was short-lived. In 2015, Pearson sold the newly merged Powerschool to Vista Equity Partners for $350 million in cash. Before the acquisition, Vista Equity Partners was buying up smaller SISs. After the acquisition of Powerschool, Vista Equity Partner's Powerschool became the single largest SIS database, holding information on over 13 million students.[36]

Implications for the Field of Special Education

There is no doubt that Maximus is greatly profiting from our government policies, including the implementation of SESIS in NYC. What is worse, is that the product Maximus is providing for the government is riddled with issues including faulty software, failure to deliver on contract promises, falsifying claims, and being charged with corruption for stealing funds from the very people they were hired to help (as in falsified medical claims in the District of Columbia's Child and Family Services Agency).[37] Despite these issues, Maximus's stock continues to rise, and the corporation continues to obtain government contracts. If the free market system was truly working, then shouldn't a business with faulty products and shady dealings be out of business? If not, then there is a definite need for more stringent oversight or regulation.

Also alarming is the packaging of student data (as in the merger of Maximus's TIENET systems and Pearson's Powerschool) and the selling of data to the highest bidder (as in the sale of Powerschool to Vista Equity Partners). Why are corporations getting rich off of student data? Why is student data so valuable?

As an educator, I believe that it is important to understand the history and rationale behind the systems that we use. Knowledge of these systems gives us power to understand practice. SESIS is not a perfect system. It crashes and it is not user friendly; however, I believe that it also filled an important void of accountability in NYC schools. A system like SESIS makes sure that schools are held accountable to the law. A system like SESIS makes it easier for students to transition from school to school, program to program, without information and services being lost. A system like SESIS allows teachers and service providers to access IEPs anywhere. A system like SESIS ensures that children like Freddie Boyce receive a fair and equitable education. But, is SESIS the right system for NYC DOE schools?

Is SESIS worth the $79 million invested in the program? I wonder what the outcomes of such a system may have been if that money had been invested directly into the DOE schools. I wonder if a better system could have been developed from within. By my calculations, that $79 million contract could have provided an NYC DOE team of 26 people a job for 30 years that paid $100,000 a year salary. Much in technology changes over 30 years. Imagine if we had a team of people constantly investing and reinvesting in the system, dedicated to the unique needs of NYC DOE school children, evolving the system with the times.

In doing this research, I was frustrated in how difficult it was to uncover any details about the contract negotiations between the DOE and Maximus. There should be more transparency in the contract negotiation process so that the consumers of the product—schools, teachers, administrators, service providers, parents, and ultimately the students, can have input into how money is spent. I am confident that by asking questions, researching connections, and following money trails, we can begin to develop a clearer picture of motives and potential misuse of power in our public education system.

Notes

1 D'Antonio, M. (2008). *The State Boys Rebellion*. Paw Prints.
2 Allen, S. (2006). The Voice of a Lost Generation. Boston.com. Retrieved August 1, 2016, from http://archive.boston.com/yourlife/health/mental/articles/2006/05/01/the_voice_of_a_lost_generation/
3 Education for All Handicapped Children Act, Pub. L. 94-142, 94th Cong., 1st Sess. (November 30, 1975).
4 Individuals with Disabilities Education Act, Pub. L. 101-476, 101st Cong., 2nd Sess. (October 30, 1990).
5 Ford, R., & Day, A. (2014, November 14). Beyond CityTime. Retrieved October 18, 2015, from www.theinvestigativefund.org/investigations/politicsandgovernment/1581/beyondcitytime
6 Cramer, P. (2011). Report links SESIS struggles and DOE's contracting practices. Chalkbeat New York. Retrieved October 10, 2015, from http://ny.chalkbeat.org/2011/11/29/reportlinks-sesis-struggles-and-does-contracting-practices/
7 Ford, R., & Day, A. (2014, November 14). Beyond CityTime. Retrieved October 18, 2015, from www.theinvestigativefund.org/investigations/politicsandgovernment/1581/beyondcitytime
8 Ibid.
9 Ibid.
10 Fundforpublicschools.org (2015). About Us—The Fund for Public Schools. Retrieved 19 October 2015, from https://www.fundforpublicschools.org/about-us
11 Kim, T. (2013). *Audit Report on The Department of Education Special Education Student Information System*. New York: Office of the Comptroller.

12 Ibid.
13 According to his LinkedIn profile, Andrew Buher worked on The Equity Project (TEP) Charter School from 2009–2010. He also was a "Governance Consultant" for the KIPP foundation in 2010. He is currently the Executive Director of Dialog—all before the age of 30.
14 Kim, T. (2013). *Audit Report on The Department of Education Special Education Student Information System.* New York: Office of the Comptroller.
15 Kim, T. (2013). *Audit Report on The Department of Education Special Education Student Information System.* New York: Office of the Comptroller.
16 Herold, B. (2015). NYC Tech Shortcomings Prompt Big Payout for Educators. *Education Week.* Retrieved October 7, 2015, from www.edweek.org/ew/articles/2013/10/09/07overtime_ep.h33.html
17 MAXIMUS, Inc. (n.d.). The Center for Media and Democracy. Retrieved October 18, 2015, from www.sourcewatch.org/index.php/MAXIMUS,_Inc.
18 Bottari, M. (2013). Meet Richard Montoni, America's Highest Paid "Caseworker." *PR Watch.* Retrieved October 10, 2015, from www.prwatch.org/news/2013/12/12348/meet-richard-montoni-americas-highest-paid-caseworker
19 Sourcewatch.org. (2015). MAXIMUS, Inc.—SourceWatch. Retrieved October 15, 2015, from www.sourcewatch.org/index.php/MAXIMUS,_Inc.
20 Bottari, M. (2013). Meet Richard Montoni, America's Highest Paid "Caseworker." *PR Watch.* Retrieved October 10, 2015, from www.prwatch.org/news/2013/12/12348/meet-richard-montoni-americas-highest-paid-caseworker
21 Ibid.
22 MAXIMUS. (n.d.). Our Services. Retrieved November 22, 2015, from www.maximus.com/our-services
23 MAXIMUS, Inc. (n.d.). The Center for Media and Democracy. Retrieved October 18, 2015, from www.sourcewatch.org/index.php/MAXIMUS,_Inc.
24 *Investor's Business Daily.* (2014, February 27). Maximus Makes Money on ObamaCare, Government Spending. Retrieved October 18, 2015, from www.nasdaq.com/article/maximus-makes-money-on-obamacare-governmentspending-cm330864
25 NASDAQ, 2016.
26 *Investor's Business Daily.* (2014, February 27). Maximus Makes Money on ObamaCare, Government Spending. Retrieved October 18, 2015, from www.nasdaq.com/article/maximus-makes-money-on-obamacare-governmentspending-cm330864
27 Fundforpublicschools.org. (2015). About Us—The Fund for Public Schools. Retrieved October 19, 2015, from https://www.fundforpublicschools.org/about-us
28 Ibid.
29 Ibid.
30 Taylor, K. (2015, May 12). Public Schools Fund, under De Blasio, is Struggling to Lure Wealthy Donors. *The New York Times.*
31 Ibid.
32 MAXIMUS Special Education Case Management System Selected by Chicago Public Schools. (2007, May 16). Press Release Distribution, EDGAR Filing, XBRL, Regulatory Filings. Retrieved September 1, 2016, from www.businesswire.com/news/home/20070516005114/en/MAXIMUS-Special-Education-Case-Management-System-Selected

33 Ibid.
34 MAXIMUS, Inc. (n.d.). The Center for Media and Democracy. Retrieved October 18, 2015, from www.sourcewatch.org/index.php/MAXIMUS,_Inc.
35 PowerSchool. (n.d.). About Us. Retrieved November 22, 2015, from www.powerschool.com/about-us/
36 MAXIMUS, Inc. (n.d.). The Center for Media and Democracy. Retrieved October 18, 2015, from www.sourcewatch.org/index.php/MAXIMUS,_Inc.
37 Bottari, M. (2013). Meet Richard Montoni, America's Highest Paid "Caseworker." *PR Watch*. Retrieved October 10, 2015, from www.prwatch.org/news/2013/12/12348/meet-richard-montoni-americas-highest-paid-caseworker

5

TURNING AGAINST (PUBLIC) ARTS EDUCATION

An Arts Perspective of the Business of Education

Robert Randazzo

In 2012, a national arts education program was launched, titled "Turnaround Arts," an initiative to support programing of arts education in America's high poverty schools. Turnaround Arts, spearheaded by First Lady Michelle Obama and the President's Committee on the Arts and the Humanities (PCAH), is reflective of education policies during the Obama Administration. These policies include "Race to the Top" and the "Every Student Succeeds Act." Within 4 years, through the collaborative efforts of First Lady Michelle Obama PCAH, the United States Department of Education, and the National Endowment for the Arts, Turnaround Arts expanded to reach 60 schools and a vast network of public and private partnerships. Additionally, professional artists and celebrities such as Yo-Yo Ma, Trombone Shorty, Sarah Jessica Parker, and Kerry Washington have been recruited to adopt schools and become mentors to students.[1] Sarah Jessica Parker, a "Turnaround Arts celebrity advocate," praised the initiative by saying, "I have seen firsthand how excited these kids are to learn through the arts."[2] Yet, as I set out to present the Turnaround Arts network, I consider not the excitement celebrity endorsements, or the advocacy of First Lady Michelle Obama, or the generous support from our nation's leading corporate and philanthropic leaders; rather, I wonder if the efforts to create arts programing in our nation's school systems is sustainable enough to undermine the sanctuary of our nation's public school system. Turnaround Arts is a federal initiative endorsed by partnerships between government agencies, corporations, foundations, and A-list celebrities.

In this chapter, I will analyze the network map titled "Turnaround Arts network" and reveal how public and private partnerships engaged in providing schools with services from non-profit and for-profit vendors. Among these partners are influential corporations, foundations, and non-profits. The implications of the Turnaround Arts network can be seen in two ways. On one hand, the private and public partnerships have collaborated in bringing arts programming to students in high-poverty neighborhoods. In some cases, students in K-12 schools are being exposed to classes in dance, theater, music, or visual arts for the first time. On the other hand, the analysis can be seen as having implications of the privatization of the education movement.

In 2016, students and groups within the Turnaround Arts network attended an annual talent show aimed to celebrate the success of the program. In the opening remarks of the talent show, host Michelle Obama praised the success of Turnaround Arts by stating, "The Turnaround Arts, program isn't just turning around schools, it's turning students' lives around as well."[3] The first lady continued to address how the program, over the course of 5 years, has made a tremendous impact on bringing arts education to schools in the US. However, what was not addressed at the Turnaround Arts talent show, or advertised in a flashy and flamboyant Turnaround Arts website, was how the policy turned to the private sector to outsource arts education jobs in schools.

Behind the bells and whistles of Turnaround Arts, the implications suggest a driving force that is aligned with the privatization of the education movement. In many cases, "No Child Left Behind (NCLB)," in 2001, opened the doors to the enabling of the private sector's involvement with public education. Since NCLB, public and private stakeholders have taken hold of the process of preserving education initiatives, and the shift can be seen in policies that have focused on increasing math and reading scores. During the twenty-first century, NCLB testing mandates, the Common Core Learning Standards, and Race to the Top created a public discourse of a perpetuated blame game placed on teachers, school administrators, and school districts on failing to reach expectations of federal and state education policy. However, the implications of such reform are to enable the privatization of education. Education reformers believe the business sector, by posing solutions of school choice, accountability, and charter schools, can magically curve the growing achievement gap and equip our students with the skills needed to compete in a global economy. Thus, the Turnaround Arts initiative, despite the enthusiasm for arts education, is in fact a "wolf in sheep's clothing," so to speak. The initiative turns arts education into a tool for assisting with closing the achievement gap or increasing skills in reading or math. The objective and background of Turnaround Arts points to implications that suggest a drive to corporatize American education.

The implications can be best explained through the theoretical paradigm of economization of education. Economization of education is referred to as the increasing involvement of economists in education research, the evaluation of the effectiveness of schools and family life according to cost–benefit analyses, and the promotion of school choice in a competitive marketplace.[4] In other words, economics is weaved into the everyday life of society, including education. Investing in education is like investing in a commodity. Over time both the student/or raw product will increase in value. In *Economization of Education*, in line with this thinking, Professor Joel Spring, writes:

> Economic education goals result in corporatization of future workers by attempting to shape their character traits, knowledge, and skills to meet the needs of the global labor market and the desires of multinational corporations. In the context of human capital, skills are divided into hard and soft with hard skills usually referring to such things as literacy instruction and numeracy and soft skills to character traits that will help the worker succeed in the workplace.[5]

The desired goal of economization is to equip the worker with the proper hard skills and soft skills needed to be a future corporatized worker. Hard skills are referred to as literacy instruction and numeracy, and soft skills as character traits.[6] The skills will enable the worker to succeed in a global labor market and adhere to the expectations of corporate organizations. Additionally, it is an expectation, through economization, for the worker to bestow the corporate doctrine to corporatized family.[7] This involves maintaining a family structure and perpetuating the same corporate values onto the children.

Additionally, embedded into the rhetoric of Turnaround Arts is a focus on how the initiative of the program has been successful in improving reading and math scores in schools where it has been implemented. This includes how Turnaround Arts schools showed a 23 percent improvement for students performing math on a proficient level, a 13 percent increase of reading proficiency for students, and how the program has been 86 percent successful in reducing disciplinary issues.[8] Among other statistics are how attendance levels increase with schools involved in the Turnaround Arts program. This can be seen as another example of how the paradigm of economization underlies the Turnaround Arts initiative.

Furthermore, the rhetoric used to describe the Turnaround Arts initiative, including the statistics that point to how students that received Turnaround Arts programming have made incredible gains in reading and mathematics skills, all fit into the paradigm of economization. Yet, what is not included is how the Turnaround Arts initiative description has the intent to outsource arts education jobs to the private sector, thus continuing to dismantle public education. Historian Diane Ravitch states,

> The deceptive rhetoric of the privatization movement masks its underlying goal to replace public education with a system in which public funds are withdrawn from public oversight to subsidize privately managed charter schools, voucher schools, online academies, for-profit schools, and other private vendors.[9]

For the case of Turnaround Arts, the rhetoric is masking the agenda to replace public-funded arts instruction with non-profit and for-profit private vendors.

It is important to make note of the problematic Every Student Succeeds Act (ESSA; 2015), signed into legislation by President Obama in 2015, and how it involves the intentions of the Turnaround arts program. ESSA was the successor to No Child Left Behind (NCLB), a controversial education bill implemented in 2001. In contrast to NCLB, ESSA emphasizes less federal control and more autonomy to the States in implementing education policy. However, ESSA also emphasizes similar measures of testing, accountability, school choice, and teacher evaluations; rhetoric that echoes the paradigm of economization. In contrast to NCLB, ESSA pushed for arts education by focusing on the arts and music to fit the definition of a well-rounded education, which comprises shared subjects such as reading and mathematics. For ESSA, the definition of a well-rounded education includes the instruction of reading, math, the arts, technology, science, etc. Thus, the emphasis of arts education pedagogy takes to the mainstage along with the pillars of reading and mathematics. As this can be music to the ears of arts advocates, however, another interpretation to consider is that arts education is a tool, along with the core subjects, in closing the achievement gap. Current US education policy, including Every Student Succeeds, supports school privatization. Additionally, Turnaround Arts is a nationwide initiative that supports privatization.

I have addressed the underlying objectives for privatizing arts education. The discussion has been a prologue to the upcoming analysis of the Turnaround Arts Network. As I begin to analyze Turnaround Arts Network, I will reveal the players involved in the public and private partnerships within the nation-wide network. What will be discovered is underpinnings of economization within each organization that advocates for arts education. To make this clearer, my analysis is not to debate the impact of arts education. I am an advocate of arts education, and subscribe to many notions of how the arts is impactful to our students. The analysis of the network map is to simply reveal the implications behind the Turnaround Arts initiative, that is, how arts education is being privatized, and jobs are being outsourced to the private sector.

Turnaround Arts Network

To recap, Turnaround Arts is an initiative led by the United States Department of Education, the National Endowment for the Arts, and the President's Committee on the Arts and the Humanities (PCAH). The objective is to revitalize arts education in our nation's high-poverty schools. To achieve this objective, funding is allocated to Turnaround Arts schools to purchase services from private sector arts organizations, including non-profit and for-profit organizations. Funding and allocations come from sources that include the US Department of Education grants, as well as donations by the public and private partnerships within the Turnaround Arts network. The implications of this initiative are underlined by the privatization of education movement. Through a network of public and private partnerships, Turnaround Arts' underlining objective is to outsource arts education to the private sector. In this section, to analyze the Turnaround Arts network, I will select various states that participate in the Turnaround schools program and discuss which private sector arts organizations are involved in schools, as well as which private corporations and foundations are involved in funding.

The Turnaround Arts network is composed of government agencies, non-profit organizations, corporations, and foundations. The leading government agencies for Turnaround Arts are the United States Department of Education, National Endowment for the Arts, and the President's Committee on the Arts and the Humanities (PCAH). Below is a list of leading private organization supports, including not-for-profit groups, corporations, and foundations.[10]

In 2015, over 60 schools were selected in the states of Connecticut, California, Hawaii, Minnesota, Louisiana, New York, North Dakota, Wisconsin, Florida, District of Columbia, and Illinois. As I deconstruct the network, it will become clear how the public and private are involved with Turnaround Arts. Some leading private sector organizations act as a funding resource for schools to use for arts organization vendors. These organizations include: AOL Charitable Foundation, Crayola, Ford Foundation, The Herb Alpert Foundation, JC Penney Cares, The Keith Haring Foundation, Robert Rauschenberg Foundation, Rosenthal Family Foundation, GIVE Steven & Alexandra Cohen Foundation, Laird Norton Family Foundation, and iTheatrics. Additionally, a few private organizations in the network are actually vendors for the Turnaround Arts schools; these include Little Kids Rock and Music Theatre International.

California has the highest number of school participants in the Turnaround Arts program. The program has been operating in ten low-performing elementary schools across California. Some of the groups that endorse Turnaround Arts are P.S. Arts, Create CA, the California Arts Council, as well as celebrity artists such

TABLE 5.1 Leading Private Organization Supports

Americans for the Arts	Music Theatre International
AOL Charitable Foundation	NAMM Foundation
Crayola	Robert Rauschenberg Foundation
Ford Foundation	Rosenthal Family Foundation
The Herb Alpert Foundation	GIVE Steven & Alexandra Cohen Foundation
JC Penney Cares	Laird Norton Family Foundation
The Keith Haring Foundation	iTheatrics
Little Kids Rock	Wolf Trap Foundation for the Performing Arts

Source: Turnaround Arts. http://turnaroundarts.pcah.gov

as Jason Mraz, Forest Whitaker, and Marc Anthony. As this propels student excitement and leads to higher attendance and academic achievement, there is less focus on an in-depth pedagogical approach to teaching the arts, and more focus on how arts education can benefit academic achievement. Turnaround Arts schools are some of the lowest academic performing schools in the state. One of the desired outcomes of the Turnaround Arts program is to raise math and reading test scores in these schools.

Like other areas in the United States, California is partaking in programs to boost standardized test scores, particularly in reading and math. Vendors, who are used to outsourcing the arts to these schools, are on the frontlines working with students one on one, and using the arts as a filter for academic achievement. For example, "P.S. Arts," a non-profit arts organization, is a vendor for Turnaround Arts schools in California Arts. Instructors, employed by P.S. Arts, provide weekly arts instruction, inclusive to the disciplines of dance, music, theater, and visual arts. P.S. Arts provides a 30-week, in-school instructional residency that focuses on integrating the arts into skills-based instruction.[11] P.S. Arts is supported by top corporate sponsors, which include Delta, Target, Tommy Hilfiger, and The Walt Disney Company. Additionally, P.S. Arts is supported by a modest list of foundations, including both The Herb Alpert Foundation and GIVE Steven & Alexandra Cohen Foundation. This is a concrete example of how an arts organization's acts are used as vendors to schools, and supported with funding through government agencies and private organizations.

Similar to P.S. Arts, Music Unites, a non-profit organization which provides after-school arts programing to Turnaround Arts schools in California, utilizes this same type of funding. The Music Unites mission statement is reflective (with underlying themes of economization) of how standardization is becoming part of this problem when describing how arts instruction is in alignment with standards for career and college readiness, or the program is dedicated to guiding youth toward planning and achieving responsible goals for their future.[12] This is similar to the privatization rhetoric discussed previously.

Participating schools in California, as well as schools across the country, purchase services from Music Theatre International (MTI) and iTheatrics. MTI is a licensing agency to a large collection to theatrical productions, including Broadway shows. Its services include granting the arts organizations, including professional theaters, community theaters, and schools, the rights to perform a production from the MTI library. In regards to education, Music Theatre International allows K-12 schools to choose from the education division, with categories ranging from Broadway Junior Collections, which adapt productions for elementary and middle schools, and School Edition collection, which adapts productions for high schools. Upon purchasing a production license, the school is issued with production materials that include scripts, an orchestration score, and a vocal book. In the case of Broadway Junior, the school will acquire what is known as the ShowKit,[13] which includes a "how to" guide on putting on a production, scripts for the students, rehearsal accompaniment CDs, a choreography instruction DVD, and a piano vocal score. The adapted scripts, rearrangement of music, and educational curriculum guides are developed by iTheatrics. iTheatrics is an organization that is identified on the Turnaround Arts network map. As iTheatrics adapts musicals for the education division, it also supports initiatives such as Junior Theater Festival, Junior Theater Celebration, and Make a Musical.[14] MTI and iTheatrics play a secondary role in the privatization movement in its endeavors of servicing schools with curricular material in the arts. As already mentioned, MTI and iTheatrics compile instructional guides and resources for putting on a production, otherwise known as the ShowKit.[15] Essentially, the kit becomes a scripted curriculum for educators to follow in putting on a production. MTI advertises slogans for the kit to be "the best theatre educational tool in the country" and "there's no way to fail." This scripted curriculum guide to putting on a production is not different from a scripted curriculum for teaching reading or math. If a non-arts educator can follow a scripted curriculum to instruct reading and math, the same instructor can follow an easy guide to putting on a production. Thus, the ShowKit[16] undermines the commitment and endeavors of higher education in preparation for teachers who seek to pursue a career as an arts educator.

On the other side of the country, in New York City, the Turnaround Arts network is managed by the New York City Department of Education, New York City Department of Cultural Affairs, and the Fund for Public Schools. Through the collaboration of these public and private agencies, the Turnaround Arts network works in a similar way to the explanation I gave for California. In New York City, the Fund for Public Schools assists in routing private organizations to support the Turnaround Arts initiative. The Fund for Public Schools was established in 2002 by Mayor Michael Bloomberg and emeritus chancellor, Joel Klein. It serves as a conduit for public and private partnerships for the advancement of programing and development in the school system.[17]

According to the Fund for Public School's website, "The organization is a primary vehicle for securing private support to advance these efforts." Through investment from foundations, businesses, and individuals, the Fund for Public Schools has raised more than $350 million for initiatives and school-focused programs.[18] The fundraising and programs goals for the Fund for Public Schools are driven by the NYC school chancellor's priority initiatives; therefore, goals vary from year to year depending on the amount of private funding that is needed for support. One example is the involvement of the Shubert Foundation, the Fund for Public Schools, the New York City Department of Education, and the Turnaround Arts network. The Shubert Foundation is an established partner with the Fund for Public Schools; thus, it holds a place card within the Turnaround Arts network. In 2014, the Shubert Foundation awarded $22,495,000 to divisions within Fund for Public Schools.[19] Among the allocations, $210,000 went to Theatre Education and $165,000 went to

Turning Against (Public) Arts Education 65

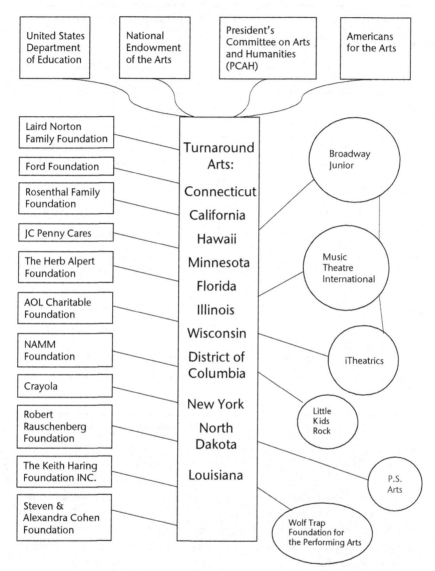

FIGURE 5.1 Structure of the Turnaround Arts Network

Broadway Junior.[20] Broadway Junior is a subdivision within Music Theatre International. The Fund for Public Schools is endorsed by an enormous amount of corporate and philanthropic support. See Table 5.2 for a short list of corporate, philanthropic, and individual supporters, as according to the 2013 annual report of the Fund for Public Schools.

TABLE 5.2 Corporate, Philanthropic, and Individual Supporters

American Council on Education	O'Melveny & Myers LLP
Bloomberg Philanthropies	Qatar Foundation
Michael & Susan Dell Foundation	International, LLC Robin
Bill & Melinda Gates Foundation	Hood Foundation
GE Foundation	Children's Foundation
Lower Manhattan Development Corporation	The Shubert Foundation, Inc.
Mayor's Fund to Advance New York City	Solomon Wilson Family Foundation
The Wallace Foundation	Target Corporation
JPMorgan Chase Foundation	Two Trees Management Company
MacArthur Foundation	United Way of New York City
National Philanthropic Trust	Exploring the Arts
Foundations, Inc.	Morgan Stanley
Bank of America	Morgan Stanley Foundation
Ford Foundation	A|X Armani Exchange
The New York Community Trust	Home Box Office, Inc.
New York Life Foundation	Ezra Jack Keats Foundation
	Public Broadcasting

Source: Creating Partnerships to Transform NYC Schools. www.fundforpublicschools.org[21]

The list in Table 5.2 is an example of the private sector involvement. A larger and completed list can been seen on the website for the Fund for Public Schools. In 2012, the Fund for Public Schools received $21,305,578 in contributions and grants.[22] In 2013, the private contributions and grants increased to $47,710,314.[23] In addition to influencing arts programing, the Fund for Public Schools is involved with programs tailored to college and career readiness, mathematics, technology, and literacy; all key themes applicable to economization.

In a broader sense, the economization paradigm extends from national to global interests. Thus, the United States' obsession with test scores, academics, and closing the achievement gap has much to do with competing with other countries. In 2010, 15-year-olds in participating countries engaged in an assessment to determine skill levels in mathematics, reading, and science. A total of 60 countries participated, including 34 members of the Organization for Economic Cooperation and Development (OECD).[24] The United States ranked 14th in reading, 17th in science, and 25th in mathematics.[25] Shortly after the test results, researchers determined that results of international tests were flawed. This swamped media and newspaper outlets with skepticism of decades of comparing the US test scores with those of countries across the globe. It raised questions as to how far behind the United States was in reading, mathematics, and science.

Researchers have long argued that the problem with educational policy is within the federal level, and reform would be most effective on a local scale. Thus, a focus on the arts in 2016 is not so much a motive to fund low-income students, it is more of a focus to move toward accountability for schools.

There is hardly an international test, or global competition to determine which country produces the most musicians, dancers, or actors; however, it is important to note that other countries place a higher value on the arts than does the United States. In Europe, in many cities there is a performing and visual arts school. These schools are funded by the government and those who qualify for them pay nothing to receive the training they need to work in the arts, much like in academics in Europe. In England, there are art schools in almost every city, as well as Scotland. There are arts performances for tourists and those who attend arts schools find employment. This is another problem with the arts in the United States. Becoming a theater or dance major often is a degree path that leads to waiting tables, with a very few elite and well-funded (mostly by family) individuals making it to the top of dance, theater, and other art forms.

Advocates of Turnaround Arts have praised the policy for its achievement in bringing arts programing to high-poverty schools across the country. Celebrity Kerry Washington stated, "I have witnessed the power of integrated arts education to move the needle on some of our toughest educational challenges, and to give all students the chance to excel and to shine."[26] *The Washington Post* hailed the program to be "One of Michelle Obama's key arts programs [which] will continue after she leaves the White House."[27] Even the United Federation of Teachers proclaimed: "a new program, the Turnaround Arts initiative, is putting the arts back into the schools that need them most."[28]

To conclude, the analysis of the Turnaround Arts network map can be seen to include both pros and cons. I wonder what will become of America's traditional education system. The privatization movement is supported by Democrats and Republicans. Will privatizing education be sustainable for generations in the future? Perhaps these answers are yet to be determined. Amongst the beginnings of our country and establishing a democracy, our founders argued that an education was a necessity in preserving a democracy. Yet, the privatization movement will remain a threat to the preservation of the rich, multi-layered thread that holds together public education.

Notes

1 Committee on the Arts and Humanities Announces Expansion of Turnaround Arts Program. The White House (2014).

2 Committee on the Arts and Humanities Announces Expansion of Turnaround Arts Program. The White House (2014).
3 Committee on the Arts and Humanities Announces Expansion of Turnaround Arts Program. The White House (2014).
4 Spring, J., *Economization of Education: Human Capital, Global Corporations, Skills-Based School*, London and New York: Routledge (2015).
5 Ibid.
6 Ibid.
7 Ibid.
8 Turnaround Arts. http://turnaroundarts.pcah.gov/
9 Ravitch, D., *Reign of Error: The Hoax of the Privatization Movement and the Danger to America's Public Schools*, New York: Knopf Doubleday (2013). Kindle Edition.
10 Turnaround Arts. http://turnaroundarts.pcah.gov/
11 Turnaround Arts. http://turnaroundarts.pcah.gov/
12 P.S. Arts. www.psarts.org
13 Broadway Junior ShowKit. Music Theatre International.
14 Ibid.
15 Ibid.
16 Ibid.
17 Creating Partnerships to Transform NYC Schools. www.fundforpublicschools.org
18 Ibid.
19 Ibid.
20 Ibid.
21 Ibid.
22 Ibid.
23 Ibid.
24 Ibid.
25 www.insidebroadway.org/our-programs/in-school-programs.html
26 https://www.namm.org/news/press-releases/turnaround-arts-announces-expansion-35-schools
27 Michelle Obama Secures a Post-Whitehouse Future for Her School Arts Program. *The Washington Post*, May 24, 2016. https://www.washingtonpost.com/lifestyle/michelle-obama-secures-a-post-white-house-future-for-her-school-arts-program/2016/05/24/e905b6aa-20fc-11e6-aa84-42391ba52c91_story.html?utm_term=.cff2ff1cec62
28 http://turnaroundarts.pcah.gov/impact/

6

POLICY NETWORKS AND POLITICAL DECISIONS INFLUENCING THE DREAM ACT

The Power of the Dreamers

Aminata Diop

Introduction

From the publishing of Ronald Reagan's Administration report "A Nation at Risk," in the 1980s to the George W. Bush Administration's passage of No Child Left Behind in 2001, the fundamental foundation of public education has shifted and taken different directions. The multiple reforms of the 1920s, geared toward the endless efforts to improve public education, have been replaced by the continuous efforts of private foundations and other venture philanthropies leading us into a transformed and remade world that looks more like a private market. These foundations and philanthropic associations' influential powers are present in the political, social, and economic arenas. These entities are slowly reshaping the landscape across the country, especially in the education world. This is leaving some of us to question the role that wealth plays and the ways it can influence education in a democratic world. As Michael W. Apple stated, "Neoliberal reforms now dominate the educational landscape in a wide range of nations."[1] These transformations affect our policies and the ways they are justified even though the actual practice more than often stays the same.

The reshaping of the landscape of education by these powerful foundations and philanthropies also influences the shift in authority. In dealing with this constant change, multiple sets of actors influence policies in different ways. These actors are usually connected to network(s) in a very discrete way. For the purpose of this chapter, I put a strong emphasis on the word networks because, as Stephen Ball puts it, "[P]olicy networks ... constitute a new form of governance, albeit not in a single coherent form, and [bring] in the policy process new sources of authority and indeed a 'market of authorities'."[2] In this process, policy itself is being privatized while schools and education in general are becoming more commodified and reaching different market values.[3]

The more education takes the center stage, the more it becomes an economic good with a higher and higher value price to everyone, particularly to the undocumented immigrant youths living in the United States. Education then becomes a product capable of being sold to those who can afford it and out of reach to those who cannot afford it. Burch argued in 2009, while presenting her own research about the new privatization, "that markets can succeed where government has failed and the role of policy is to cheerlead and stimulate demand."[4] This is an interesting shift as Burch (2009) calls it the "new privatization" where "education policy and the market have become more closely linked."[5] This paradigm shift is leading education to be more expensive and less affordable to some. For immigrant youths, the inaccessibility to education is not only due to its high cost, but for a variety of reasons, one of which can be immigration status. These immigrant youths living in the US give us, as a nation, a completely new reason to create social ways to influence political projects and change the way we educate in a democratic society.

The Undocumented Immigrant Youths

Many things are sources of a significant public and political debate, especially the topic of immigration in the US. According to the US Government, as of January 2011, there were about 11.5 million illegal immigrants inside the US.[6] Zong and Batalova found that "some 42.4 million immigrants lived in the United States in 2014."[7] Undocumented immigrants comprise about 30 percent of the country's estimated population of 40 million immigrants.[8] Undocumented immigrants present in the United States are, broadly, of two categories: those who have illegally entered the country; and those who, having entered legally (such as with a tourist or student visa), are nonetheless now present illegally (visa "overstayers").[9] Each year, more and more undocumented students graduate from the US high schools system and many of these students graduate at the top of their class. Those who graduate high school, however, face the challenge of not being able to attend college or, in some cases, join the military.

When an undocumented immigrant graduates from high school, college does not become the next step in their process of furthering their education. The life after high school, in or outside of college, brings about its own challenges for these graduates by either a lack of access or resources. Those who are able to attend college sometimes cannot afford it. Others face the reality of being denied admissions into their colleges of choice. These anticipated challenges drive some immigrant students to drop out after high school. As a result, they take life on a day-to-day basis. Some are afraid to set certain goals for their future because they fear those dreams might never come true. A lot of these students tend to be bicultural, although, for some, English is the only language they speak. Most grew up in the US and are not familiar with their birth countries at all. Many of them usually do not even realize the true meaning of their immigration status until they start applying for colleges or attempting to get a driver's license. The lack of Social Security Numbers is usually the first encounter they face related to their immigration status. Often, they are left with the feeling of an uncertain future because both college and occupation options are greatly limited.

From the Simpson-Mazzoli to the DREAM Act

The US is a country that has always had immigrants and will continue this great tradition. Thus, it is only reasonable that from time to time politicians give proposals that would benefit these undocumented immigrants. Of course, like anything else, there will always be those who advocate for such proposals and others who will oppose them for various reasons. In 1986, Congress passed an amnesty bill. The 1986 Immigration Reform and Control Act, a.k.a. the Simpson-Mazzoli Act[5] was meant to be a once and for all solution to the illegal problems the country was facing. The Simpson-Mazzoli Act allowed millions of immigrants in the US to get their rights to become citizens, however, there were many fraudulent actions people took to become citizens. The required provisions were mainly ignored or bypassed and led to a lot of fraud. Therefore, the answer to the problem of undocumented immigrants living the US turned into an even bigger problem.

Immigration acts in the US lack a successful and comprehensive history. Historically, immigration bills have always been challenging to be passed into laws. Looking at the history of immigration proposals and their approval rates, it could be anticipated that this was not going to be different when the Development, Relief, and Education for Alien Minors (DREAM) Act was proposed in 2001. Various senators presented the DREAM Act to the House from 2007–2011. However, each time, it failed to pass the 60 required votes to become a law.[11] The DREAM Act is strictly for young undocumented immigrants who have finished high school in the US and wish to go to college. The DREAM Act bill requires that immigrant youth must: enter the US before age 15 to be able to obtain lawful employment; spend 5 years in the US; be a high school graduate or equivalent; complete 2 years of college or military service; obtain conditional residence; have a good moral character.[12]

Supporters of the DREAM Act believe it will lead to more college graduates, future taxpayers, new soldiers, and economic benefits. However, those opposed to the bill argue that passing the DREAM Act would make the US a magnet to other illegal immigrants and will encourage more illegal immigration, which in turn will lead to more problems to deal with in the future. Furthermore, they argue that the DREAM Act does absolutely nothing in terms of securing the US borders, nor does it help US workplace enforcement. Therefore, passing the DREAM Act into a law could really hurt the US economy in the end. Those opposed to the DREAM Act always refer to the 1986 amnesty and its failure. The one thing they fail to consider is that every policy has its ways of being lived and needs to be carefully considered from every aspect possible. The benefits of course should be positive and outweigh the negative effects.

The Lifespan of the DREAM Act in Congress from 2001–2013

In 2001, a number of immigration reforms were happening (state and federal). The DREAM Act left the Senate with no concrete resolution. Between 2001 and 2002, recommendations were made to re-write the Act to consider other politicians' suggestions. In the end, nothing was enough and in May 2011, when Senator Majority Leader Harry Reid re-introduced it to the senate, some Republican senators like John Cornyn (TX), Jon Kyl (AZ), John McCain (AZ), and Lindsey Graham (SC) decided to object to the bill, and the Act was amended.[13] The reason being they wanted immigration enforcements to be reinforced first before they would consider voting for the bill (even though they had voted for the bill before).

In 2007, Richard Durbin put the DREAM Act high on his list of the bills to be discussed. On September 7, 2007, Durbin proposed the DREAM Act as an amendment and it was in the hands of the Department of Defense (DOD). The DOD all along was very supportive for the DREAM Act to be passed into law because, in 2005, there was a big downfall in recruitment. The DOD would benefit from the passing of the DREAM Act as it would serve as another pool for potential American soldiers. As a recruitment strategy, the DOD in 2007 promised residency status to undocumented persons who enlisted in the military. Most people who qualified for enlistment needed different requirements from those originally proposed by the DREAM Act (e.g., graduate from 2-year community college; complete at least 2 years toward a 4-year degree, or serve 2 years in the US military).[14] If someone met two of the three requirements and enlisted in the military, they would be eligible for Permanent Resident Status, which would make them eligible for some state aid. However, many undocumented immigrants lacked the educational credentials to join the DOD. The DOD is still one of the biggest advocates for the DREAM Act to be passed into a law. It was all for the bill to pass into a law just so it could meet its recruitment numbers. The bill was presented as an amendment at that time and never got voted for despite the enthusiasm of the DOD.

On October 18, 2007, Durbin, along with Charles Hagel and Richard Lugar, introduced the DREAM Act again, but the Senate kept making the same argument regarding the language.[15] On October 24, the bill went up yet for another vote.[16] It failed to reach the 60 yes votes it needed to be passed into a law. By this time, some senators saw the actual Act as a distraction from more serious issues that could be dealt with. After the DREAM Act failed to be voted as a law in 2011, President Obama, against Congress's approval or wishes, acted on his own authority and decided in June 2012 to sign the Deferred Action for Childhood Arrivals (DACA). DACA would grant residency to the now called "Dreamers." These "Dreamers" are none other than the kids brought to the US by their parents. This policy's intent was to allow some undocumented immigrants

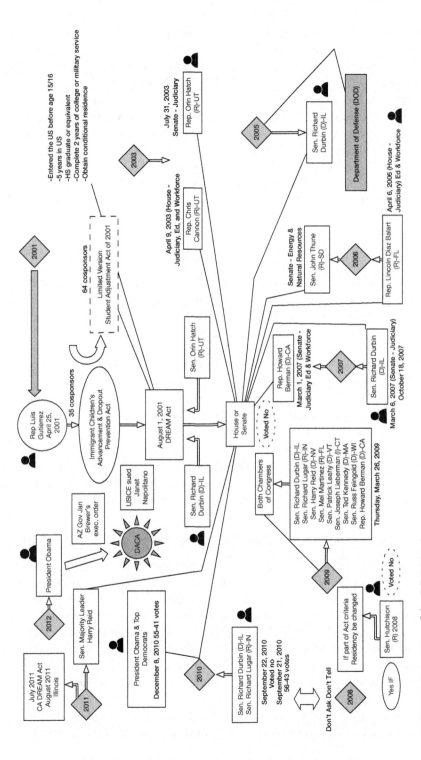

FIGURE 6.1 Structure of the DREAM Act

who have continuously resided in the US since June 12, 2007 to remain in the country.[17] Those who qualified would not only be able to receive a renewable 2-year work permit, but they would also be exempt from deportation.[18] The senators who always refuted the DREAM Act and thought it was controversial now really needed to pay attention to Obama's DACA program. If the DREAM Act were to be passed into a law, some advocated that it would have a positive economic impact, which would mean new jobs would be created and more state and federal taxes would be collected from more households. Yet, despite the energy and enthusiasm of the 2006 mobilizations, Congress failed to enact a progressive immigration reform that year. When the DREAM Act came up for an important vote in October 2007, it failed to gather the 60 votes needed to proceed to a debate on the Senate floor.

The Power of the Dreamers Coming Together

In the early 2000s, many young immigrant youths who qualified for the DREAM Act decided to organize and support each other. Congressmen John Bernstein and Mike Berman were very involved in the advocacy process. The National Immigration Law Center (NILC) and the National Council of La Raza (NCLR)'s staff first joined the immigrant youth and advocated for them. Shortly after the year 2001, more and more immigrants started telling their stories. Cristina Jimenez, Managing Director of United We Dream, originally from Ecuador, came to the US at the age of 13 and attended high school and college as an undocumented student, and, as many others, started sharing her story with the media. According to Leslie Rojas Berestein,[19] "on the morning that an electronic monitoring device was placed on his ankle, Matias Ramos, an undocumented youth, and co-founder of United We Dream, turned to Twitter, posting a photo of himself and announcing that he had been given two weeks to leave the country."[20] More youth started to tell their stories until they connected with United We Dream (UWD).

The Power of Online Networks, Foundations, and Philanthropies

Many of the DREAM Act supporters turned to social media such as Twitter, Facebook, Flickr, Vimeo, and YouTube to build an online community, which often led to a faster connection and interaction. Social media, especially microblogging, can have a huge impact on causes like the DREAM Act. Some of the young DREAM Act supporters focused on using these social media platforms, leading to new online activist websites like DreamActivist.org.[21] These undocumented immigrant youths chose to turn to these online platforms for better organization, networking, and mobility. DreamActivist.org was founded primarily by a group of chat room youths, but was first set up by a Nigerian-born immigrant student who moved to the US when she was very young. She was a great student in high school, especially in math and science. While exploring her options for attending college before finishing high school, she realized her immigration status might not allow her to get to college. She turned online for resources, as the people around her had no answers. Though the site lacked scholarship information, it did become a platform for an online forum. The discussants had such a strong bond that they came up with the website. Many of the founders met only virtually and managed to stay connected and eventually became the biggest advocates of the DREAM Act.

According to their website, United We Dream (UWD) is the largest immigrant youth-led network in the United States. UWD started in 2000 as a national youth-led organization. Part of its mission is to achieve equal access to higher education for all people, regardless of their immigration status. UWD has more than 50 affiliates in over 25 states.[22] It partners with many other networks to get local, national, and regional support. This helps provide the necessary tools and resources to the ever-growing immigrant youth advocates. Their hope is to empower youth to organize and grow with powerful leadership development skills; bringing people together to fight a common cause and ensuring they are capable of using community building skills. In doing this, UWD hopes to create strong and meaningful alliances with other groups who are fighting for education rights for all. In a word, UWD guides, nurtures, and educates these immigrant youth who are documented and undocumented.

UWD is a major supporter of emerging groups advocating for education for all and might need guidance to make its goal happen. A big part of donations from private foundations such as Ford, Open Society, Ford Freedom Fund, and Unbound Philanthropy Fund is from members' contributions. UWD also receives gifts from other networks not necessarily involved in working with undocumented immigrant youth. Unbound was the first institutional funder. When founded in 2008, UWD's board of directors had seven members who were mostly from group members or other affiliates. The UWD board is appointed by members for a 2-year term and can serve up to two terms. Thus, all board members serve a total of 4 years before moving on to other jobs. The board members are a combination of men and women who are mostly undocumented immigrants. At the end of their 4 years, they choose to continue to stay connected with UWD via online and other local organizations in their communities and work on other issues of interest.

Today, UWD has 13 board members. UWD's governance, finance, and fundraising leaders include three members at minimum with at least one designated as a Chair. The Development, Relief, and Education for Alien Minors (DREAM) Act brought many advocacy groups together. In 2008, United We Dream created United We Dream Network (UWDN). UWDN is a nonpartisan network with the largest immigrant youth-led organization in the US. The network has more than 100,000 immigrant youths and 55 affiliate organizations in 26 states. The organization and networks are much stronger because of the online connections.

"I have a Dream" Foundation was founded in 1981 and currently has over 200 programs around the US. The network is composed of 16 affiliates that are currently operating 36 programs across the US. What makes this unique is that they welcome all students at the time of program inception. All the programs support children from elementary school all the way to college. The "I Have a Dream" Foundation always looks for strategic partnerships at the local and national levels just to make sure they have a continuum of support for these Dreamers and hope to get them onto a pathway to college. Evaluations found that the Dreamers showed improvements in their grades and their school attendance. These young people handle peer pressure well and show a high level of aspiration and positive attitudes toward school, life, and their future in general. About 90 percent of the Dreamers affiliated with the "I Have a Dream" Foundation do complete high school. Among these 90 percent high school graduates, 67 percent go on to enroll in college. People and other organizations that are supporting the "I Have a Dream" Foundation see them as exemplary agents making a difference in the lives of disadvantaged students. On an individual level, the "I Have a Dream" Foundation is providing opportunities for success to Dreamers who thought they could never achieve much. On the broader impact, the Foundation's programs have impacted many other supporters. Some of these supporters even launched or led many education-focused initiatives. For instance, the federal Gaining Early Awareness and Readiness for Undergraduate Programs (GEAR UP) program was a replication of the "I Have a Dream" Foundation programs.[23]

According to the Los Angeles Trial Lawyers' Charities' (LATLC) website, part of its mission is to make a positive difference in the quality of life for people who live within the greater area of Los Angeles. The issues the organization focuses on include those related to children, education, and persons with disabilities. Seven lawyers founded the organization in 2007, whose practice mainly focuses on plaintiff personal injury. LATLC now has close to 1,800 supporters and draws membership from the Consumer Attorneys Association of Los Angeles (CAALA), California Employment Lawyers Association (CELA), California Applicants Attorneys Association (CAAA), and Consumer Attorneys of California (CAOC).

The Junior Statesmen Foundation is a nonprofit educational corporation that provides administrative and educational support for the Junior State of America. They support the DREAM Act bill. According to their website, their mission is to strengthen American democracy by educating and preparing high school students for life-long involvement and responsible leadership in a democratic society. One of their funders is the US Department of the Interior, and the Office of Insular Affairs has some relationships. The Assistant Secretary for Insular Affairs carries out the administrative responsibilities of the Secretary of the Interior in coordinating federal policy for the territories of American Samoa, Guam, the US Virgin Islands, and the commonwealth of the Northern Mariana Islands.

The Melody Robidoux Foundation is also a supporter of the DREAM Act, but little information could be found on their website regarding their support of the Act. The Hurlbut-Johnson Charitable Trusts is an advisement fund of the Silicon Valley Community Foundation. They have grants and some are used to support community develop in education like the educating of girls who will become the next generation of women educators.

The mission of the Minkwon Center for Community Action, according to their website, is to meet the concerns and need of the Korean American community. They partner with grassroots organizations involved in education and different advocacy initiatives to address mainly immigration policies at the state and national level, but also other important community issues. They provide much-needed assistance to the marginalized Korean Americans, more specifically the more recent immigrants with limited English proficiency. After the organization was founded in 1984, it took almost 10 years for the *Washington Post* to make an ad campaign for immigrant rights, which the organization was involved in. Then, in 2001, with the DREAM Act campaign, the organization became very involved in advocating for the passing of the bill into a law. For 4 years, they focused on the evolution of the Act. Their website shows that in 2009, they not only created an Immigrants Rights Legal Clinic, but also changed their name from YKASEC (Young Korean American Service and Education Center) to Minkwon Center for Community Action. In 2010, they rallied in Washington DC to support the Immigration Reform. In 2012, they launched the legal services for Deferred Action for Childhoods Arrivals (DACA). On top of all this community work, in 2014, the organization was able to reach 60,000 new immigrant voters and have them register to vote. One of the top funders of the Minkwon Center for Community Action is the Single Stop USA/Robin Hood Foundation.

Since 1988, the fund has created programs and schools that assist families in New York's poorest neighborhoods. Single Stop has three different kinds of partners: leadership, event, and the Co-Op. Some of Single Stop leadership partners include J.P. Morgan, Hyatt, Morgan Stanley, and Sony & BMG Music Entertainment. By leadership partners, Single Stop means those involved "on all levels: program pilotage, high-value contributions and endless commitment to results are just some of the ways these corporate partners are making it possible for us to help more low-income New Yorkers than ever before."[24] The event partners are described as those who "demonstrate their corporate commitment to giving back through cash and in-kind contributions on exclusive Robin Hood events."[25] Some of their event partners include Ralph Lauren Foundation, Uber, Equinox, Guggenheim, and JetBlue.[26] Their Co-Op partners "make every dollar count by donating a portion of proceeds to Robin Hood's year-round campaign against poverty."[27] Some of their Co-Op partners include Ermenegildo Zegna and Major Food Group.

The Minkwon Center for Community Action supporters include the New York State Division of Housing & Community Renewal, which is responsible not only for the supervision and maintenance of, but also the development of, affordable low- and moderate-income housing in all New York State. Many of its affiliates are supportive of the DREAM Act bill and have posted numerous articles on their websites about its failure to become a law since 2001. Another organization that supports the Minkwon Center for Community Action is the Rockefeller Brothers Fund, which is a private family foundation with a major goal of helping to advance social change that contributes to a world that will be just, peaceful, and sustainable. These private foundations share commonalities, including that they are both philanthropists and grant-making institutions.

There are many colleges and universities that strongly support the DREAM Act. The CUNY schools have groups of undocumented immigrants called the CUNY Dreamers. They all meet periodically to share their fears and worries, and get professional advice from lawyers who volunteer to help. Some politicians, on the other hand, have gone on record nationally to support the DREAM Act—people like President Obama, ex-US Secretary of Homeland Security, Janet Napolitano, and New York City Mayor Michael Bloomberg. There are also organizations such as Microsoft that went public along with the US Conference of Catholic Bishops, and the National Association for College Admissions Counseling about their strong support to see the DREAM Act bill passed into a law.

It is very encouraging to see how many people and organizations are supporting the DREAM Act. However, personally, looking at the way the House and Congress handled the proposal of the DREAM Act, I am not at all positive that the bill will turn into a law anytime soon, especially after reading in the *National Review* that Paul Ryan "hinted strongly that he will not bring an immigration bill to the House floor." Ryan "agreed to prevent a floor vote on the issue his party's base most fears being brought to the floor."[28]

Opponents of the DREAM Act bill have been consistent in criticizing the Act from the time it was proposed until now. The broadest objection is to the general notion of "amnesty" for illegal immigrants, and concerns that passage of the DREAM Act would reward illegal behavior and result in a flood of illegal immigration. A related concern is that the Act would allow many more than just the best and the brightest of undocumented immigrant children to gain legal status, either because the provisions are too lenient or because of the potential for fraud. They also argue that once these individuals receive legal status in the United States, they will be able to petition for the admission of their relatives, regardless of whether those relatives would qualify under the provisions of the Act. In addition, they also feel that the Act would grant beneficiaries access to certain higher education benefits and other public benefits at the expense of deserving legal residents. There is disagreement over whether the DREAM Act would boost the economy or whether it would ultimately cost the government money. Finally, some object not to the substance of the bill, but to the passage of any immigration provision that is not part of a comprehensive immigration overhaul. Drafters of the 2010 DREAM Act tailored its provisions to address many of these concerns, but there are still loopholes that may contribute to the continuous resistance to pass the bill into a law.

There are some organizations that are not currently supporting the DREAM Act such as NumbersUSA and the Center for Immigration Studies. They are both non-profit organizations in favor of immigration reduction. They constantly seek to reduce immigration levels in the US to pre-1965 levels without country of origin quotas as established in the Immigration Act of 1924. These organizations want to see fewer immigrants in the country. Former Republican co-sponsors of the DREAM Act, including Orrin Hatch and John McCain, vowed to vote against the bill.[29] Senator Kay Bailey Hutchison (RTX), who had suggested that she would support the bill with some small changes, also voted no (Edward Schumacher-Matos, Op-Ed.,). Senator Kay Hagan (D.N.C.), one of five Democrats to vote against the bill, opposed the DREAM Act on the grounds that it lacked adequate enforcement measures.[30] Underlying much of the opposition to the DREAM Act is the belief that "at its fundamental core 'the DREAM Act' is a reward for illegal activity."[31] It is a plausible argument to question that the DREAM Act would, to some extent, sanction illegal immigration, no matter how faultless its immediate beneficiaries are. It is not absurd to suggest that parents may see this as an incentive to bring their children to the United States illegally and try to get them enrolled in school or the military as an alternative to pursuing protracted, and often fruitless, legal channels of immigration. However, the DREAM Act requirements are clear and specific to those undocumented immigrants who have already lived in the US almost all of their lives, and know nowhere other than the US.

Immigration hawks like Congressman Lamar Smith (RTX) are not the only ones who question the wisdom and justice of allowing certain illegal immigrants to remain in the United States while others are deported, and while legal immigrants must pursue citizenship through protracted application processes. Some immigrants oppose the measure on the grounds that everyone should have to apply for citizenship through the same channels no matter how hard working they are or how much potential they show.[32] To refuse to address these criticisms at face value, and instead argue that the DREAM Act is a no-brainer, is a mistake and ignores valid concerns about how the United States should deal with undocumented immigrants.

In addition to expressing concerns about the specific provisions of the DREAM Act, several lawmakers have made it clear that their support for the bill is contingent on its inclusion as part of a larger overhaul of the immigration system. For example, Senator Arlen Specter (DPA) opposed passage of the DREAM Act in 2007 because he believed it would "weaken our position to get a comprehensive bill."[33] The Bush administration opposed the 2007 DREAM Act at the last minute in part on the grounds that "the Nation's broken immigration system requires comprehensive reform."[34] Yet, at the time of writing, it is almost 2017 and we are still having the same conversation. It is worth noting that undocumented immigrant youths should feel proud of the work achieved so far and changes that have been made since 2000. When compared with other social movements, it is imperative to note that these undocumented youths did not let their immigration status hold them down. By sharing their stories leading to a coalition meeting in Washington DC (with the help of the National Immigration Law Center), they accomplished a lot. In 2008, when the House Republicans stalled on immigration reform, with the help of UWD, more than 500 Dreamers came together in Phoenix, Arizona, to call on President Barack Obama to provide deportation relief to millions of Dreamers and their families. These immigrant youths have been politically active. They stood up together and created opportunities for those in need to have access to deportation relief information and also higher education opportunities.[35] They are currently gaining different streams in social justice work while strongly building a movement on the principles of social inclusion and justice that could change the landscape of the undocumented immigrant youths' education in the US.

Though DACA did not help the adults, it did provide options for the youngsters. DACA has been one of the movements that achieved the most significant victory in such a short period of time. We should hope, in the year 2016, not to be doing work for policy change to keep families together or protected families against deportation, but it is the reality we are still living and this becomes even more real with the approach of the November 2016 election. Donald Trump already threatened to get rid of DACA, build walls, and stop Muslims from moving to the US. If Trump gets elected and keeps his promises, it will be arguably fairly difficult for these immigrant youths to gain more victories and possibly change history. Hillary Clinton did state a commitment to keeping DACA, protecting families from deportation, and avoiding kids and parents being separated. The outcomes of the 2016 election could have a big impact on the future of the undocumented immigrant youths living the US. However, we should always remember that the stories of these immigrants arouse in us the possibility for a profound transformation as they get tied to political conversations, including those not only of systems of oppression, but also unbalanced distribution of resources. As one of the most powerful countries in the world, those responsible for voting the DREAM Act bill into a law must keep in mind that these immigrants' stories are like all Americans'. As Oh and Cooc state, these immigrant youths' "stories, like those of previous generations, add to this country's founding, and continuing, legacy of immigration."[36]

Notes

1 Apple, Michael, *Mapping Corporate Education Reform: Power and Policy Networks in the Neoliberal State* (New York: Routledge, 2015), xvii.
2 Ball, Stephen, *Global Education Inc.: New Policy Networks and the Neoliberal Imaginary* (New York: Routledge, 2012), 9.
3 Ibid., 8.

4 Burch, Patricia, *Hidden Markets: The New Education Privatization* (New York: Routledge, 2009), 83.
5 Ibid., 5.
6 Hoefer, Michael et al., Office of Immigration Statistics, U.S. Department of Homeland Security. Estimates of the Unauthorized Immigration Population Residing in the United States: January 2011, at 4 (2012), available at http://www.dhs.gov/estimates-unauthorized-immigrant-population-residing-united-states-january-2011
7 An "illegal immigrant" (or "unauthorized resident") is defined as a foreign-born noncitizen who is not a legal resident. Id. at 2. A legal resident immigrant is defined to include "all persons who were granted lawful permanent residence; granted asylum; admitted as refugees; or admitted as nonimmigrants for a temporary stay in the United States and not required to leave by January 1, 2011."
8 Michael Jones-Correa, Migration, Policy Institute, Contested Ground: Immigration in the United States 13 (2012), available at www.migrationpolicy.org/pubs/TCM-UScasestudy.pdf (noting that there are approximately 11.5 million illegal immigrants and slightly under 40 million total immigrants).
9 Hoefer et al., supra note 23, at 2.
10 See: https://gringaofthebarrio.wordpress.com/2015/07/27/1986-immigration-reform-and-control-act-a-k-a-the-simpson-mazzoli-act/
11 Preston, Julia, Bill for Immigrant Students Fails Test Vote in Senate, *The New York Times* (October 25, 2007).
12 See: https://whitehouse.gov and https://dreamact.info/students
13 See: https://projects.propublica.org/represent/votes/111/senate/2/278
14 See: http://archive.defense.gov/news/newsarticle.aspx?id=61928
15 See: https://www.congress.gov/bill/110th-congress/senate-bill/2205
16 Ibid.
17 See: https://www.dhs.gov/deferred-action-childhood-arrivals
18 See: https://www.uscis.gov/humanitarian/consideration-deferred-action-childhood-arrivals-daca
19 See Leslie Rojas Berestein, "A High-Profile Challenge to the White House's New Deportation Guidelines," *Multi-American*, September 22, 2011 (www.scpr.org/blogs/multiamerican/2011/09/21/7425/a-high-profile-challenge-to-the-white-houses-new-d/).
20 Zimmerman, A. M., "A Dream Detained: Undocumented Latino Youth and the DREAM Movement." *NACLA*, November/December 2011 (https://nacla.org/article/dream-detained-undocumented-latino-youth-and-dream-movement). See also, Zimmerman, A. M. (2012). "Documenting Dreams: New Media, Undocumented Youth and the Immigrant Rights Movement. Confessions of an Aca-Fan. MAPP Working Paper." Available at: http://henryjenkins.org/2012/07/documenting_dreams_new_media_u.html (accessed July 19, 2012).
21 See: DreamActivist.org, "Our Stories" (www.dreamactivist.org/about/our-stories/).
22 Ibid.
23 See: www.ihaveadreamfoundation.org
24 See: https://www.robinhood.org/corporate-partners#section-1
25 Ibid.
26 Ibid.
27 Ibid.

28 See: Chait, Jonathan, "Paul Ryan Says He Will Serve as House Speaker, Maybe," http://nymag.com/daily/intelligencer/2015/10/paul-ryan-has-conditions-for-serving-as-speaker.html#
29 Hennessey, supra note 114.
30 NUMBERSUSA, supra note 104. See: https://www.numbersusa.com/content/my/congress/1336/votingrecord#tabset-5
31 See:http://abcnews.go.com/Politics/dream-act-senate-republicans-block-act-for-illegal-immigrant-students/story?id=12429589
32 See: http://articles.latimes.com/2010/dec/24/local/a-me-1224-
33 See: CONG. REc. S 13,300-02.
34 See: www.aila.com/content/default.aspx?docid=23685
35 Cristina Jiménez, Managing Director of United We Dream (UWD) interviewed on July 6, 2016.
36 Soojin S. Oh and North Cooc. Immigration, Youth, and Education. Editors' Introduction. (Fall, 2011). *Harvard Educational Review,* http://hepg.org/her-home/issues/harvard-educational-review-volume-81-number-3/herarticle/editors'-introduction_826

7

THE CALL FOR FACULTY PREPARATION

Diane Price Banks

Introduction

This chapter will discuss the need for a formal, potentially mandatory, faculty preparation program for new hires to higher education institutions. I will highlight voices from newly hired faculty to assist in the call for a mandatory faculty development policy on pedagogy and classroom management skills for new hires. I will use my own story to further demonstrate the need for faculty development as well as propose a policy with the intent of introducing it to City University of New York's (CUNY) Board of Trustees and the Union, PSC CUNY Welfare Fund. The hope is to begin the conversation and transition from first-year faculty struggling in their classrooms to being better prepared to educate their students on day one. In no way should this be taken as a cure for all that ails new faculty hires but, at the very least, a step in the right direction towards modifying the current business of higher education.

The Business of Higher Education

Since the inception of colleges and universities in this country, it has been the business of higher educational institutions to hire faculty who are leaders in their field, those who possess practical industry and research knowledge, who could lead and teach from experience rather than theoretical knowledge. Case in point, in 2013, CUNY hired General Petraeus, former director of the Central Intelligence Agency (CIA), to teach a course on public policy titled, "Are we on the threshold of the (North) American Decade?"[1] He was hired not on his ability to teach public policy from a pedagogical standpoint but rather, as a "distinguished leader with experience in international security, intelligence and nation-building."[2] However, the knowledge expected in the classroom encompasses more than just practical knowledge acquired from the field. To appropriately educate students in every discipline, faculty in academia must demonstrate not only practical knowledge but pedagogical and theoretical knowledge as well. The current and pre-existing hiring strategy of filling faculty ranks with those who demonstrate practical knowledge and leadership should not be void of theoretical and pedagogical support needed upon employment. To accompany the approach of hiring distinguished faculty it is imperative that institutions implement a policy that includes on-the-job training for new hires educated outside of teacher preparation programs like Teachers College at Columbia University. Training should encompass, but not be limited to, pedagogy and classroom management skills. On-the-job training for newly hired faculty should be a national standard and not a policy solely implemented within CUNY. Dr. Petraeus is certainly not the only faculty member hired mainly on his practical expertise; I was too. This practice happens to be the culture and business of higher education institutions.[3]

Profoundly notable, this hiring practice may contribute to achievement gaps with students instructed by professors who lack pedagogy and classroom management skills. In recent years, several higher education institutions developed *Teaching Strategy* courses to help first-year and veteran faculty improve and implement pedagogy in their classrooms. Such institutions include CUNY's Graduate Center in New York City and Washington University in St. Louis, Missouri. However these courses are not mandatory nor well-known by faculty, at least within CUNY institutions. A good number of new faculty admitted they are *too busy* focusing on content knowledge and developing their teaching skills and consequently cannot find time to attend professional development courses tailored to enhancing teaching strategies.[4] It has become common practice for faculty to develop pedagogical and classroom management skills over time. Typically, new faculty tend to find support during teacher observations. Upon employment at CUNY, faculty members are evaluated and observed once a semester for seven consecutive semesters by veteran faculty in their respective departments. This gives veteran faculty the opportunity to correct and suggest better teaching techniques to novice instructors while in the classroom.[5] This common practice requires new faculty to learn by fire and not by structured training. The vast majority of new faculty are overwhelmed and bombarded with content knowledge and without proper training subsequently have difficulty translating that content in a way that engages student learning and understanding.[6]

The White House, in 2015, emphasized the need to increase underrepresented minority groups of students into academia. The published report recognized that the demand for college-educated workers in America is growing.[7] The report acknowledges that besides increasing and diversifying student enrollment, it is equally important to ensure their success once admitted. In 2009–2010, the National Center of Education Statistics (NCES) reported that 69 percent, or 7 out of 10 first-year Science, Technology, Engineering, and Mathematics (STEM) college students dropped out or switched their major within the first year.[8] There are many factors that contributed to this outcome. Notable reasons included lack of financial aid, family issues, having to choose work over school, lack of student support, lack of college preparation and, most importantly for the purpose of this chapter, poorly instructed science, math, and technology courses.[9] As an institution for learning it is imperative, at the very least, that we implement the development of pedagogy and classroom management skills to newly hired faculty.

Boice conducted a mixed methods study on the experiences of new faculty hired to academia.[10] From 1987–1989 he documented the voices of new faculty from two separate and intellectually different campuses as they explained the nuances of teaching in academia. He documented that on both campuses pressure was on promotion and tenure rather than being a better educator in the classroom.[11] New faculty often felt a lack of collegial support, often stating they wished someone would give them advice about teaching.[12] During interviews, new faculty explained that veteran faculty tended to speak to them about gossip and politics 52 percent of the time as opposed to teaching related topics, which rated 3.5 percent.[13] Notwithstanding, from a personal standpoint this practice continues now in 2016. One participant stated during an interview,

> No, no one has said much about teaching. Mostly, I've been warned about colleagues to avoid. A lot of it is gossip and complaining. I can only think of two specific things that have been said about teaching here. One is how bad the students are ... and how unprepared and unmotivated they are. The other one, that maybe two people mentioned, was a warning about the need to set clear rules and punishments on the first day of class. All in all, I'm pretty disappointed with the help I've gotten.[14]

Boice also noted that "inexperienced and returning faculty were not confident that they knew how to teach (although their senior colleagues seemed to assume that they did)."[15] Oftentimes, many newly hired faculty felt that old faculty were incompetent at teaching, which explained the lack of guidance. Another novice faculty member stated,

> One thing I worried about in returning to a campus job was whether I could handle the teaching. I guess I didn't presuppose that I would get lots of help but I certainly didn't expect to be surrounded by colleagues who don't seem to care about teaching. When I talk about it in the department I feel like I am violating a rule of silence.[16]

There should be a clear level of concern when new faculty are introduced to the profession only to realize there is no support. It's sink or swim! Boice recommended two main suggestions for improving teaching in the classroom: One, exempt new faculty from student evaluations for the first 2 years of teaching. This should help alleviate any negative pressures during teaching and allow them to try different teaching styles without punishment. And, two, get new faculty involved in faculty development programs that will enhance pedagogy and classroom management skills.[17]

My Story—The Quest for Pedagogy!

In December 2010, I was officially hired as a full-time sub lecturer at a community college in a moderately sized city in New York. I was given a start date, congratulated, and handed a textbook and a copy of the syllabus from the previous semester. My initial excitement was trumped by the overwhelming fear of, "Well, how do I teach?" With a start date of less than 30 days away, I felt totally unprepared for classroom interaction. I was dumbfounded to learn that on-the-job training was not available for my new profession. Thirty days is an insufficient amount of time to pedagogically prepare to teach three courses of microbiology, especially for a novice educator who lacked a teacher education background. Given the amount of time, I read and dissected as much as I could to enhance my theoretical, content-based knowledge on the subject matter. As a consequence, I completely omitted content from the lecture that I personally felt was too difficult to explain, given the lack of preparation time. I thought, "I'll focus more on this topic next semester when I have enough time to fully own the material." Initially, I had no one to turn to, no one to bounce ideas off of, and no experienced professor providing on-the-job training or mentorship. I felt alone.

I was under the false assumption that teaching was all about content knowledge. I was totally unaware that there was an art and science to teaching. To assist with background knowledge I reviewed my old microbiology notes from college. I repeatedly rehearsed my lessons with the publisher-provided PowerPoint slides. As a timesaving technique, I decided to master the first three chapters in their entirety before school began. I surmised this was a more practical approach to gaining content knowledge over reviewing, with complete understanding, 23 chapters in 30 days. I projected that every week once school began I would master each lesson chapter by chapter.

As aforementioned, it has become the business of education in academia to hire faculty primarily on their practical knowledge. Needless to say, most faculty in the first 3 years of teaching lack pedagogy, classroom management skills, and/or collegial support while in the classroom.[18] This has led to dissatisfaction within the profession, faculty burnout, and moderate attrition rates.[19] As an infectious disease researcher and a certified Clinical Laboratory Scientist in the state of New York, I was just what the institution needed. My field experience qualified me for a lecturer position instructing microbiology. I achieved close to a decade of work experience as a clinical laboratory scientist, nevertheless I quickly recognized I lacked pedagogical skills. Pedagogy, a term I would become acquainted with much later in my career, is the methods and practices used in class by educators to help create an atmosphere of learning.[20]

Initially my lectures were the facts and principal style of teaching.[21] This consisted of me talking and regurgitating everything I knew about the microbes around us. There was no interaction with students other than me talking and them listening. I never even checked throughout my lesson whether they understood or were even following along. When exam time came my students flunked miserably. I was stumped. The content on the test was exactly what I lectured on. I couldn't fathom how the students failed. At first, I thought they weren't studying; then I thought maybe they didn't know how to study. I repeatedly looked outward for reasons why they failed, similar to the faculty in the Boice 1991 study. Eventually I thought, what am I doing wrong? As I became more comfortable and familiar with my colleagues I would ask them about their classes. Through these inquires I realized I wasn't applying techniques used to help students understand lecture material and, in fact, I wasn't alone. I heard several professors talking about pedagogy and Bloom's taxonomy yet I had no clue what they were. Eventually, I realized these were something I needed and was desperately lacking. My research background and knowledge of microbes were not the only knowledge I needed to teach these young minds. I also needed pedagogical skill and effective classroom management techniques. My experience led me on a journey to become a better educator. Several department meetings were reserved to share classroom strategies, knowledge, and pedagogical style. I quickly realized this was an issue that many of my colleagues shared but were reluctant to be the first in a crowded room to attest to it.

The Call for Faculty Preparation

There are several articles published that address and bring to light the need for a faculty preparation program. A leading source of publication are the fields of pharmacy and nursing. Several articles address the dire need to transform clinicians and field experts to professors. The articles claim newly hired faculty lack pedagogy and suggest MD and PhD programs must better prepare their graduates for faculty roles.[22]

Paul Ramden, author of *Learning to Teach in Higher Education*, wrote a profound book describing the nuances of being a faculty member at the college level. He noted,

> the average university teacher is now expected to be an excellent teacher … who can expertly redesign courses and methods of teaching to suit different groups of students, deal with large mixed-ability classes, apply information and communicate technology and inspire students with zero tolerance for delay whose minds are probably on their part-time jobs rather than the pleasures of learning.

He further stated, "It is not enough to be an exceptional clinician, advocate or designer" rather he or she "must be a distinguished teacher as well."[23] He suggested that institutions who want to develop their faculty must do so by providing direct resources, rewards, and incentives.[24]

Dr. Bob Emiliani, author of *Lean Teaching: A Guide to Becoming a Better Teacher* and scholar in Lean Management implementation, explained his rationale for the pedagogical struggles of faculty in academia.

> A research degree such as Ph.D ... is greatly valued in higher education. Though there is some coursework to complete, the emphasis is on doing research and completing one's doctoral dissertation. ... Despite some teaching experience, the doctorate trains students to do research. A student who completes traditional masters and doctoral degrees typically spends far more time doing research than teaching. So, it should be no surprise that professors can't teach—many, maybe most, but certain[ly] not all.[25]

Dr. Emiliani emphasized that professors who wish to improve their teaching have to be self-motivated, as the business of higher education incentivizes being a researcher rather than a better educator. He echoes the call for colleges and universities to take greater responsibility in preparing their future and current faculty. To further highlight the call for faculty preparation, Dr. Emiliani goes on to answer the question as to why K-12 teachers also have problems with teaching despite being particularly trained to teach. The answer, simply put, is due to teachers being taught by faculty who can't teach.[26] Thus teachers are reproducing learned behaviors from higher education faculty who may also lack pedagogy and classroom management skills.

The National Science Foundation (NSF) released a program solicitation grant in June 2015 and June 2016 titled, "Improving Undergraduate STEM Education: Education and Human Resources (IUSE: EHR)."[27] This federal grant is currently offering $300,000 over a 3-year period to explore, design, develop, and implement courses to engage student learning and provoke institution and community transformation in the education of STEM students. On one hand, the grant is offering funding to help improve STEM curricular with the hopes of improving student engagement and increasing minority participation. On the other hand, the grant is looking to fund the development and implementation of pre-service faculty preparation courses to better prepare faculty and teachers who teach STEM-related courses. NSF also acknowledged in the call for proposals the crucial need to increase and diversify the STEM field; notwithstanding, recognizing the need to develop the STEM curriculum as well as its educators.

Answering the Call: The Price Prep Policy

Ineffective teachers are a disadvantage to students and society at large. The current status quo with the business of higher education has become ineffective and a call for improvement is long overdue. Here, I propose a policy for further discussion and future implementation. The Faculty Development and Preparation Policy for Higher Education, conveniently coined the Price Prep Policy, is designed to assist novice faculty in becoming effective educators in year one as opposed to year four or five, which seems to be the trend documented by Boice. The faculty preparation program will mimic CUNY's mentorship program as senior faculty will be assigned as mentors to newly hired faculty.[28] Veteran faculty will mentor novice faculty on policy and procedures of the department and college at large with a main focus on the development of pedagogy and effective classroom management skills.

The Mentors

The assignment of senior faculty for the Price Prep Policy program will consist of three factors: a candidate's application for participation, recommendation from the department chair, and approval from the department's Personnel & Budgets (P&B) committee. Potential mentor candidates must meet at least three eligibility criteria. They must have: instructed the course for a minimum of three consecutive years; received three consecutive satisfactory peer observations in that particular course; and received no less than 3.3 on three consecutive student evaluations.

Once senior faculty are accepted as mentors, they must complete a one-year training course that reinforces classroom management dynamics and pedagogical implementation. Ideally, training should be conducted by respective campus professional development departments. The Price Prep Policy program for mentors consists of three phases. In phase one of the mentorship program each candidate will participate in a full 2-day training seminar. Day one will orient mentors to the Price Prep Policy program, policies, and expectations. Day two will consist of defining pedagogy, having an open discussion on pedagogical techniques, and how to implement them in order to effectively evaluate their mentees. This day will also focus on paperwork for the evaluation process. Phase two will provide the mentor with field evaluation experience. Mentors will participate in mock evaluations and shadow veteran mentors during the evaluation process where applicable. Phase two mentors will be given one semester to create, adjust, personalize, and prepare paperwork, lesson plans, etc. for the incoming mentees. This should be a staggered and ongoing process for preparing mentors. Documents developed in phase two should be specific to the subject matter being taught. During the training process, the professional development department is expected to be supportive of mentoring faculty. The last phase will consist of the mentor's assignment to a mentee for a full academic year. The mentor will be fully supported and documentation generated will be evaluated by the professional development department for effectiveness and critique. The professional development department will oversee the entire process, record relevant data for statistical purposes, and evaluate the entire program for effectiveness and faculty retention. Once phase three is successfully completed, each faculty mentor will receive a certificate of completion and certification as a faculty preparation mentor. This status will provide mentors with the opportunity to mentor new faculty as they arise in their respective departments for years to come.

The Mentees

Upon confirmation of employment, the department chairs and institutional human resource departments should direct new hires to the professional development department. The professional development department should keep an up-to-date list of new faculty hires. The professional development department is tasked with assigning the new hiree to an available mentor within their respective departments. Phase one should begin during the mentees' first employed semester. In phase one, mentees will co-teach the assigned course with their assigned mentor. The mentor will work with the mentee in establishing lesson plans and implementing pedagogy in the classroom. The mentee will play a supportive role in the classroom while learning through observation and interactions with the mentor and students. The mentor and mentee will meet weekly to discuss lessons and in-class expectations. In phase two—the second semester—the mentee will teach the course independent of the mentor. The mentor is expected to be available as needed to fully support the mentee. During phase two, both participants will meet daily to discuss in-classroom experiences, establish goals, and review future lesson plans as well as provide guidance toward tenure and promotion. The mentor will evaluate their mentee once every five weeks, totaling three evaluations at the conclusion of phase two. The final evaluation will include the mentors' recommendations for the mentee.

The Toledo Plan, formerly known as the Peer Assistant & Review (PAR) program, was implemented in 1982 in Toledo, Ohio. The program provides on the job training for novice teachers in the K-12 profession. The recommendations of the Price Prep Policy will mimic those of the PAR program: recommended without continuation in the program; recommended with continuation; or dismissal.[29] A recommendation without continuation means the mentee satisfied or exceeded all program goals and expectations. A recommendation with continuation means the mentee showed promise of effectiveness but failed to meet all program goals and thus needs improvement. The mentee will participate in one additional semester at phase two and be assigned a new mentor, if available. A recommendation of dismissal indicates that the mentee continuously failed to meet program goals, failed to implement suggested pedagogical techniques, and/or was ineffective in the classroom. Supporting documentation and interim corrective action reports must accompany this recommendation as well as signed documentation of union acknowledgement. All recommendations are reported to the department's P&B committee. The committee will make the final decision regarding the mentee's employment to which an on-campus union representative must be present.

It is also recommended that all faculty teaching a course for the first time participate in the Price Prep Policy program beginning at phase one. Faculty teaching existing courses that feel they need additional support may apply for the Price Prep Policy program as a mentee. Volunteer participants will be assigned a mentor and begin at phase two of the mentee process. Letters and certificates of completion should be distributed to mentees who were deemed recommended with no continuation in Price Prep. The letters and certificates should be transferable from institution to institution for the particular course deemed recommended.

Faculty Development: Continuing Education (CE) Credit

Faculty preparation programs should include two main courses that all new faculty are encouraged to enroll tuition free. The two courses should include, but are not limited to, *effective teaching strategies* and *purposeful pedagogy*. It is also recommended that unions and campuses implement a continuing education program whereby faculty can receive continuing education credit (CE) for each course they complete within a year. This credit would count toward the professional development criterion for faculty promotion, tenure, and reappointment. This practice is currently underway in the clinical settings. Case in point, clinical laboratory staff participate in proficiency testing and employee training yearly. Each staff member must complete 12 continuing education (CE) credits a year by participating in a combination of lectures, seminars, and online courses.[30] Laboratories are penalized when their respective staff are unsuccessful in completing their summed credits within a given year. CE credit is a useful way to track and monitor faculty professional development training and should be implemented in all CUNY campuses. Faculty should complete six CE credits a year in professional development. Each course could range anywhere from one to six CE credits. Types of professional development may vary as well as credits assigned. If faculty attend conferences pertaining to their field of study it can be supplemented for CE credit pending departmental approval. CE credit for conferences will be at the discretion of each department. Departments and campuses at large must bear the initial burden of implementing, monitoring and enforcing this policy.

Policy 5.28: Faculty preparation and development
Created: October 17, 2015

Preamble: A good portion of faculty within the CUNY system were hired based on field/industry experience and for this they are knowledgeable but lack pedagogical techniques and course content depth. Many newly hired faculty are forced to learn by trial and error. This may result in student failures during primary teaching years as well as students feeling they are not getting anything out of the course; their feeling of not being taught anything; decrease student retention or ultimately poor graduation rates[1]. On a case by case bases new faculty once hired are handed textbooks and syllabi and simply told the class start date and time. The faculty preparation program should be considered an on-the-job training program[2]. The pairing of new faculty with trained veteran professors will most certainly assist novice lecturers with the development of pedagogy and teaching strategies.

Contents:
A. Definitions
B. Policy
C. Process/Procedure
D. Contact Information
E. Forms

A. Definitions.
a. Mentor. Experienced/Senior faculty member approved to mentor mentees.
b. Mentee. Newly hired junior Faculty or existing faculty members instructing a course for the first time.

B. Policy
a. **General:**
  i. CUNY will provide on-the-job training for all new faculty employees as well as existing faculty who will teach a course for the first time.
  ii. CUNY employees will review and follow this policy and procedure.
b. **Mentors:**
  i. The assignment of senior faculty for the mentoring program will consist of a candidate's application for participation, recommendations from the department chair and approval from the departments' P & B.
  ii. Potential candidates must meet eligibility criteria that will consist of:
    1. instructing the course at a minimum of three consecutive years;
    2. received three consecutive satisfactory peer observations in that particular course and;
    3. Receive no less than 3.3 on three consecutive student evaluations.
  iii. Once accepted in the mentor program faculty must complete a one year training course to qualify as a mentor.
  iv. The training will be conducted by the campus professional development department.

The Call for Faculty Preparation   93

    c. Mentee:
- i. Newly hired junior faculty and all faculty teaching a course for the first time will co-teach their assigned course with their assigned senior faculty mentor.
- ii. Faculty teaching existing courses that feel they need additional support may apply to the program as a mentee.
    1. Volunteer participants will be assigned a mentor and begin at phase two

C. Process and Procedure
  i. Mentors:
    1. Phase 1:
- a. In phase one of the mentorship program each candidate will participate in a compensated full two day training seminar
- b. Day one will orient senior faculty to the mentorship program, policies and expectations.
- c. Day two will consist of pedagogy implementation in the classroom, and how to effectively evaluate their mentees.
    - i. This day will also focus on forms for the evaluation process.

    2. Phase 2:
- a. Phase two will provide the mentor with field experience in effectively evaluating a mentee.
- b. They will participate in a mock evaluation or shadowing event of a fellow mentor where applicable.
- c. Mentors will be given one semester to create, adjust, customize and prepare paperwork, and lesson plans for their incoming mentees.
- d. The professional development department is expected to be supportive of the mentoring faculty member for the full year of training.

    3. Phase 3:
- a. The last phase will consist of the mentor's assignment to a mentee when applicable.
- b. The mentor will be fully supported and documentation generated will be evaluated by the professional development department for effectiveness and critique.
- c. Upon successful completion of phase 3, each faculty mentor will receive a certificate of completion from the professional development department that will be recognized University-wide.

d. In accordance with existing CUNY policy 5.01 section 1.1 of the Academic Personnel Practice: Senior faculty responsibility[3]. The mentor will serve the department by providing on-the-job training to newly hired faculty and colleagues recommended or volunteered to the program.

ii. **Mentees:**
   1. **Phase 1**
      a. The mentees first employed semester should begin in phase one.
      b. Mentee will co-teach their assigned course with their assigned senior faculty mentor for one full semester.
      c. The mentee will play a supportive role in the classroom while learning through observation and interactions with their mentor and students.
      d. The mentor and mentee will meet daily to discuss lessons and in- class expectations.
   2. **Phase 2**
      a. mentee will teach a course (full semester) independent of the mentor
      b. The mentor is expected to be available as needed to fully support the mentee.
      c. Both participants will meet daily to discuss in- classroom experiences, establish goals and review future lesson plans as well as provide guidance towards tenure ship.
      d. The mentor will evaluate their mentee once every five weeks totaling three evaluations at the conclusion of phase two.
      e. The final evaluation will include the mentors' recommendations of the mentee.

iii. **Recommendations**

Recommended without continuation	☐ Satisfied or exceeded all program goals and expectations. ☐ Recommended for reappointment.
Recommended with continuation	☐ Shows promise of effectiveness but failed to meet all program goals and thus needs improvement. ☐ Recommended for reappointment. ☐ The mentee will participate in one additional semester in the mentee program at phase two and assigned a new mentor, where applicable.

Dismissal	☐ Continuously failed to meet program goals, failed to implement suggested pedagogy and/or was ineffective in the classroom. ☐ Not recommended for reappointment. ☐ Supporting documentation and interim corrective action reports must accompany this recommendation as well as signed documentation of union acknowledgement.

iv. Professional development department
1. Conduct faculty mentorship training
2. Will oversee the entire process, record relevant data for statistical purposes and evaluate the entire program for effectiveness and faculty retention.
3. Distribute certificates of completion to mentors and mentees.
4. Conduct faculty professional development courses that will serve as continuing education credit.

v. Department P & B
1. Will recommend and refer viable candidates for the mentorship program
2. May recommend and refer existing faculty in need of pedagogical development to mentee program.
3. All recommendations are reported to the departments P & B and professional development department for evaluation and tracking.
4. The P&B will make the final decision regarding the faculty's employment to which an on campus union representative must be present.

vi. PSC CUNY union representative
1. In accordance with CUNY policy 5.07 Excluded titles, applicability of professional staff congress-CUNY Collective bargaining agreement this policy shall apply to all employees[4] unless otherwise directed.
2. Union representative must be available and attend a meeting with mentor(s) and mentee alongside the P & B to discuss a candidate's recommendation of dismissal.
3. All attendee's will conclude on the final recommendation of the mentee in question.

vii. Faculty Professional Development

1. Courses which all new faculty are encouraged to enroll include but are not limited to: effective teaching strategies and purposeful pedagogy.
2. It is recommended that unions and campuses implement a continuing education program whereby faculty receive continuing education credit (CE) for each course they complete within a year[5].
3. Credit would count towards the professional development criterion for faculty promotion and reappointment.
4. Faculty should complete 6 credits a year in professional development.
5. Each course could range anywhere from 1–6 continuing education credits.
6. Types of professional development may vary as well as credits assigned.
7. Faculty attending conferences pertaining to their field of study may supplement it for continuing education credit pending departmental approval.
   a. Substitution of CE credit for conferences will be at the discretion of each department.
8. Departments and campuses at large must bear the initial burden of implementing, monitoring and enforcing this policy.

D. Contact information

a. The originator of this policy is Diane Price Banks, Faculty member at Bronx Community College and doctoral student with CUNY's Graduate Center's Urban Education program. She could be reached at Diane.Price@BCC.CUNY.EDU and 718-289-5536 (office).
b. Upon adoption of this policy the point person will be the professional and development department on each respective campus.

E. Forms

a. To be developed.

References:

[1] Hyman, Jeremy, and Lynn Jacobs. 2015. "10 Warning Signs of a Bad Professor." *US News & World Report*. Accessed September 27. http:// www. usnews. com/education/ blogs/ professors - guide/2010/01/ 06/10 - warning-signs-of-a-bad-professor.

[2] "Teacher Quality and Student Achievement: Research Review." 2015. Accessed September 27. http://www. centerforpubliceducation.org/Main-Menu/Staffingstudents/ Teacher-quality-and-student--achievement-At- a- glance/ Teacher-quality-and-student-achievement-Research-review.html.

3 "CUNY > Policy > Manual of General Policy." 2015. Accessed October 17. http://policy.cuny.edu/manual_of_general_policy/#Navigation_Location.
4 Ibid.
5 "Online Compliance and CE Courses for Clinical Labs." 2015. Accessed September 27. https://www.medialabinc.net/ continuing_ education_ and_ compliance_ courses_for_laboratories.aspx.

FIGURE 7.1 Policy 5.28

The Cost

The overall cost of the Price Prep Policy program is inexpensive when compared with the PAR program.[31] Mentoring faculty should be paid $1,000–$2,000 as a bonus and incentive to enroll as mentors. After completion of phase one, $500 should be distributed to the mentor. At the end of phase two, $250–$500 should be paid, and the remainder of the funds should be distributed at the end of phase three. Mentors who sign up for an additional year of mentoring—providing a new hire is available—should receive no less than $1,000/annum/mentee dispensed at $500/semester. During the mentoring process mentors should receive release time for meeting and supporting their mentee. The staff of the professional development department, if outsourced, will be paid a stipend to accommodate the initial training and year of oversight. If the staff are full-time then no additional cost will apply as this falls within current services they provide. This cost will vary from campus to campus. The mentee will receive no additional pay other than what they were hired to receive. However, some campuses may opt to provide incentives to encourage new faculty to participate in the program. The overall cost for the Price Prep Policy program will vary from campus to campus and year to year. The hiring of new faculty and the training of mentoring faculty will vary in number and potentially fluctuate in cost from time to time. In addition, each institution is financially independent of one another. Faculty wages vary from person to person. The listed factors make it difficult to determine the total cost at this time. A ballpark figure is estimated at $5,425 for one mentor and one mentee at phase one and two of the Price Prep Policy program. This figure includes the one-and-a-half year mentor training and one-year mentee training. If the mentor recommends the mentee for continuation in the Price Prep Policy program then the total cost would increase to include one additional semester totaling $6,460.

Funding Sources for the Price Prep Policy

Currently, CUNY's operational cost is $3 billion annually; 46 percent of which is covered by New York State and 10 percent comes from the New York City budget.³² The remaining 44 percent is covered by grants and donations. Additionally, in 2015 CUNY was awarded $3.5 million of Race to the Top (RTTT) funds for faculty professional development through its teacher preparation programs.³³ Lastly, PSC CUNY, the union for faculty and staff, handsomely awards scholarships of $3,500–$12,000 toward professional development.³⁴ With funds from the RTTT grant, scholarships offered by PSC CUNY, and possible appropriations from the CUNY Board of Trustees, this project is financially feasible for implementation.

Networks of Power

The major organizations that impact this area of interest are CUNY at large and its faculty, students, and Board of Trustees. In the K-12 grade levels the major organizations of power are teacher preparation programs like: Peer Assistance and Review (PAR) in Toledo, Ohio; National Council on Teacher Quality (NCTQ); EdTPA; American Association of Colleges for Teacher Education (AACTE); and Pearson, to name a few.

Generally, the power in higher education is wielded by faculty in their classrooms, in their departments and as active members of the Union in regards to content taught in classrooms. It is most certainly wielded by College administration through its committees, Deans, Vice Presidents, and Presidents. Students in the vein of student government and participation in college committees also wield power. However, power is ultimately wielded by CUNY's Board of Trustees, which consists of 17 members.

Of the 17 members, 15 were appointed by former Mayor Michael Bloomberg, current Mayor Bill Di Blasio, and current Governor Andrew Cuomo. Of the 15 members, Mayor Di Blasio and Governor Cuomo recently appointed 13 within the last 4 years. Of the full 17-member Board, one is a current faculty member for CUNY while the other is a current student representing all students within the CUNY system. The policy and purpose of CUNY's Board of Trustees, as stated on their website is,

> To preserve, enhance, and improve the University as an institution of the highest quality and standards, with a faculty and administration charged to fulfill both the general and specific missions of the University: to educate and serve the people of New York City, to constitute an urban-oriented institutions of higher education, and to engage persistently in the search for knowledge and truth.³⁵

The new Board of Trustees, in accordance with their policy, must in good conscience look to ways that will improve its faculty and better its students.

William C. Thompson, newly appointed Chair of CUNY's Board of Trustees and former Comptroller for the City of New York, as well as former five-term

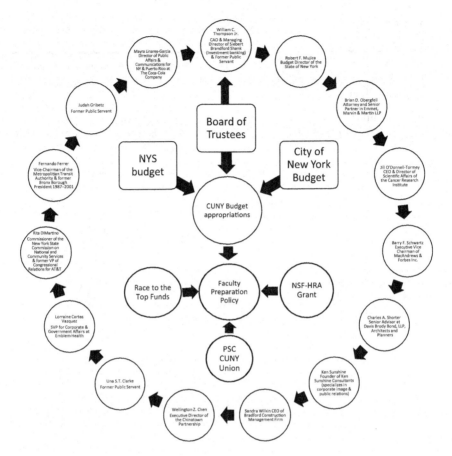

FIGURE 7.2 Structure of CUNY

president of New York City Board of Education, is a person of particular interest in the implementation of this policy. As Board chair, he has the power and authority to add the faculty preparation policy to upcoming meeting agendas for discussion, notwithstanding, his background in education gives him the personal insight of how to effectively implement a policy of this magnitude to CUNY at large. The question is, does this policy fit the political agenda of the new Board?

The Chairperson for CUNY's University Student Senate is the only student member of the Board. Students generally hold this seat for one academic year. Fall 2016 will usher in a new student senator. As a student tasked with speaking to the Board on behalf of all 274,357 CUNY students,[36] this person can also present the faculty preparation policy for addition to the agenda. The University Student Senate at large would ultimately find comfort in this policy as it provides much needed structural training for incoming faculty, many of whom had classes instructed by novice faculty who lacked pedagogical and classroom management

TABLE 7.1 The City University of New York (CUNY) Current Board of Trustees as of June 15, 2016

Mayor Michael Bloombergs appointees (Date)	Mayor Bill de Blasio appointees (Date)	Governor George Pataki appointees (Date)	Governor Andrew Cuomo appointees (Date)
Rita DiMartino (July 2003 & 2010)	Una S.T. Clarke (June 2015)	Wellington Z. Chen (2000 & 2005) term ends June 2017	William C. Thompson Jr. (June 25, 2016)
Judah Gribetz, term ended June 2014 (still listed as trustee to date)	Lorraine Cortes-Vazquez (June 16, 2016)		Brian D. Obergfell (June 2012) – Nominated by governor and unanimously confirmed by NYS senate
Charles A. Shorter (2008 & 2013) term ends in 2020			Mayra Linares-Garcia (June 15, 2016)
			Robert F. Mujica (June 15, 2016)
			Fernando Ferrer (June 15, 2016)
			Jill O'Donnell-Tormey (June 25, 2015)
			Barry F. Schwartz (May 6, 2014)
			Ken Sunshine (June 15, 2016)
			Sandra Wilkin (June 15, 2016)

skills. This should be thought of as a great movement toward the progressive betterment of classroom instruction for all learning types.

The Chairperson for the University Faculty Senate serves as a member of the Board for 2 years. This individual is usually an active member of the teaching body of CUNY and represents all 6,700 plus faculty members within the system. As a member of the teaching body this individual ideally comes with first-hand experience as a faculty member, new or veteran. Possessing knowledge of the trenches may provide support for services desperately needed on the front lines. Faculty, both veteran and novice, would appreciate the faculty preparation program. Participating veteran faculty will have the opportunity to share their knowledge and earn extra capital per annum. New faculty will have the opportunity to better prepare, manage, and instruct a variety of different learning styles and abilities in the classroom.

There are many powerful and influential people at CUNY and beyond who may help needed services get into the right hands. However, for the purposes of this chapter I focused on the above members as they may have a stake in the need for faculty preparation. As for the remaining members of the Board, and as potential employers of CUNY graduates, they may come to appreciate the policy as graduates would be better prepared and workforce ready.

Conclusion

Many newly hired faculty learn pedagogy and classroom management skills by trial and error as they acquire years of experience. A good percentage of CUNY faculty were hired based on practical experience and for this they are knowledgeable but may lack pedagogical techniques and course content depth. This may result in student achievement gaps and the loss of seven out of ten STEM majors during the first year of college. As the business of higher education, and on a case-by-case basis, new faculty once hired are handed their textbooks, along with the course syllabi, and simply told the class start date and time. The faculty preparation program should be considered as an on-the-job training program. The pairing of new faculty with trained veteran professors will most certainly assist novice lecturers with developing classroom management skills and pedagogy. The three-phase mentorship program will afford veteran faculty needed instructions in preparation for a mentee. In addition, the two-phase mentee program will afford new faculty the time and attention needed to acclimate to the teaching profession despite the lack of previous teaching experience. The Price Prep Policy model can also be effective in removing ineffective faculty from classrooms regardless of tenure or union status. Overall, the policy encourages faculty to improve upon their pedagogical skills and form effective teaching strategies.

Unsurprisingly, CUNY's Board of Trustees largely consists of non-faculty and student based individuals. The Board members are mainly composed of industry personnel and entrepreneurs from marketing and public relations sectors to construction management firms and cellphone moguls. This practice seems to mirror the traditional hiring approach for higher education institutions. It is not surprising that an institution for learning would have a minimal number of faculty and students on its Board and instead an overwhelming amount of industrial contributors. Unfortunately, this is the business of education. The true power-holders are those who are not educators and lack teaching skills in the classroom yet possess outstanding organizational and management skills. There is a complete disconnect in terms of what is needed in the classroom and what is provided by boards of trustees. The authors in this book have reiterated one salient point. The best problem-solving approach to policy should not be top-down but, rather, bottom-up. The insights possessed by those in the trenches are the best practices worth implementing. However, the voices of the front line consistently fall on deaf ears and quite often are overlooked. College administrators and boards of trustees have created a seemingly impenetrable bubble around the caucuses that create and implement policies, to which the effected have little to no say regarding its development and oftentimes even its implementation.

In reading the excerpts from the RTTT grant for faculty professional development awarded to CUNY's teacher preparation programs, CUNY proclaimed themselves as leaders in educator preparation, and further stated they were currently engaging in groundbreaking work to enhance its preparation programs. This moment proves to be great timing for the introduction and implementation of the Price Prep Policy plan.

Despite the dynamics involved in the business of higher education, it is essential to incorporate faculty preparation for the advancement of our college students and our country. Faculty preparation is necessary as it ensures students receive proper and effective instruction. It is imperative that America does all that it can to maintain its status as a world leader in all things within STEM and the liberal arts. The Price Prep Policy should not be seen as a change from the business of higher education but rather a much needed improvement.

Notes

1 "Visiting Professor David Petraeus's Spring 2014 Course." 2013. *Macaulay Now.* November 5. http://macaulay.cuny.edu/community/now/2013/11/visiting-professor-david-petraeuss-spring-2014-course/
2 Dobuzinskis, Alex. 2013. "David Petraeus Gets New Job After Resignation." *The Huffington Post.* April 23. www.huffingtonpost.com/2013/04/24/david-petraeus-cuny_n_3144059.html
3 Boice, Robert. 1991. "New Faculty as Teachers." *The Journal of Higher Education,* 62(2): 150–173. doi: 10.2307/1982143
4 Ibid., p. 169.
5 Braskamp, Larry A., and John C. Ory. 1994. *Assessing Faculty Work: Enhancing Individual and Institutional Performance.* San Francisco, CA: Jossey-Bass.
6 Boice, Robert. 1991. "New Faculty as Teachers." *The Journal of Higher Education,* 62(2): 150–173. doi: 10.2307/1982143
7 The Executive Office of the President. 2014. "White House Report on Increasing College Opportunity for Low-income Students" January. https://www.whitehouse.gov/sites/default/files/docs/white_house_report_on_increasing_college_opportunity_for_low-income_students_1-16-2014_final.pdf
8 Chen, Xianglei. 2013. "STEM Attrition: College Students' Paths into and out of STEM Fields. Statistical Analysis Report. NCES 2014-001." National Center for Education Statistics. http://eric.ed.gov/?id=ED544470
9 Ibid.

10 Boice, Robert. 1991. "New Faculty as Teachers." *The Journal of Higher Education*, 62(2): 150–173. doi: 10.2307/1982143
11 Ibid., p. 154.
12 Ibid.
13 Ibid.
14 Ibid., p. 155.
15 Ibid.
16 Ibid., p. 159.
17 Ibid., p. 173.
18 Ibid., p. 155.
19 Ibid., p. 156.
20 Hall, G. Stanley. 1905. "What Is Pedagogy?" *The Pedagogical Seminary*, 12(4): 375–383. doi:10.1080/08919402.1905.10534667
21 Fink, Dee L. 1984. *The First Year of College Teaching (Jossey Bass Higher and Adult Education)*. San Francisco, CA: Jossey Bass.
22 Wanat, Matthew A., Marc L. Fleming, Julianna M. Fernandez, and Kevin W. Garey. 2014. "Education, Training, and Academic Experience of Newly Hired, First-Time Pharmacy Faculty Members." *American Journal of Pharmaceutical Education*, 78(5): 92. doi: 10.5688/ajpe78592
23 Ramsden, Paul. 2003. *Learning to Teach in Higher Education*. New York: Routledge, p. 4.
24 Ibid., p. 9.
25 Emiliani, Bob. "Why Professors Can't Teach." The Lean Professor Lean Teaching in Higher Education (blog), February 9, 2014. Accessed September 30, 2016. www.leanprofessor.com/2014/02/09/professors-cant-teach/
26 Ibid.
27 Boylan, Myles G., Teri Jo Murphy, Ellen Carpenter, and Abiodun Ilumoka. 2015. "Improving Undergraduate STEM Education: Education and Human Resources (IUSE: EHR)." National Science Foundation – Where Discoveries Begin. June 29, 2015. https://nsf.gov/publications/pub_summ.jsp?org=nsf.
28 "Faculty Mentoring Program – Internal Funding Programs – CUNY." 2015. Accessed September 1, 2015. www.cuny.edu/research/faculty-resources/internal-funding-programs/FacultyMentorshipProgram.html
29 Ohio Department of Education. 2011. "Ohio-S-Model-Peer-Assistance-and-Review-PAR-Program.pdf.pdf" May 27. https://education.ohio.gov/getattachment/Topics/Teaching/Educator-Standards-Board/Ohio-s-Model-Peer-Assistance-and-Review-PAR-Program.pdf.aspx
30 Forsetlund, Louise, Arild Bjørndal, Arash Rashidian, Gro Jamtvedt, Mary Ann O'Brien, Fredric M. Wolf, Dave Davis, Jan Odgaard-Jensen, and Andrew D. Oxman. 2009. "Continuing Education Meetings and Workshops: Effects on Professional Practice and Health Care Outcomes." In Cochrane Database of Systematic Reviews. John Wiley & Sons. http://onlinelibrary.wiley.com/doi/10.1002/14651858.CD003030.pub2/abstract
31 Papay, John P., and Susan Moore Johnson. 2012. "Is PAR a Good Investment? Understanding the Costs and Benefits of Teacher Peer Assistance and Review Programs." *Educational Policy*, 26(5): 696–729. http://epx.sagepub.com/content/26/5/696.short
32 City University of New York. 2011. "2011 Budget." https://www.budget.ny.gov/pubs/archive/fy0910archive/eBudget0910/agencyPresentations/pdf/cuny.pdf

33 Chancellor's letter. 2016. "FY2016BudgetRequest.pdf." www2.cuny.edu/wp-content/uploads/sites/4/page-assets/about/trustees/FY2016BudgetRequest.pdf
34 "PSC-CUNY Grants | PSC CUNY." 2015. Accessed October 12, 2015. www.psc-cuny.org/our-benefits/psc-cuny-grants
35 City University of New York. Board of Trustees (2016). *Manual of General Policy*. http://policy.cuny.edu/manual_of_general_policy/article_ii/policy_2.01/text/#Navigation_Location
36 City University of New York. Board of Trustees (2016). www.cuny.edu/irdatabook/rpts2_AY_current/ENRL_0019_UGGR_FTPT_HIST.rpt.pdf

8

EXPLORING FEDERAL FINANCIAL AID NETWORKS

Who Cares and Why?

Corie A. McCallum

Original Insight and Background

The United States federal government has long-established rules and regulations for the disbursement of federal financial aid funding to students dating back to the Higher Education Act of 1965. Initially, I had planned to explore a small section of the 1998 Amendments to the Higher Education Act of 1965 that enforced a new law in regard to Title IV funding for students who were convicted of a drug offense by state or federal government—a law that is still very much in practice today. That new amendment from 1998 stated that students would not be eligible to receive Title IV federal funding if they were "convicted of any offense under any Federal or State law involving the possession or sale of a controlled substance" (Civic Impulse, 2015). As a higher education professional working in conjunction with financial aid at one of the colleges in a large, urban university system, I am very involved with the Title IV process and this amendment piqued my interest. Additionally, as the primary conduct officer at the college, it seemed fitting that I might come across some of the students who could be affected by the 1998 HEA amendments. However, once I began the research, many of my ideas about the 1998 amendments and others changed. While the importance of changing that particular aspect of the 1998 HEA amendments still resonated with me, the impact of those restrictions touched far fewer students. So, I would not say I had a change of heart, but a change of focus.

Instead of creating a sort of exposé on those who *cannot* receive federal financial aid and why they cannot receive it, I decided that I would focus on Title IV Federal Financial Aid policy in general and how it is created, changed, and administered by the federal government. Who makes the decisions about the amount of Pell Grants to be dispersed in a given year? Are there major corporations, like Sallie Mae, that play a role in the decisions of the Department of Education? Who are the people lobbying for more (or less) financial aid availability, especially loans, for students? Additionally, in my quest for answers to the questions about the overall function of Title IV funding, more specific questions arose around education policies that shape the way financial aid decisions are made. While financial aid and Title IV funding remained a focus for this research, I could not ignore the intersection of economic policies and education in the United States. How would increasing the minimum wage and poverty indicators affect Pell funding? How many students utilize Title IV funding? Can the United States have free college for all, too? How would the recent presidential candidates' plans for education impact financial aid? Those are the questions that guided my thinking and for which I attempted to provide some answers. I have also provided my own insight into the world of financial aid as a Student Affairs professional entrenched in the current system.

Financial Aid Funding: Origins and Processes

Origins

Similar to nearly every ideal we have in place about education in this country, financial aid was not established by the good people of the United States or even the original 13 colonies. Financial Aid, more appropriately called "pious" giving in its very early days, was among the first kinds of financial aid established in the medieval times. Needless to say, there have been a plethora of changes since the original ideas of student-paid, church-paid, or crown/state-paid financial aid of the medieval times. However, the underlying principal of "pulling yourself up by your bootstraps" that originated with those early years in education, where religion and piousness undergirded the pursuit of education, are still in effect today (Fuller, 2014).

The University of Bologna has also played a significant role in the construction of the original forms of financial aid. The students, who hired professors directly, would form together to insure that they could keep receiving instruction even when some students could not pay. Fuller (2014) described this process as the first need-based institute of financial aid; students not able to pay would have to receive funds from senior students who maintained their "nation's" funds as loans (Fuller, 2014). Fast forward 900+ years and we have a seemingly completely different system in place today in the United States. Although our current processes and how we determine needs have changed, the barebones structure of state-paid giving has remained intact.

Moving into the twentieth century, in 1965, President Lyndon B. Johnson signed the Higher Education Act (HEA) of 1965 into law.[1] The HEA was originally created "to strengthen the educational resources of our colleges and universities and to provide financial assistance for students in post-secondary and higher education".[2] The HEA provided stipulations and directives for how federal money would be distributed to the states and ultimately to the students. Essentially, the HEA provided the basis for the formulation of student loan programs like Federal Family Education Loan (FFEL) and the Pell grant. Since its inception, the HEA has been amended at least half a dozen times (Kantrowitz, 2015a). In addition to amendments, in 2008 the Higher Education Opportunity Act (HEOA) was enacted, which reauthorized the original HEA and extended the provisions of the HEA (ACE NET, 2016). With the enactment of the HEOA, the original HEA was extended until 2013, though recently Congress has extended the law through 2016 (ACE NET, 2016). However, a complete overhaul of the law is expected to occur in the following months as Congress's recent extension was set to expire in September 2016. Ironically, the importance of these laws and the influence of lawmakers, lobbyists, and the general public goes unnoticed to those not directly impacted by the effects. In the not too distant past of the 1990s when many of the amendments to the HEA were passed, the complicated language and hundreds of pages of information, as well as extended periods of time that lawmakers wasted fighting over other, often unrelated, issues, prevented financial aid issues in higher education from coming to the forefront. However, with the proliferation of student loan debt and the ability for students and parents to voice their opinions about it now, financial aid issues, especially around access and the cost of access are certainly at the forefront today.

Processes

American tax dollars and a federal budget, created years in advance, provide the funding for federal financial aid and, specifically, Title IV funding. What might be a more accurate statement is that the HEA defines and directs the taxes of the American people along with some government subsidy to supply federally based financial aid. In the 2014–2015 school year alone, taxpayer dollars and government subsidies supplied over 150 billion dollars in federal financial aid to students across the country (Federal Student Aid, n.d.). The president's allocations for a given year determine the way in which the funding will be disbursed. These allocations are made years in advance though, sometimes disabling a current president from making changes immediately to the next year's funding scheme. Whatever federal aid is available for students is then distributed by the United States Department of Education. These resources include loans, grants, and work-study programs. Within each of those sources are multiple varieties of each kind of aid, which I will explain in detail later.

There are four major federal grant programs, including the Federal Pell Grant (Pell), Federal Supplemental Educational Opportunity Grant (FSEOG), the Teacher Education Assistance for College and Higher Education (TEACH) Grant, and the Iraq and Afghanistan Service Grant (Grants and Scholarships, n.d.). While all of these grants are needs-based, the TEACH grant and Iraq/Afghanistan service grants come with additional qualifying stipulations for students to receive them, including service post-graduation and stringent timelines of eligibility for those whose parents were serving in the military after the 9/11 tragedy (Grants and Scholarships, n.d.). In order for students to receive these grants (or even loans, which I discuss later), they must complete the Free Application for Federal Student Aid or FAFSA. In the past, students completed the FAFSA at the beginning of the calendar year in January, to determine their eligibility to receive funds for the upcoming academic year. However, recent changes by President Obama have significantly changed and improved the FAFSA process.

As a result of changes made by the Obama Administration of the Department of Education, the FAFSA now will now be available three months earlier—beginning in October 2016 students can file for aid around the same time as college application processes begin (Fact Sheet, 2015). Not only will the FAFSA be available significantly earlier, the president has allowed prior, prior-year tax information to be considered in determining students' eligibility for funding (Fact Sheet, 2015). The changes will allow students to apply earlier and also to apply with fewer obstacles or complications that changing tax information from the previous year can sometimes create. For example, a student intending to enroll in college under the previous iteration of FAFSA regulations would need to apply for aid using FAFSA in January of the year they would attend, so January of 2015 for enrollment in Fall of 2015. Under the new regulations, a student intending to enroll in college for the Fall 2017 semester would need to file the FAFSA beginning in October of 2016. This change allows students to meet college and universities' "priority deadlines," which allow the students to be eligible for additional funding (FAFSA, n.d.). In the older iteration of FAFSA regulations, most colleges and universities accepted applications until mid-March for priority deadlines, but this left a very small window of time for students to update their or their parents' tax information, which is now a moot point, thanks to the prior-prior year tax information. In other words, students can use tax information (theirs and or their parents) for the year prior to which they apply. Additionally, the priority deadlines for additional funding, like Federal Supplemental Educational Opportunity Grants (FSEOG) or additional monies awarded to the school through the state (TAP for New York State) or other agencies would become even more pressing (FAFSA, n.d.). Again with the new regulations governing FAFSA, the final deadline for FAFSA will remain the end of June, with all corrections (corrections can include changing marital status or parental information) being due in early fall (Student Aid Deadlines, n.d.).

The Department of Education uses FAFSA and the financial information students provide on the application in combination with complicated metrics for determining student eligibility. These metrics are composed of multiple answers that students report on their FAFSA about topics from tax information to savings to investments, among other things. From that information, FAFSA metrics assign the student a specific dollar amount known as the Expected Family Contribution. The Expected Family Contribution (EFC) represents the student and his or her family's portion of financial responsibility for a college education. Further, the EFC is based on all the financial, tax, and in some cases living situations, of the students. For example, in the 2015–2016 academic year, a student whose parents earned less than $24,000 for the 2014 tax year and received some form of needs-based benefits (like SNAP or TANF in New York state) would receive a zero for their EFC for the academic year (EFC Formula Guide, 2016). In other words, the family would not be expected to contribute any funds to the student's college expenses. While some may argue that this is a positive and generous program, it does not negate the fact that some students must live in poverty, endure unfair obstacles to accessing colleges and universities, and basically ensure massive loan accrual for students with zero EFC scores. However, there is at least one positive benefit of using the EFC formula and that's the simple fact that the United States Department of Education does not use the federal poverty guidelines to make a determination of the amount of money families can expect to pay out of pocket for higher education expenses (FAQs, 2015).

While the disuse of federal poverty guidelines does not seem to further the economic disparity among citizens of the United States, a look at the National Center for Education Statistics' report on Student Financial Aid Estimates for 2011–2012 showed that of the students living in poverty (poverty as defined by the EFC guidelines as having an automatic EFC of 0) more than half, or 56.6 percent, are still using loans to finance their education (NPSAS: 12, 2013). More strikingly, the study showed that seemingly middle-class students (the federal government makes no determination of "middle-class" or "wealthy"), or in this case students whose parents earned more than $40,000 ($40,000–59,999) but less than $80,000 ($60,000–79,999) annually, had the highest percentages of students borrowing at 63.6 percent and 58.3 percent, respectively (NPSAS: 12, 2013). The fact that at least half of students, whether in poverty or not, are using loans to supplement their education costs is a cause for major concern. Whether students are borrowing to pay their room and board while living on campus or using loans to provide childcare for their children while taking night classes, education is costing us significantly more than it ever has, with what seem like fewer and fewer job opportunities to show for it. To be fair, though, fairness and equity seemingly have no place in the financing of education; there have been some important changes to the way federal loans and grants are distributed. For review, the following list from Federal Student Aid (2015) explains all the categories of aid and then lists the kind of aid each category provides. As I discussed previously, students must complete the FAFSA to be eligible for any of the kinds of aid listed below:

- Loans
  - Direct Loan
  - Federal Perkins Loan
- Grants
  - Federal Pell Grant

- Teacher Education Assistance for College and Higher Education (TEACH) Grants
- Federal Supplemental Educational Opportunity Grant (FSEOG)
• Federal Work-Study (FWS) (Federal Student Aid, n.d.).

As students continue to enroll in colleges and universities, the recent changes in the way students apply for aid have helped, from my perspective, in being able to afford college while they are attending. But, as is the case for many, myself included, affording the debt associated with college continues to be a struggle—particularly for those with loan debt. In recent years, through the Obama administration, there has been a major focus on fixing student loan debt, increasing the Pell Grant, and the destruction of the Federal Family Education Loan (FFEL)—all of which were impacted by the Health Care and Education Reconciliation Act. With the passing of the Health Care and Education Reconciliation Act of 2010, the Federal Family Education Loan was terminated (Kantrowitz, 2015a). This means that the federal government has effectively cut the financing of loans by "middlemen" and now only offers loans directly to the borrowers. Prior to the act, student loan borrowers had a choice between Direct Loans, which are funded directly through the Department of Education, or FFEL, which were funded through banks and other financial institutions that received subsidies from the government for providing student loans (Kantrowitz, 2015b). The act, described below, meant more funding for Pell and other small programs as well as an increase in the loan servicing business of Sallie Mae, now Navient, and other big name servicers, like Nelnet. Kantrowitz (2015a) describes the changes as follows:

> The Health Care and Education Reconciliation Act of 2010 (P.L. 111-152) was passed by the House and Senate on March 25, 2010 along party lines and signed into law by President Obama on March 30, 2010. The bill eliminates the federally-guaranteed student loan program (FFELP), with all new federal education loans made through the Direct Loan program starting July 1, 2010. The savings are redirected to the Pell Grant program, deficit reduction, improvements in income-based repayment and a variety of smaller programs. Most of the Pell Grant funding was used to backfill a funding shortfall from the American Recovery and Reinvestment Act of 2009 (stimulus bill) and to make permanent the increased maximum Pell Grant from that legislation.

While the Higher Education Act and all its amendments have been instrumental in governing the programs and funding streams of federal financial aid, there are several constituents both in government and the private sector that wish to influence the law and the creation and/or flow of funding from the federal government. Some of these organizations and individuals are well known, while others are behind-the-scenes tech gurus and lobbyists. Organizations such as

American Council on Education (ACE) boasts of its 1,600-person membership that represents presidents of colleges and universities across the country (American Council on Education, n.d.). ACE, an advocacy group that hails itself as the "convener of higher education associations," has lobbied for a dozen issues in 2015 including tax acts, the HEA renewal, and federal budget and appropriation issues (American Council on Education, n.d.). But ACE is just one of many education-based organizations that hope to influence educational policy by engaging those who are directly involved—college presidents, higher education officers, and even some faculty. However, there are other organizations that include constituents from both public and private sectors, which seemingly hope to influence higher education trends, though I am arguing, their benevolence comes with a price.

Influential Organizations and Leaders

The aforementioned tech gurus and behind-the-scenes lobbyists include people like Bill and Melinda Gates, Mark Zuckerberg, and Priscilla Chan, and others like Wendy and Eric Schmidt. These individuals and their foundations are almost famous for donating funding to research and other charitable enterprises, but to what end? How do these people, among many others, impact financial aid and higher education? For example, let's talk about Eric Schmidt of New America Education Central and EdCyclopedia. Both Education Central and EdCyclopedia, the organization and web resources, are parts of New America Foundation's Education Policy Program, which was founded in 1999 by Ted Halstead. Eric Schmidt, the Chair of the Board of Directors for New America and Executive Chairman at Google, was (at the time of the research for this article) on the Board of Directors at Apple, and also was a member of the Board of the popular publication *The Economist* (Schmidt, 2015 via Crunchbase). Interestingly, New America Foundation has another arm—their policy analysis tool known as "Atlas."

While Atlas provides important information about the effects of financial aid on students and the economy, it is important to note that Eric Schmidt's personal investments might play a role in those statistics. Furthermore, Dr. Schmidt recently invested $18 million into WibiData, a "software company that provides big data applications for enterprises to deliver personalized experiences across channels" (Schmidt, 2015 via Crunchbase). Considering that Atlas is a subsidiary of New America, it seems less than ironic that Atlas is where the information about financial aid sources, specifically federal aid, and funding streams abounds. I am not arguing that Eric Schmidt or the Zuckerbergs or the Gates are inherently evil people. But, the amount of money they are able to donate does allow for some questions about the influence of those donations. Do they have undue influence on policies and procedures because of the sheer volume they are able to give? Does their work in numerous corporations and companies cause conflicts

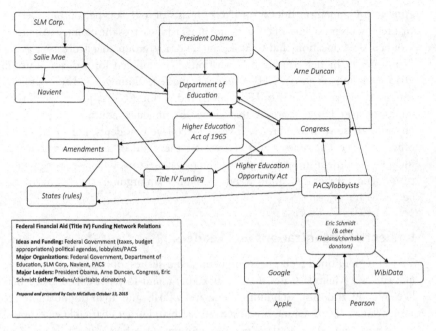

FIGURE 8.1 Structure of the Higher Education Act of 1965

of interest? I think we would be remiss not to consider those questions and the fact that most donations come with their own tax benefits—be they for the individual or the foundation.

As I have discussed, key players for federal financial aid ideas do not stop at individuals. There are multiple advocacy groups, lobbyists, and politically inclined foundations that have interest in financial aid, and the way in which it is dispersed (Kantrowitz, 2015c). Some of those key players include Sallie Mae, Nelnet, and other political entities like education unions and even private donors. In short, these players made and still make money from student loans. In the long version of this story, these corporations know that less funding for Pell and other grant money equates to need for students. That need is then supplemented by loans. The *types* of loans are of significant interest to Sallie Mae, Nelnet, and other loan-related corporations. Now that the FFEL program has ended and effectively eliminated banks and other financial institutions from dispersing funds to students directly and therefore also eliminated the subsidies those financial institutions received from the federal government, it would seem that these corporations have a lot more to contribute to the discussion about financial aid and loans (Kantrowitz, 2015b).

Sallie Mae, whose parent company is SLM Corporation, was the principal government-affiliated agency that provided public, government-guaranteed student loans for over 30 years. Since its inception in 1973, Sallie Mae has been first a public loan originator, then a private loan originator for student loans, and now is a servicer for the government in addition to keeping its own private loan business for students (Sallie Mae, 2016). Recently, though, in 2014, Sallie Mae split into two companies, Navient and Sallie Mae (Stratford, 2014). Sallie Mae's association with the government still maintains about $550 billion in contracts to service federal direct loans (Kiersh, 2009). And while Sallie Mae may have lost some of its ability to lend directly to the student loan borrower population with the changes in law and in their business practices, Sallie Mae has still given substantial campaign funds and other donations to Republican and Democratic party members of the House and Senate. They too know the importance of their influence on individuals. Most notably John Boehner, former Republican Speaker, received in 2009, just before the elimination of the government's indirect or Federal Family Education Loan in 2010, the maximum amount of $250,000 in the 2009–2011 session of Congress (Kiersh, 2009). However, Senator Boehner was not alone. In 2014, over 80 percent of lobbyists for SLM Corporation, the parent company of Sallie Mae, were former government employees connected to the Department of Education and other federal-level positions (Opensecrets.org, 2014). While SLM and Navient as corporations saw increases in their budget and contracts with the federal government, one would be remiss not to mention one other particular individual: former Secretary of Education, Arne Duncan.

Although Duncan's contributions to the state of education in the US today are most distinctly tied to his work with the K-12 sector with Common Core initiatives and increased testing mandates, he has played an important role in the increased funding of Title IV, specifically Pell Grants. Both Duncan and President Obama worked to relieve middlemen in the higher education loan funding processes and discontinued FFEL. But Duncan and President Obama's collaboration on this initiative should not come as a surprise, as Duncan and President Obama were friends during President Obama's time in the Senate and Duncan's time as CEO of Chicago Public Schools—where Duncan was notorious for closing public schools and reopening them as charters. The key players are not just politicians though—as I have examined in previous sections, they can be any people or corporations with money to give and something to gain. The public must be scrupulous and diligent in the investigation of relationships to private sector donors and philanthropists who tout influencing and ultimately changing education policies "for the better."

As I have explained, there are several players that are involved in funding programs, whether financial aid related or not, within the federal government. The lobbyists, PACS, and foundations that have interest in education in general are innumerable and range from small, grassroots groups like Grassroots Education Movement to superpower "philanthropists" like the Gates' Foundation. Political parties, candidates, and private individuals all have a stake in education as business and as a tool to control future economic and capital development in the United

States. Unfortunately, it seems that most of these groups (individuals as well) have one major focus—education as a means to a capitalistic and monetized end.

Can Free College Fix It All?

At a time in which K-12 education seems to be suffering through test-and-punish standards, a series of ineffective legislation initiatives like No Child Left Behind and Race to the Top, and now Every Student Succeeds Act, as well as a lack of funding, it seems nearly impossible to consider the effects of funding for higher education. Still, it seems that the United States as a country values higher education and often considers attaining a college degree a symbol of wealth and prosperity. As an educator, seeing terms like "college readiness" and "grit" becoming more popular leads me to believe that the idea of employability and the ability to make money are beginning to define what we think of as happiness and even success. Further, common mantras like "stay in school," "keep your grades up," and "graduate and get a good job," flow easily from adults to high school students as they prepare to officially enter adulthood. There seem to be deeply held beliefs about what it means to be successful in this country. These well-meaning people often forget to mention that even if a student gets a "good job" after college or even scholarships while in college, that they will likely be burdened by a large debt as the rising cost of college, in addition to potential loan issues, constrict finances for students after graduation. Not only do current students use loans, but they also struggle to find jobs, even with a degree. It seems like now, more than ever, making college tuition free would positively impact the country. Everyone from President Obama to Democratic Senator and former presidential candidate Bernie Sanders has a plan to make that happen. When Senator Sanders lost the party nomination, he and Secretary Clinton appear to have collaborated, as Secretary Clinton's plan echoes ideas from Senator Sanders' plan. President Obama too has taken strides to address college affordability and debt. And then, unfortunately, there is the case of Mr. Trump. What is missing from any plans addressing higher education and the funding for it is the impetus to examine what role higher education plays in the United States. We should question whether that role was defined by the people, for the people, and how might the people want to change its role. Whether it's the New College Compact plan proposed by Secretary Clinton, Senator Sanders' College for All Act, or Trump's plan (at the time of publication, he had not indicated a formal platform on higher education policy), we should be taking a broader look at the purpose of education outside of capitalistic endeavors. So yeah, free college would be great. But, to what end?

Parting Thoughts

Throughout this work I have argued that there is a continual push to fund higher education and that the idea of degrees equating to jobs remains unquestioned.

Further, I have argued that although there are both Republicans and Democrats alike lining their pockets with donations from Sallie Mae, Navient, and Google, there is again little to no mainstream critical thought about higher education and the purpose of it. From my perspective as a Student Affairs professional in higher education, as a society, we do not consider how $20,000 in student loan debt (a modest amount by any standards) positively impacts a student or their ability to be a happy and productive citizen. Instead, what we measure is the number of years it will take a person to pay off that debt, and how quickly they do so depends on how "good" a job they get with their degree and in many cases multiple degrees.

The idea that education is an economic stimulant affected by education policies alone has been debunked, though politicians, policy-makers, and even laymen have negated that finding with neoliberal thinking and promulgation of the "pull yourselves up by the bootstraps" mentality. To combat the "American Dream," ideology that is so pervasive in mainstream culture today, I look to the work of Jean Anyon, Joel Spring, and Stephen J. Ball, among few others. Perhaps most infamously, Anyon focuses on small, "winnable" battles in the community. Specifically, she touts going door-to-door to discuss school reforms with parents in a local community as an example of mobilizing and building a coalition of parents. In regard to federal financial aid policy, it is not as simple as mobilizing one school district, or rallying a particular PTA group. The work for this kind of reform must begin early, move forward with small steps, and prepare others for the long-haul as *indirect* policies are the key to effecting change in federal aid and higher education overall.

I am not from the K-12 sector of education, but I do realize that primary schooling is essentially the beginning of a student's college career. Access to pre-K, bilingual education, and other early education reform are some of the keys to ensure access to underrepresented minorities in higher education and essentially the end of the whitewashing of higher education as an institution. The following quote from Anyon's *Radical Possibilities* (2005) outlines my thinking and propels me as I continue the daily work of an educator. "Education is an institution whose basic problems are caused by, and whose basic problems reveal, the other crises in cities: poverty, joblessness and low-wages, and racial and class segregation" (Anyon, 2005, p. 177). Financial aid is an important factor in higher education, but it should not be a determining factor. Free college, student loan forgiveness, and charitable foundations might be the solutions to the problems in education, but only if we want to continue the pursuit of our capitalistic notions of success.

Notes

1 Mark Kantrowitz, "History of Student Financial Aid," FinAid, accessed October 2, 2015 from www.finaid.org/educators/history/.phtml

2 "H.R.—105th Congress: Higher Education Amendments of 1998," Civic Impulse, accessed October 2, 2015 from www.govtrack.us/congress/bills/105/hr6

References

ACE NET. (2016). Higher Education Act 2016. Retrieved September 3, 2016 from www.acenet.edu/advocacy-news/Pages/Higher-Education-Act.aspx

American Council on Education. (n.d.) Retrieved October 2, 2015 from www.acenet.edu/about-ace/Pages/default.aspx

Anyon, J. (2005). *Radical possibilities: Public policy, urban education, and a new social movement.* New York: Routledge.

Civic Impulse. (2015). H.R. 6—105th Congress: Higher Education Amendments of 1998. Retrieved from https://www.govtrack.us/congress/bills/105/hr6

EFC Formula Guide, 2015–2016. (2016). Information for financial aid professionals. Department of Education. Retrieved from http://ifap.ed.gov/efcformulaguide/090214EFCFormulaGuide1516.html

Fact Sheet. (2015). The President's plan for early financial aid: Improving college choice and helping more Americans pay for college. The White House, Office of the Press Secretary. September 13. Retrieved from https://www.whitehouse.gov/the-press-office/2015/09/14/fact-sheet-president's-plan-early-financial-aid-improving-college-choice

FAFSA (n.d.) Applying for aid. Retrieved September 20, 2016 from https://studentaid.ed.gov/sa/fafsa

Federal Student Aid. (n.d.). Retrieved October 1, 2015 from https://studentaid.ed.gov/sa/types#federal-aid

FAQs. (2015). Frequently asked questions related to the poverty guidelines and poverty. U.S. Department of Health and Human Services, Office of the Assistant Secretary for Planning and Evaluation. September 13. Retrieved from http://aspe.hhs.gov/frequently-asked-questions-related-poverty-guidelines-and-poverty#programs

Fuller, Matthew B. (2014). A history of financial aid to students. *Journal of Student Financial Aid*, 44(1): 4.

Grants and Scholarships. (n.d.) Retrieved November 29, 2015 from https://studentaid.ed.gov/sa/types/grants-scholarships

Kantrowitz, M. (2015a). History of student financial aid. Retrieved October 2, 2015 from www.finaid.org/educators/history.phtml

Kantrowitz, M. (2015b). Direct loan vs. the FFEL Program. Retrieved October 3, 2015 from www.finaid.org/loans/dl-vs-ffel.phtml

Kantrowitz, M. (2015c). Student aid lobbying and advocacy groups. Retrieved October 2, 2015 from www.finaid.org/questions/advocacy.phtml

Kiersh, A. (2009), Capital Eye Report: Direct or indirect loans? Either way, it's win-win deal for major political contributor Sallie Mae. Open Secrets Blog. July 23. Retrieved from https://www.opensecrets.org/news/2009/07/direct-or-indirect-loans-eithe/

National Postsecondary Student Aid Study 2011–12 (NPSAS: 12). (2013). Student Financial Aid Estimates for 2011–12. National Center for Education Statistics. Retrieved from http://nces.ed.gov/datalab/tableslibrary/viewtable.aspx?tableid=9064

OpenSecrets.org. (2014). "Profile for 2014 Election Cycle." The Center for Responsive Politics, 2014. Retrieved from https://www.opensecrets.org/orgs/summary.php?id=D000022253&cycle=2014.

Sallie Mae. (2016). History. Retrieved October 2, 2015 from https://www.salliemae.com/about/who-we-are/history/

Schmidt, Eric. (2015). Retrieved October 2, 2015 from Crunchbase: https://www.crunchbase.com/person/eric-schmidt#/entity

Stratford, Michael. (2014). Sallie Mae splits in two, names new loan servicing program "Navient." *Inside Higher Education.* February 26. Retrieved from https://www.insidehighered.com/quicktakes/2014/02/26/sallie-mae-splits-two-names-new-loan-servicing-unit-navient

Student Aid Deadlines. (n.d.) Retrieved November 29, 2015 from https://fafsa.ed.gov/deadlines.htm

9

A POLITICAL ECONOMY OF INCARCERATION

Race, Schooling, and the Criminal Justice System

Sakina Laksimi-Morrow

Introduction

"One of the few things that really work well in the Boston schools is the punitive trip downwards. The upward route is ten times harder and more obscure."[1]

The cumulative effects of Zero Tolerance policies enacted in public urban schools have led to a trajectory of institutionalized marginalization and disenfranchisement for youth of color. Research around the effects of Zero Tolerance policies on students in urban public schools has produced an extensive collection of data documenting the discriminatory patterns in disciplinary action enacted on youth of color. Findings indicate patterns of disparity as black and Latino/a boys and girls are disproportionately punished in comparison with their white counterparts. In fact, difference in punitive measures between black and white students begins as early as preschool.[2] The overwhelming narrative that the data around Zero Tolerance policies constructs is that there is a crisis within American public schools where racial and social inequalities are perpetuated and exacerbated through the dominant disciplinary regime that filters the (mis)behaviors and infractions of children and youth of color through a "crime control prism."[3] This term was coined by Paul Hirschfield, a sociologist and criminal justice expert, who presented a compelling theoretical framework for understanding an institutionalized form of social control. The crime control prism is a useful device by which to make meaning out of the historical relationship between black people and white society. This chapter positions schools' Zero Tolerance policies as part of the crime control paradigm that theorizes and enacts a particular kind of social order that maintains iterations of racial hierarchy. I make a case that the underpinning logic of the neo-liberal market economy in the United States has further influenced the political environment that continues to inscribe criminality on communities of color. These policy practices (suspension, expulsion, and arrest) subsume and consume youth into a system that is punitive not only to their present infractions but leads to a longer and more permanent punishment economy.[4] They are fed into the burgeoning carceral state that commits them to a trajectory of systemic institutional marginalization and disenfranchisement.

Arrest, Disruption, and Labeling: Zero Tolerance Policies

> The rule was there. It was relaxed for white children. It was enforced rigorously for Negroes. In this way the color line grew firm and strong.[5]

While conventional thought on the school to prison pipeline focuses on youths' referral to detention centers as the primary place of contact with criminalization, some theories present an even earlier intervention point that is critical to this process. In "Juvenile Arrest and the Collateral Educational Damage in Transition to Adulthood," Kirk and Sampson evaluate the effects of official intervention on school completion for youth.[6] They categorize arrest as a form of official intervention in which youth are stopped, handcuffed, and detained by police officers, often in front of peers, teachers, and staff. This enactment of Zero Tolerance policy brings the crime control paradigm into direct proximity with the school. The school becomes an extension of the processes of marginalization that happen in the realm of housing and labor, to name a few institutions that segregate, isolate, and marginalize communities of color.

When schools enact Zero Tolerance policies, they are replicating a form of social control that began in the 1980s with the drug war. Disciplinary action is shifted away from school personnel like teachers and principals, and given to police officers. Immediately, the behaviors and infractions of the children are filtered through crime control prism. In fact, arrest on school grounds is rather common. According to the U.S. Department of Statistics, 92,000 students nationwide were arrested in school between 2011 and 2012. In places like the New York City public schools, 74 percent of these arrests were for misdemeanors or civil violations.[7] Three quarters of these official interventions would not have been deferred to the domain of the juvenile criminal justice system had it not been for the widespread enactment of Zero Tolerance policies and the burgeoning expansion of school resource officers. These criminal justice officials have become a more pervasive part of the urban public school landscape since the 1994 Gun-Free School Act.[8]

The increased criminalization of youth behavior in school spaces through these policies has created barriers to student success and school completion. Kirk and Sampson assert that data findings indicate that arrests mark a disruption in the students' educational trajectories, and that such a disruption is highly correlated to school drop out and push out. Their research finds that the social stigma and consumed time in the system create collateral educational damage that has reverberations throughout students' academic lives.[9] Generally, sociologists have categorized three main frameworks to explain school dropout: social control theory, rational choice theory, and labeling theory. Social control theory posits that negative interactions at school weaken the social bonds between youth and the school community. This leads youth to resist returning to school and viewing school as a hostile and threatening environment. Second, rational choice theory explains that youth make the decision to drop out as future prospects for academic and social success seem increasingly dim in context of negative interactions with the police. They may see that their time and efforts are best invested elsewhere when they witness or experience negative interactions between criminal justice officials. Labeling theory asserts that when youth are labeled as criminals that signals a shift in perception by school staff and the community, and self-perception. The label carries a stigma, and the stigma mediates the relationship between the youth and public institutions that have branded the youth's behavior as delinquent or even criminal.[10]

There are several mechanisms by which labeling deviance and criminality generates negative effects on youth of color. First, being labeled deviant or criminal will influence a youth's self-perception. For youth of color that label is especially harrowing because it reflects and fulfills the racial stereotypes of mainstream media and discourse on black and brown criminality.[11] Studies find that labeling deviance has a stronger effect on disadvantaged youth because of the pre-existing negative stereotypes associated with these youths in mainstream culture: "[s]tructural location, such as race or social class, may provide people with differential means to resist deviant labeling in the face of official intervention."[12] In other words, these youth exist in a world ordered by social roles in which deviance and criminality are inscribed into their identity through images, television, film, music, and literature. Compounded by a lack of social capital, youth of color and poor youth are less able to resist these labels. These stereotypes increasingly become the markers by which youth navigate adolescence and, later, adulthood. These representations are especially pertinent in schools. "The criminalization of urban youth that results from these pervasive images and information bites also influences social policy relative to public schools and teacher education."[13] Public discourse about crises of school violence in the early 1990s fits into an overarching narrative on black pathology, and the stereotypes of deviant and delinquent black youth became useful archetypes for re-invigorating this discourse on violence and crime control.

The 1994 Gun-Free School Act exemplifies the ways in which perceptions of school safety culminated into nationalized Zero Tolerance policies that began with criminalization of guns at schools and increasingly became applicable to other illicit practices such alcohol, tobacco, drugs, and violence.[14] Interestingly, the epidemic of school shootings was neither an urban problem nor a black problem. However, as the policies were rolled out they became congruent with popular perceptions and stereotypes of poor urban youth of color, and the implementation of these policies was most vigorously enacted in urban schools. The popularized views on the urban ghetto fit easily with the rhetoric of school violence.

> According to this perspective, jarring media constructions of the "crisis" of school violence unite the public, stakeholders (e.g. teachers' unions), and public officials in a stance of righteous indignation towards marginalized "folk-devil". Often emerging from this emotional and political mobilization are quick-fix, punitive solutions that are disproportionate to actual threats of violence.[15]

The narrative of delinquent and deviant youth of color further re-enforces dominant views of communities of color stemming from the "culture of poverty" ideology formalized and popularized in the mid-1960s by Daniel Patrick Moynihan.[16] This approach to understanding "black culture" is premised on pathologizing the black family and the ghetto environment as deficient. The blame for abject poverty is shifted away from sustained structural inequalities enacted and maintained by dominant society to the sets of behaviors, values, and interactions of the black urban poor. In this schema, the view of youth of color as deviant and delinquent is congruent with "culture of poverty" ideology that inscribes pathology onto the lives of black folk. Zero Tolerance policies are then a logical conclusion to dealing with youth of color.

As such, official intervention such as arrest will signal to school professionals and criminal justice officials a well-established narrative on juvenile deviance and delinquency.[17] The label will further alter the perception of these officials, both in and out of school, resulting in more severe responses to student misconduct and misbehavior:

> [o]fficial intervention may negatively affect educational attainment by triggering stigma and exclusion in school ... students defined as having a delinquent character by school officials are subject to harsher disciplinary procedure, such as temporary suspension, transfer to another school, or even expulsion.[18]

In this way, popular stereotypes and perceptions of youth of color are ossified into informal practices and public policies that indiscriminately sweep youth into the criminal justice net.

The disparity in treatment between black and white students begins as early as preschool. Almost half of preschool children suspended more than once are black, and black students are three times more likely to be suspended than their white counterparts.[19] In addition, studies have proven that students of color are punished more severely for less serious and more subjective infractions than their white counterparts.[20] From a very early age, children of color are subject to disciplinary action that is relatively disproportionate to their actual infractions, furnishing their trajectory in life with incidences of reprimand and exclusion in America's institutions. A significant portion of the black population is subsumed into a permanent punishment economy in which behaviors and actions are consistently policed and reprimanded. Accumulated disadvantage begins with early interventions: "official intervention increases the probability of involvement in subsequent delinquency and deviance because intervention triggers exclusionary processes that have negative consequences for conventional opportunities."[21] In other words, the twin-mechanism of self-perception and public perception of deviance and criminality create a complex condition of mutually reinforcing and escalating behaviors, interactions, and practices that push youth of color into a trajectory of institutionalized marginalization and criminalization. Cumulative disadvantage through labeling and disruption of educational trajectories increasingly shuts out many opportunities to youth as the social, psychological, and institutional barriers increasingly narrow the life trajectories of these youth.[22]

De-Industrialization and the Crime Control Paradigm

> To be born Black within the US [still] means to be disproportionately represented among the poor, the incarcerated, the unemployed, the sick, the undereducated and under-nourished; and, among those awaiting state sanctioned execution on death row.[23]

De-industrialization, disinvestment in urban public infrastructure, the expanding criminal justice system, and the privatization of correctional facilities create the nexus in which the school-to-prison pipeline is the logical outgrowth. The relationship between urban public schools and the criminal justice system was fostered by a variety of forces and factors that systematically excluded black populations from participation in economic and social development. The economization of incarceration has further influenced a political environment where crime control is the reigning logic of governance of the urban poor. Residential and school segregation spatially and socially marked the urban poor; the black population was targeted as an object of social ill.

De-industrialization of inner cities in the 1940s marked a new era in racial and social disparity. Facilitated and accelerated by government subsidies, the movement of resources out of urban centers was a precondition of poor urban isolation.[24] As manufacturing jobs shifted out into the suburbs, and later abroad, employment opportunity for inner city folks dwindled. Federal subsidies such as FHA and VA facilitated suburbanization beginning in the late 1940s, creating a mass exodus of middle-income and white households. There is an established pattern of discretionary action on behalf of banks and public institutions that excluded black folks from partaking in these opportunities to move out into the suburbs. Access to superior living conditions, better funded schools, and higher-paying work was significantly limited. White flight signaled the beginning of a systemic disinvestment in public urban institutions. With homeowners now mobilized in America's suburbs, local politicians were advocating for resources that privileged their propertied constituents.[25] Meanwhile, in cities, high unemployment rates compounded with low performing urban schools further ossified the color line.[26] City schools as public institutions are thus situated within a larger political economy of post-industrial urban change. In *Ghetto Schooling*, Jean Anyon writes:

> In the years between 1945 and 1960, a number of developments coincided to lay the foundation for the isolation and alienation of the urban poor that characterize our cities—and our city schools—today: the migration to cities of southern blacks fleeing poverty, segregation, inadequate education; federally subsidized suburbanization of white families and manufacturing firms leaving these same cities, federal and state policies that did not adequately address the problems festering in urban neighborhoods; corporate disinterest; and local political patronage and corruption.[27]

Within two decades, major American cities had drastically transformed from predominantly manufacturing to white collar industry. In the early 1940s, New York's manufacturing industry employed a little over 40 percent of the total working population. By the 1960s, the vast majority of those jobs had been displaced by employment opportunities in the corporate, real estate, banking, financial, legal, and insurance industries, as well as civil service jobs in the growing bureaucracy of New York.[28] Under the auspices of Fiorello LaGuardia and Robert Moses, New York was transformed from an industrial working-class city to a corporate center with a booming middle-class.[29] Investments shifted from the funding and supporting of urban infrastructure, including city schools, to financing middle-class housing and a growing service industry.[30] Meanwhile, in 1950s New Jersey, the dispersal of manufacturing jobs from urban centers to the suburbs (and later abroad) accelerated in pace. The relocation of the manufacturing sector outside the reach of poor urban communities of color was aided by federal subsidies worth a little over 120 billion dollars.[31] Resources for sustaining a viable community in poor areas, many of which were predominantly black or Latino, were increasingly scarce. White flight and deindustrialization shifted good jobs away from them, creating a socially isolated superfluous population without the means to access white-collar jobs.[32]

The effects of white flight and urban disinvestment would have generational reverberations; many youth of color were effectively shut out from jobs in the high-tech industry through the lack of educational preparedness available to them. Public schools in poor urban communities did little than warehouse children in poor conditions. The institution funneled these youth into positions of subordination in the new economy.[33] Urban schools prepared youth for low-wage service sector jobs through a curriculum that emphasized discipline and conformity. They also pushed insubordinate youth into the juvenile criminal justice system. City schools just did not have the adequate resources to provide a contemporary and quality education for its poor children.

> Urban schools where adolescents of color are concentrated and isolated are slow to come to terms with the fact that society is no longer based on an industrial economy organized around capital and labor. As such, these schools primarily promote a curriculum that resembles factory assembly lines. ... The pedagogies on these schools emphasize control, rigidity, and conformity, subjecting students of color to mindless drills and exercises solely to prepare them to raise their standardized test scores.[34]

Social control began to effectively be synonymous with crime control and, for many students, being referred to the criminal justice system became a quick fix for deteriorating schools. As Hirschfield explains,

> schools' altered disciplinary and security regimes can be traced largely to deindustrialization, which shifted impacted schools and their disciplinary practices from productive ends towards a warehousing function. Aided by a crime-fixated and punitive political climate, these changes helped reorient school actors more towards the prevention and punishment of crime, and less towards the preparation of workers and citizens.[35]

The economization of incarceration has contributed to the proliferation of this logic. Today, the number of people incarcerated or under criminal justice control is unprecedented, and the rates of recidivism have proven that more often than not these measures enacted upon youth are disproportionately punitive and have detrimental long-term consequences. With very little political representation, poor communities of color were often left with deteriorating and insufficient services in schools and other public institutions as public monies were funneled into other areas that service middle- and upper-class whites. De-industrialization and white flight had not only taken work and resources out of major cities, but also a property tax base and a strong constituency.[36]

The criminal justice system filled the vacuum where other public institutions were insufficient. As state discretionary funds go to prison construction and expanding the criminal justice system, this institution had the most amount of means to govern poor urban communities. The crime control paradigm had already inscribed a particular view of these populations and subsuming them into processes of governance and control in the juvenile and criminal courts was aligned with a tradition of practices enacted on people of color since the mid-1850s. Black Codes that were instituted to control newly freed slaves were a predecessor for many of the ways that contemporary policing and social control have developed. Through a variety of ways, the prison sector has become an industry that offers work for many communities as well as a cheap labor pool for both private and public prisons:

> The prison-industrial complex is a legacy of 20th-century partial solutions to a central problem—the color line or "race relations"—that promises to haunt the 21st century. ... It meets the ever-increasing profit demands of capitalism and a variety of jobs, both "Negro jobs" on the inside and respectable ones on the outside that absorb white workers displaced by the prevailing high-technology, service-oriented. For instance, in Kankakee, Illinois, where the unemployment rate in 2000 is nearly 30%, the county's community college restructured its curriculum to provide training residents in anticipation of the 950 jobs to be generated by a new women's prison to be opened by the Department of Corrections in 2002.[37]

Masses of youth of color are pushed into a permanent punishment economy in which the cumulative disadvantage of school punishment (suspension and expulsion), official intervention (arrest), and interaction with criminal justice officials enhanced by pre-existing racial stereotypes (labeling) create the conditions for a significant institutional marginalization and disenfranchisement.

Navigating the Prison-Industrial Complex: Narrowing Trajectories

> For a great many poor people in America, particularly poor black men, prison is a destination that braids through ordinary life, much as does high school and college for rich white ones.[38]

The latest available data indicates that, as of 2014, a little over 2 million individuals are incarcerated in U.S. prisons. Nationally, black men and women are incarcerated at a rate five times that of their white counterparts, making up 40 percent of the prison population while only being 13 percent of the total United States population. For every 100,000 black individuals, 2,603 are in prison. Latinos only make up 16 percent of the U.S population but 19 percent of the prison population, with 831 incarcerated for every 100,000. Meanwhile, whites make up 64 percent of the population and 39 percent of the prison population, with a relatively low 450 incarcerated per 100,000.[39] Moreover, including incarceration, parole, and probation, more than 6 million individuals are under correctional supervision.[40] Therefore, the scope of the criminal justice system is far wider than incarceration rates.

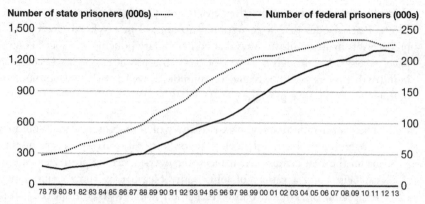

FIGURE 9.1 Total State and Federal Prison Populations, 1978–2013

Census Bureau data for 2010 confirms the stark racial disparity and overrepresentation of individuals of color in prison or on parole. The disproportionality of the prison population mirrors a strikingly similar disproportionality of official intervention on school ground. Nationally, across all grade levels, black students are up to 42 percent of students who receive out of school suspensions. For preschoolers that number is as high as 50 percent. Furthermore, black students make up an additional 31 percent of students who experience school-related arrest. However, black students only make up 16 percent of the K-12 student population.[41] As such, while the *volume* of incarcerated individuals of color, particularly black men, is much higher than the rate of school suspension, expulsion, and arrest, the *rate and proportion* of students who face punitive measures reflect the proportion of individuals in prison. In both school and in prison, the black population represents only about 15 percent of the total population, and up to half the population that is subject to punitive measures. In the age range between 18 and 19, black males were nine times more likely to be incarcerated.[42] This is a crucial point when many youth should be graduating from high school. Instead, many end up in the criminal justice system. More than half of black men without a high school diploma go to prison at some time in their lives.[43] This makes arrest and referral to juvenile facilities particularly damaging, interrupting school completion and boosting the odds of incarceration. Meanwhile, with cuts in education programs in prisons, incarcerated youth are less likely to obtain a GED or higher education. "Detention offers few opportunities to earn a general Equivalency Diploma (GED) and, with the denial of access to Pell Grants for those incarcerated in 1994, opportunities to access post-secondary education while incarcerated are seriously limited."[44] The cumulative effects of educational disruption, disinvestment in education, and criminalization bind these youth to a narrow trajectory of institutionalized disenfranchisement.

Several factors have led to the sustained growth of the carceral state. On the one hand, selective drug and sentencing policies have been particularly punitive, absorbing a disproportionate amount of youth and adults of color into the criminal justice system. On the other, the move toward privatization of prisons has commodified inmates, making incarceration an increasingly profitable industry. While violent crime rates have drastically dropped over the past 30 years, prisons have tripled in size.[45] Data indicates almost half the prison population is convicted for nonviolent drug offenses. Meanwhile, violent crimes account for only 2.9 percent of incarcerated population.[46] Federal law stipulates a minimum of 5 years' imprisonment for the possession of 3.5 ounces of heroin or 5 grams of crack, and 10 years' imprisonment for the possession of 2 ounces of rock cocaine or crack. These specifications do not apply to cocaine powder, a drug similar in composition but more expensive and utilized by white, middle- and upper-class individuals. To be imprisoned for powder cocaine, the individual must be found with one hundred times the quantity criminalized for rock cocaine. The additional three-strikes policy mandates life in prison for individuals convicted of two prior felonies, relegating these individuals to a permanent punishment economy.[47]

These punitive measures have particularly become attractive to correctional corporations as monetization of inmates has grown over the past three decades. While private for-profit prisons only make up 8 percent of the total facilities nationally, their influence and practices are significant. The multi-million dollar industry is one of the fastest growing in the U.S., making profit not only from government contract with occupancy rate stipulations but also from inmate labor.[48] Additionally, the opening and operating of prisons has created jobs in rural communities with high unemployment rates.

> The prison-industrial complex [...] curbed the decline of many white rural areas and, more broadly, pacified the white working class. Criminal justice expansion artificially tightens the labor market, stimulates the economy of ailing rural communities and affords residents greater electoral representation and population-based federal appropriations. Accordingly, many rural politicians stake their political careers on the location of juvenile and adult prisons in their districts and the hundreds of stable, well-paying jobs that they promise to generate for their constituents.[49]

The revenue stream from the prison-industrial complex thus has many stakeholders and, as such, the expansion and maintenance of the carceral state is deeply embedded in the contemporary American economy.

As of 2014, there are reportedly 100 private prisons housing over 62,000 inmates who are in turn contracted out to private corporations in the manufacturing industry. Prison workers supply virtually all military bullet-proof vests, ammunition, and helmets, along with 98 percent of the domestic equipment assembly services, and 21 percent of office furniture. Companies

TABLE 9.1 Federal and State Prison Population in Private Facilities (2000–2012)

Year	Total Federal Prison Population	Federal Population in Private Facilities	% Federal Population in Private Facilities	Total State Prison Population	State Population in Private Facilities	% State Population in Private Facilities
2000	145,416	15,524	10.7%	1,248,815	75,291	6.0%
2005	187,618	27,046	14.4%	1,338,292	80,894	6.0%
2010	209,771	33,830	16.1%	1,404,032	104,361	7.4%
2011	216,362	38,546	17.8%	1,382,606	101,730	7.4%
2012	217,815	40,446	18.6%	1,352,582	105,674	7.8%
Average annual % change, 2000–2010	3.3%	7.1%	n/a	1.1%	3.0%	n/a
Average annual % change, 2010–2012	1.3%	6.0%	n/a	−1.2%	0.4%	n/a
Percent change, 2011–2012	0.7%	4.9%	n/a	−2.2%	3.9%	n/a

Sources:

Total Federal and State Prison Population Data (2011, 2012): U.S. Department of Justice, Bureau of Justice Statistics, *Prisoners in 2012*, December 2013, p. 39, http://goo.gl/9J305J (accessed May 4, 2014).

Total Federal and State Prison Population Data (2000–2010): U.S. Department of Justice, Bureau of Justice Statistics, *Prisoners in 2011*, December 2012, p. 2, http://goo.gl/DkPcDg (accessed January 23, 2013).

Federal and State Private Prison Population Data (2011, 2012): U.S. Department of Justice, Bureau of Justice Statistics, *Prisoners in 2012*, December 2013, p. 40, http://goo.gl/9J305J (accessed May 4, 2014).

Federal and State Private Prison Population Data (2000, 2010): U.S. Department of Justice, Bureau of Justice Statistics, *Prisoners in 2011*, December 2012, p. 32, http://goo.gl/DkPcDg (accessed January 23, 2013).

Federal and State Private Prison Population Data (2005): U.S. Department of Justice, Bureau of Justice Statistics, *Prisoners in 2010*, February 2012, p. 30, http://goo.gl/73pVs (accessed January 23, 2013).

Percent Federal and State Population in Private Facilities (and related percent changes): Authors' calculation.

such as IBM, Microsoft, and Pierre Cardin all contract out services to private prisons. Meanwhile prison-workers receive anywhere between 17 cents and 50 cents an hour, in comparison with state inmates and federally run prisons who work for 1.25 cents an hour. "Thanks to prison labor, the United States is once again an attractive location for investment in work that was designated for Third World labor markets,"[50] as the criminalization and incarceration of youth and adults of color becomes an integral part to the economy in many areas nationally.

Post-Incarceration: Political Participation and Recidivism

> It may be helpful, in attempting to understand the basic nature of the new caste system, to think of the criminal justice—the entire collection of institution and practices that comprise it— not as an independent system but rather as a gateway into a much larger system of racial stigmatization and permanent marginalization.[51]

Release from prison does not indicate an end to the trajectory of social and economic marginalization and political disenfranchisement, but rather, its logical conclusion. Once a person has been incarcerated with a felony conviction there are several formal and informal mechanisms of exclusion that take place, which cause long-term consequences. This is especially pertinent to communities of color who come to represent a vastly disproportional part of the incarcerated population. While state and federal laws differ, more broadly speaking the disenfranchisement of felons is a common practice across the United States. Disenfranchisement specifically refers to prohibition from voting in political elections. For felons, state laws limit political participation at various degrees. This essential right of citizenship is not only symbolic but effectively positions felons as voiceless in the political process. With no representation, legislation and reform is difficult to negotiate and the carceral state continues to flourish.

> In 1980, fewer than two million individuals were either incarcerated or on probation or parole; in 2011, that number was over seven million … the overall disenfranchisement rate has increased dramatically in conjunction with the growing U.S. corrections population, rising from 1.17 million in 1976 to 5.85 million by 2010. The growing incarceration rate has been mirrored by the disenfranchisement rate, which has increased by about 500% since 1980. The fact that felony disenfranchisement is so wide-reaching is deeply disturbing, and indicates that these laws undermine the open, participatory nature of our democratic process.[52]

Furthermore, while political disenfranchisement has implications on the long-term chances of reform, social and economic disenfranchisement have more immediate consequences on the life chances of felons. Other forms of exclusion and marginalization include job and housing discrimination, the prohibition from licensure in particular careers, various degrees of disqualification from grants and loans for higher education, and disqualification from a number of social services, including public housing and food stamps.[53] Felons who get out of prison frequently find themselves in even more precarious conditions than they started in. They are officially branded as ex-convicts, and excluded from basic rights and opportunities to create a life for themselves. Often for those who have spent a long time institutionalized within the criminal justice system, and for many who grew up in the system as teens and young adults, mainstream society is a particularly problematic space for them to navigate. Their lives are punctuated with various forms of formal and informal marginalization. The intergenerational reverberations of these accumulated disadvantages place families in cycles of social and economic isolation. Children often witness their family members, neighbors, and peers being hauled off to the courts and prison. As official interventions become more pervasive on school grounds, the practices and policies that have engendered the growing carceral state are brought into proximity with vulnerable children:

> Over the course of the twentieth century, attitudes towards criminality have gradually come to include recognition of the possibility of the rehabilitation and reintegration of former prisoners into society upon their release. However, there has not been a corresponding realignment of felony disenfranchisement laws to make them consistent with more contemporary goals of the criminal justice system—increasing public safety and reducing reoffending. ... Disenfranchisement, on the other hand, is likely to have the opposite effect by further marginalizing and alienating formerly incarcerated individuals from civil society.[54]

Meanwhile the barriers to rehabilitation and viable social or economic participation are enormous. In fact, what these "correctional" facilities accomplish is not the rehabilitation of "criminals" into mainstream society, but permanent impairment to autonomy and full participation in society. This is further evidenced by rates of recidivism. Felons are likely to be re-arrested between 1 and 3 years following release. Rates of recidivism are between 50 and 75 percent in the first 3 years.[55] The reintegration of people institutionalized within the criminal justice system is impeded by policies and practices that are disproportionately punitive.

Schools have become subsumed into this larger and most disturbing system. From an early age, children of color and poor children are dealt with by referring them to the criminal justice system. City schools face particularly difficult challenges; often classes are overcrowded, facilities are understaffed, and support services like counselors and social workers are not sufficient. Larger social ills like poverty, homelessness, mental and physical health problems, and abuse can have great effects on children, and often schools are not equipped or resourced to deal with these issues. As outlined throughout this chapter, city schools exists in a complex political economy: de-industrialization, white flight (which encompasses federal subsidy policies that facilitated further segregation), disinvestment in urban public institutions, and an expanding criminal justice system have shaped institutions and practices that perpetuate marginalization and disenfranchisement. Movement towards restorative justice tactics to replace punitive measures has gained some traction over the past couple of years. But these tactics operate in a vacuum that does not address the larger issues and obstacles that have historically created the conditions for marginalization and disenfranchisement. This represents an acknowledgement of the detrimental effects of Zero Tolerance policies, and presents a new ethos by which we may think and relate to children in schools.

Restorative Justice: Challenges and Debates

It is difficult to pin down exactly when and where Restorative Justice (RJ) practices first came about because the approach and politics to social/community remediation has its roots in societies globally. In fact, RJ practices have had a significant history in indigenous and Aboriginal communities.[56] In the Western world, RJ was used in a variety of ways from the criminal justice system to conflict resolution in community and school contexts. The term Restorative Justice came about much later in the 1970s when programs were developed to bring offender and victim together, establishing a model for conflict resolution that would emerge out of Canada and over the next two decades become instituted in experimental programs in the United States, the UK, and beyond.[57] It is important to note though, that while the term was not used nor was there a unified theory of RJ, non-punitive conflict resolution practices and philosophy pre-dated the 1970s. The history of RJ is thus complex, long, and wide in scope. This section will look at its enactment in school contexts. In the UK, as early as the 1980s, some schools began using RJ with children as young as 3 years old.[58] In the United States, RJ has held great promise in the area of the juvenile criminal justice system and the ways in which schools deal with student misbehavior. This has been especially significant considering the climate of penal policy that has been especially punitive in the United States.[59]

Restorative Justice programs are rather common in the U.S., though that has not always been the case. In 2004, almost three-quarters of jurisdictions reported having offender education programs. Specifically, the Victim-Offender Dialogue (VOD) has been used as an alternative model to incarceration for minor crimes and offenses. The budget to run programs under the auspices of RJ has gone from volunteer basis to state funded. Research in this area is growing, and current findings indicate that the programs are cost-effective and have had significant impact on reoffending.[60] In the last few years, some schools have reported success in their efforts at RJ as a practice to replace Zero Tolerance policies and punitive disciplinary action in general.[61] However, these programs have yet to be institutionalized, and as such face challenges and limitations in context of the larger economy of punishment and Zero Tolerance policies. Rather, they operate in the domain of grassroots movements that function in school and community contexts with youth. RJ is not merely a strategy of dealing with behavior, but a philosophy and approach to governance that is based in starkly different principles from the current penal climate. The key principles of RJ are:

1. Providing everyone affected by the action/behavior/conflict the space to vocalize their concerns and their feelings.
2. Mediating an acceptable way forward for all parties involved.
3. Ensuring that all parties involved are accountable for their actions.[62]

Restorative Justice focuses on communication, healing, and building bridges between the parties involved. It is therefore a much more involved, engaged, and holistic process that can lead to great strides in addressing conflict. But it is also a more costly and taxing process on schools that are already over-extended. The lack of adequate funding, resources, and training are great challenges when compared with existing systems and structures that deal with student misbehavior (suspensions, expulsions, and arrest). Sound RJ practices are embedded in a "Whole-School Approach" that enacts multi-faceted and dynamic processes of mediation, mentoring, conferencing, and support.[63] But it also operates within a larger context that maintains a culture of violent policing, significant social ills such as segregation, poverty, and homelessness, and a culture of punitive measures that is historically rooted for communities of color. As such, while successes in various contexts are beneficial and uplifting, the question remains of how to institutionalize RJ as a core part of community governance and societal policies and not merely in individual schools. Can RJ truly have wide-spread success when it is limited to individual schools? These questions are crucial and pressing as schools re-evaluate their practices in light of crises in discipline and the detrimental effects that Zero Tolerance has had on schools and students.

Today, the United States continues to be the leader in incarceration globally. This is due in large part to the relationship between social/penal policy and politics.[64] In a culture of fear, politicians have leveraged the legal system and how it deals with offenders to champion law and order. As outlined in this chapter, the War on Drugs is a major example of this relationship; the waging of this war at a period when crime rates were going down, the publicization of drug-related crime in inner-city neighborhoods (used largely as code for poor communities of color), and the ensuing laws and policies that came out of this campaign (three-strikes, for example) have shaped how governance is enacted. What remains are these questions: how to divorce status quo politics that have traditionally been "tough on crime" on both ends of the spectrum from the criminal justice system? How do we envision a system of governance that is restorative and not punitive? How do we begin to address the underlying social ills that isolate communities of color in spaces that are ill-resourced and marginalized? The question of Restorative Justice is not merely about enacting better practices in schools but in engaging with and investing in a sustained, self-reflexive, informed, and inclusive process of healing communities that have suffered from violent policing, exploitation, and isolation in urban centers.

Notes

1. Jonathan Kozol, *Death at an Early Age* (New York: Penguin Books, 1967), 48.
2. U.S. Department of Education and Justice "The School Discipline Consensus Report: Strategies From The Field To Keep Students Engaged in School and Out of the Juvenile Justice System," Justice Center, The Council of State Governments (2014).
3. Paul Hirschfield, "Preparing For Prison?: The Criminalization of School Discipline in the USA," *Theoretical Criminology*, 12(1): (2008), 89.
4. Erica R. Meiners and Maisha T. Winn, "Resisting the School to Prison Pipeline: The Practice to Build Abolition Democracies," *Race, Ethnicity and Education*, 13(3): (2010), 271.
5. Kozol, *Death at an Early Age*, 24.
6. David S. Kirk and Robert J. Sampson, "Juvenile Arrest and the Collateral Educational Damage in Transition to Adulthood," *Sociology of Education*, 86(1), (2013), 36.
7. Justice Center, The Council of State Governments, "The School Discipline Consensus Report, 2014."
8. Ibid., 18.
9. Kirk and Sampson, 36.
10. Ibid., 37.
11. Jon Gunnar Bernburg and Marvin D. Krohn, "Labeling, Life Chances, and Adult Crime: The Direct and Indirect Effects of Official Intervention in Adolescence on Crime in Early Adulthood," *Criminology*, 41(4), (2003), 1289.
12. Ibid., 1290.
13. Garrett Albert Duncan, "Urban Pedagogies and the Ceiling of Adolescents of Color," *Social Justice*, 27(3), (2000), 38.
14. Hirschfield, 82.
15. Ibid., 85.
16. Douglas S. Massey and Nancy Denton, *American Apartheid: Segregation and the Making of the Underclass* (Massachusetts: Harvard University Press, 1993), 5.
17. Kirk and Sampson, 38.
18. Bernburg and Krohn, 1290.
19. Justice Center, The Council of State Governments, "The School Discipline Consensus Report, 2014."
20. The Advancement Project, "Test, Punish and Pushout: How 'Zero Tolerance' and High-Stakes Testing Funnel Youth Into the School-to-Prison Pipeline," (March 2010), 15.
21. Bernburg and Krohn, 1287.
22. Kirk and Sampson, 38.
23. Cleveland Hayes and Brenda Juarez, "There Is No Culturally Responsive Teaching Spoken Here: A Critical Race Perspective," *Democracy and Education*, 20(1), (2012), 2.
24. Hirschfield, 89.
25. Jean Anyon, *Ghetto Schooling: A Political Economy of Urban Educational Reform* (New York: Teacher's College, 1997), 77.

26 Anyon, 77.
27 Anyon, 98.
28 Jerald Podair, *The Strike That Changed New York: Blacks, Whites, and the Ocean Hill-Brownsville Crisis* (New Haven: Yale University Press, 2002), 9.
29 Ibid., 9.
30 Ibid., 10.
31 Anyon, 77.
32 Duncan, 37.
33 Ibid., 30.
34 Ibid., 38.
35 Hirschfield, 81.
36 Anyon, 92.
37 Duncan, 36.
38 Adam Gopnik, "The Caging of America: Why Do We Lock up So Many People?" *The New Yorker* (January 30, 2012).
39 Leah Sakala, "Breaking Down Mass Incarceration in the 2010 Census: State by State Incarceration Rates Race by Race/Ethnicity," *Prison Policy Initiative* (May 28, 2014).
40 Gopnik.
41 U.S. Department of Education For Civil Rights, "Data Snapshot: School Discipline," Civil Rights Data Collection (March 2014).
42 E. Ann Carson, "Prisoner in 2013," U.S. Department of Justice, Bureau of Justice Statistics (September 2014).
43 Gopnik.
44 Meiners and Winn, 272.
45 Gopnik.
46 Federal Bureau of Prisons, "Offenses," Inmate Statistics (April 25, 2015).
47 Vicky Pelaez, "The Prison Industry in the United States: Big Business or a New Form of Slavery," Center for Global Research, March 2014.
48 Pelaez.
49 Hirschfield, 89.
50 Pelaez, 2014.
51 Michelle Alexander, *The New Jim Crow* (New York: The New Press, 2012), 12.
52 "Democracy Imprisoned: A Review of the Prevalence and Impact of Felony Disenfranchisement Laws in the United States," *American Civil Liberties Union* (September 2013), 2.
53 Michelle Alexander, *The New Jim Crow* (New York: The New Press, 2012), 13.
54 Ibid., 3.
55 Office of Justice Programs, "Recidivism," National Institute of Justice (June 17, 2014).
56 Abbotsford Restorative Justice and Advocacy Association, *The History of Restorative Justice* (2010).
57 Ibid.
58 John P. J. Dussich and Jill Schellenberg, *The Promise of Restorative Justice: New Approaches for Criminal Justice and Beyond* (Colorado: Lynne Rienner Publisher, 2010), 163.
59 Ivo Aertsen, Tom Daems, and Luc Robert, *Institutionalizing Restorative Justice* (Portland: Willan Publishing, 2006), 3.
60 Dussich and Schellenberg, 13.

61 Melinda Anderson, "Will School Discipline Reform Actually Change Anything?" *The Atlantic* (September 14, 2015).
62 Dussich and Schellenberg, 164.
63 Ibid., 165
64 Aertsen, Daems, and Robert, 30.

References and Further Reading

Aertsen, Ivo, Tom Daems and Luc Robert. *Institutionalizing Restorative Justice*. Oregon: Willan Publishing, 2006.
Andrews, Dorinda Carter. "The Construction of Black High-Achiever Identities in a Predominantly White High School." *Anthropology and Education Quarterly*, 40(3), (2009): 297–317.
Alexander, Michelle. *The New Jim Crow: Mass Incarceration in the Age of Colorblindness*. New York: The New Press, 2012.
Anyon, Jean. *Ghetto Schooling: A Political Economy of Urban Educational Reform*. New York: Teacher's College, 1997.
Carson, E. Ann. "Prisoner in 2013." *U.S. Department of Justice, Bureau of Justice Statistics*, September 2014.
Clark, Kenneth. *Dark Ghetto: Dilemmas of Social Power*. Connecticut: Wesleyan University Press, 1965.
"Democracy Imprisoned: A Review of the Prevalence and Impact of Felony Disenfranchisement Laws in the United States." *American Civil Liberties Union*, September 2013.
Duncan, Garrett Albert. "Urban Pedagogies and the Celling of Adolescents of Color." *Social Justice*, 27(3), (2000): 29–42.
Dussich, John, and Jill Schellenberg. *The Promise of Restorative Justice: New Approaches to Criminal Justice and Beyond*. Colorado: Lynne Rienner Publishers, 2010.
Garrett, Albert Duncan. "Urban Pedagogies and the Ceiling of Adolescents of Color." *Social Justice*, 27(3), (2000), 33.
Gopnik, Adam "The Caging of America: Why Do We Lock up So Many People?" *The New Yorker*, January 30, 2012.
Hayes, Cleveland and Brenda Juarez, "There Is No Culturally Responsive Teaching Spoken Here: A Critical Race Perspective." *Democracy and Education*, 20(1), (2012): 1–14.
Kozol, Jonathan. *Death at an Early Age*. New York: Penguin Books, 1967.
Massey, Douglas S. and Nancy Denton. *American Apartheid: Segregation and the Making of the Underclass*. Massachusetts: Harvard University Press, 1993.
Meier, August and Elliot Rudwick. *From Plantation to Ghetto*. New York: Hill and Wang, 1966.
Moynihan, Daniel Patrick. "The Negro Family: The Case for National Action." *Office for Policy Planning and Research, United States Department of Labor*, (1965): 1–78.
Office of Justice Programs. "Recidivism." *National Institute of Justice*, June 17, 2014.
Pelaez, Vicky. "The Prison Industry in the United States: Big Business or a New Form of Slavery." *Center for Global Research*, March 2014.
Podair, Jerald. *The Strike That Changed New York: Blacks, Whites, and the Ocean Hill-Brownsville Crisis*. New Haven: Yale University Press, 2002.
Roediger, David R. *Working Towards Whiteness: How America's Immigrants Became White*. New York: Perseus Books Group, 2005.

Sakala, Leah. "Breaking Down Mass Incarceration in the 2010 Census: State by State Incarceration Rates Race by Race/Ethnicity." *Prison Policy Initiative*, May 28, 2014.

"Test, Punish and Pushout: How 'Zero Tolerance' and High-Stakes Testing Funnel Youth Into the School-to-Prison Pipeline." *The Advancement Project*, March 2010.

U.S. Department of Education and Justice. "The School Discipline Consensus Report: Strategies From the Field to Keep Students Engaged in School and Out of the Juvenile Justice System." *Justice Center, The Council of State Governments*, 2014.

U.S. Department of Education for Civil Rights. "Data Snapshot: School Discipline." Civil Rights Data Collection, March 2014.

10

A SHARED PATH TO SUCCESS

The Promise and Challenge of Special Education in New York City

Melanie Waller

New York City Public Advocate, Letitia James, has had enough of the city's failing special education system. In February of 2016, James filed a lawsuit against New York City for failing to meet the needs of students with disabilities. James argued that the failure of New York City's special education system has resulted in widespread educational neglect and a significant loss in Medicaid funding for the city. James is demanding judicial inquiry that will force the New York City Department of Education to consider and share a plan that attempts to heal this broken system.[1] James is the face of this lawsuit, but she is not alone in demanding justice for New York City's underserved special education students. Parents, administrators, policy makers, students, and stakeholders around the city are relying on New York to improve its special education system and protect the educational needs of all students.

Letitia James is the most recent advocate to sue the city and demand a stronger special education system, but she is certainly not the first. In February 1979, almost 40 years before James' lawsuit, plaintiffs filed a class action suit against New York City. This case, *Jose P. v. Ambach*, argued that the city had neglected to provide "free and appropriate public education" to students with disabilities. The court ruled for the plaintiffs and charged the department of education (DOE) with reforming its special education policies.[2] Today, James' work is part of the tradition of using the courts to demand that the city "see" their underserved special education students. Educational opportunities for students with disabilities depend on their visibility, the voices of their advocates, and the educational political agenda of the moment. In 2016 New York City schools serve 1.1 million students in 1,800 schools and 16 percent of these students are classified as requiring "special education." As is required by federal law, special education students receive annually reviewed individualized education plans that detail student needs. Special education students often require more services than the "average" student, both by the nature of their "special" status and the laws that mandate their educational protection.

This chapter will explore the most recent iteration of New York City's response to the needs of special education students, "A Shared Path to Success" (aSPtS; NYC Dept. of Education, 2012). This 2012 policy seeks to give students access to the least restrictive environment, while still honoring Individualized Education Plans, at the student's zoned school. "A Shared Path to Success" attempts to improve upon the unsuccessful New York City special education policies of 2003. Federal mandates, student needs, budget restrictions, parental concerns, private consultants, foundations, and corporate interests have all informed these revisions. So far, aSPtS has earned mixed responses from stakeholders. New York City special education students, who in many ways require more support and educational protection than other students, are at the whims of these intersecting interests.

In particular, this chapter will focus on how aSPtS is impacting high schools and their students. New York City serves as a unique example of a district that uses a "deferred acceptance algorithm" to match students with a high school. Ideally, students are matched with the high school of their choice, although this is not always the case. This model creates a highly competitive environment, in which high schools exist in an accepted and celebrated hierarchical system. New York City High Schools range from specialized, where students must take exams to gain entry, to screen schools where students undergo a review process, to open admissions. aSPtS disrupts this hierarchy, by allowing special education students' access to high schools that were previously not accessible. This shift creates new opportunity for students, and new demands on schools that must be considered in order to fully understand the impact of aSPtS.

The first section of this chapter will explore the local foundations of aSPtS, the policy itself, and the funding streams that inform the implementation of the policy. Part II will discuss aSPtS's relationship to the federal agenda and the current national focus on testing. Part III will discuss implementation of the policy and its impact on stakeholders. Part IV will focus on outcomes of the policy and recommendations.

Part I: The Foundations of Special Education Reform in New York City

"A Shared Path to Success" was a response to the failed special education reforms of 2003, 2010, and 2012. The Individuals with Disabilities Education Improvement Act (IDEA) is a federal law that protects the education of students with disabilities and, although this law does not explicitly state that inclusive education is a requirement for students, interpretations of the law imply that inclusion is the best way to meet the mandates of IDEA. In 2004 Congress concluded that the best way to support children with disabilities was to ensure "their access to the general education curriculum in the regular classroom, to the maximum extent possible."[3]

Conversely, in 2003, according to a comprehensive survey given by *EdWeek*,[4] a well-read and respected publication in the education field, 29 percent of New York City students aged 6–21 reported spending more than 60 percent of their day outside of the "regular" classroom. In 2003 New York and Rhode Island were tied for the highest percentage of students who spent more than half their day segregated from the rest of their classmates. Efforts by aSPtS to change this alarming trend were both an attempt to meet federal mandates and turn the educational tide for students with disabilities toward greater inclusive opportunities.

Special education advocates had long recommended the shift toward inclusion, even if New York City was slow to adopt the policy. In 2009, the Harries report, written by then city official Garth Harries, helped to prompt the reshaping of the Department of Education to meet the needs of special education students. Harries emphasized the importance of integrating special education students into mainstream classrooms, while still providing "specialized focus responsive to need."[5] Harries' challenge to the city was supported by research that revealed a range of benefits of inclusion; higher academic responses, higher test scores, fewer absences, fewer behavior issues, and stronger instructional experiences.[6] Ultimately, Harries' report helped to push the city to restructure the Department of Education's bureaucracy to implement inclusion policies. Harries himself, however, would not stay in New York to support the implementation of these recommendations. Harries left the city the same year as his report to take on a top role in the Connecticut school system, and would later become the New Haven Superintendent.

The same year of the Harries report, under Chancellor Klein, Laura Rodriguez became the city's first Chief Achievement Officer for Special Education and English Language Learners. The creation of this position, and the direct access to the Chancellor that it came with, increased the visibility of special education students and their needs. In 2010, under Rodriguez's leadership, the city began a rollout of inclusion policies, starting with 260 schools in 10 Children's First Networks. These schools represented all five boroughs and were composed of 100 elementary schools, 60 middle schools, and 100 high schools.[7] The data, although scattered and difficult to locate, indicate that Phase One was a successful venture that resulted in fewer referral rates for special education students.

At the end of 2010 the city planned to "continue training and (providing) technical support" for participating schools and to finalize funding, enrollment, and accountability.[8] However, Cathy Black, the 2011 ill-fated New York City Chancellor, delayed special education reforms during her brief tenure, halting the progress of the previously quick moving reform. The city would wait an entire school year to move forward. And, in 2012, under Chancellor Walcott, and a new head of special education, Corinne Rello-Anselmi, special education reform, now branded "A Shared Path to Success," began to be implemented on a widespread scale.[9]

"A Shared Path to Success" sought to accomplish three tasks: "close the achievement gap between students with disabilities and their peers without disabilities; provide increased access to and participation in the general education curriculum; and empower all schools to have greater curricular, instructional, and scheduling flexibility to meet the diverse needs of students with disabilities."[10]

It was intended that aSPtS would accomplish its goals by:

- Ensuring that every school educates and embraces the overwhelming majority of students with disabilities that they would serve if the students did not have IEPs;
- Holding schools and students with disabilities accountable for standards-based goals that reflect the Common Core standards and long-term educational outcomes;
- Leveraging the full continuum of services and curricular, instructional and scheduling flexibility needed to meet the diverse needs of students with disabilities;
- Aligning school accountability measures, funding formulas and enrollment policies and practices with these principles.[11]

The undergirding philosophy of aSPtS is that inclusion is the best practice for supporting special education students. The aSPtS version of inclusion, or the "least restrictive" learning environment, most often manifests as Integrated Co-Teaching, or ICT.

In the list above, aSPtS mandates that schools must "[educate] and [embrace] the overwhelming majority of students with disabilities that they would serve if the students did not have IEPs." In 2016, city schools are being celebrated for quickly adopting greater inclusion and fulfilling the goals of aSPtS by embracing larger percentages of special education students. Historically, top performing high schools have avoided serving special education students. Consultant David Rubel cites that in 2012 the cities' top performing schools had a special education population of 1.5 percent. However, in 2016 top New York City High Schools have increased their percentage of special education students by 92 percent.[12] And although these schools are still far behind other high schools in embracing a "fair" percentage of special education students, the trend is shifting toward greater access to schools for special education students.[13] However, it is essential to note the influence that funding streams have had on this shift. Increased enrollment of special education students in specialized and screened schools was certainly promulgated by the DOE creation of new funding formulas that came along with aSPtS.

In 2012, the Panel for Education Policy approved a budget formula intended to hasten the implementation of inclusion reform. This formula, a part of the Fair Student Funding (FSF), applies funding weights to students with additional needs, like special education or students in poverty. The intention of FSF is to "improve student achievement." FSF acknowledges that "in order for students to excel in the classroom they must have access to the necessary resources to help them succeed."[14] The money allocated to each student follows that student to the high school they attend, theoretically enabling students to choose the environment that is best suited to their needs, without worrying about the cost of their services, modifications, or additional supports. FSF aligns with the goals of aSPtS by enabling students to be fully integrated in the school community, and by allowing schools the flexibility to meet the needs of their special education students.

Critics of FSF's role in special education highlight the way that FSF allocates funding. FSF prioritizes students who are in Integrated Co-Teaching (ICT) settings for the majority of their day, rather than a self-contained or pull out environment. Students in ICT for 60 percent of the day, or all of their core academic courses, receive $7,142.20 of FSF funding, as opposed to students in a self-contained environment who receive $2,397.30. Students who receive services for less than 60 percent of their day are funded at a rate of $5,132.86.[15] This allocation clearly pushes school to embrace ICT settings as the premier option for students. From the outset, critics rightly worried that this financial consequence would push schools to move too quickly, without the necessary training and research to justify such a quick shift.[16] The predictions of the critics almost immediately realized, and the city needed to readjust the formulas just a year later, after the "60%" rule was discovered to be nonsensical for schools on an 8-period day.[17] Ultimately, FSF catalyzed the pace of implementation of aSPtS, but pace of the reform does not necessarily indicate the success of the policy.

Part II: Special Education and Accountability

"A Shared Path to Success" has helped to align New York State to the federal mandates of IDEA. It has also placed special education in line with the national push toward results, accountability, and testing. New York City policy makers are heavily influenced by educational trends and policies happening on the federal level. In 2012, Arne Duncan led the U.S. Department of Education and Melody Musgrove ran the Office of Special Education Programs. Both of these individuals, and the bureaucracies they ran, were undergoing a paradigm shift toward Results Driven Accountability (RDA) on the federal level that would ultimately influence state policies. This shift prompted schools to focus on results-driven indicators to improve *outcomes* for special education students, rather than on compliance to student needs and Individualized Education Plans.

Federal and State focus on outcomes for special education students were finalized in 2014 with official federal policy that would link RDA and the Individuals with Disabilities Education Improvement Act (IDEA).[18] Reliance on outcomes, rather than compliance, pushed schools to demonstrate measurable results for students in a quantifiable way. Schools were now asked to extend their scope beyond just providing services to students, and schools had to produce data. FSF, which helped to catalyze the rapid implementation of aSPtS in New York, includes language that aligns the state and federal governments' educational policy in the pursuit of measurable outcomes. The language of FSF clearly states that its goal, and therefore the goal of aSPtS, is to "hold schools and students with disabilities accountable for goals that are standards based and reflect Common Core standards and long-term educational outcomes."[19] This demonstrates a clear link between funding streams for students with disabilities and the goals of Common Core and those who support it.

"A Shared Path to Success" is a reform that seeks to both hold students accountable and prioritize inclusion. These ideas are not mutually exclusive, but there is a paradox in this approach. Special education advocates call for inclusion on the basis that it will improve the educational experience of all children. Reformers hope to measure the progress of special education students and, in doing so, raise the expectations and accountability of students with disabilities and the schools that serve them. The goals of these two groups are not the same, and there is an inherent tension in trying to achieve both. Reformers hope to measure and gauge outcomes and, in doing so, change and improve the child. Advocates seek to change the environment of schools, and in doing so, create a space that is beneficial for all. Both camps influenced aSPtS, but the funding allocations provided by the city demonstrate a clear preference for goals of reformers that want to measure, standardize, and test students.

The focus on measuring outcomes in order to gauge the progress and "accountability" of special education students was heavily influenced by the work of Chester E. Finn Jr. in his book, *Rethinking Special Education for a New Century*, published by the Thomas B. Fordham Institute, a conservative think-tank.[20] Finn is a former United States Assistant Secretary of Education and currently serves as the president of the conservative Fordham Institute. The Fordham Institute has funded a number of other publications supporting the move toward RDA. The Fordham Institute is funded by a number of large donors who are heavily involved in shaping educational policy, including The College Board and the Bill & Melinda Gates Foundation.[21] The research produced by the Fordham Institute promotes the shift toward outcomes rather than compliance. This shift requires schools to be accountable for providing more than just individualized services to special education students. Schools are now responsible for special education students' progress in high stakes testing environments.

RDA and the measurement of students "outcomes" is a subtext for Common Core and standardized exams. The Gates Foundation, which provided funding for some of the original research that ultimately led to the Special Education Reform, is invested heavily in the success of Common Core. The Kellogg Foundation, which also supported early research for the 2012 reforms, supports Common Core in a number of ways, most notably in the digital educational arena.[22] The attempt to standardize special education students is one that seems to be in direct conflict with individual needs, which are protected under 2004's IDEA. New York City's current answer to this paradox is the "safety net" option,

A Shared Path to Success **143**

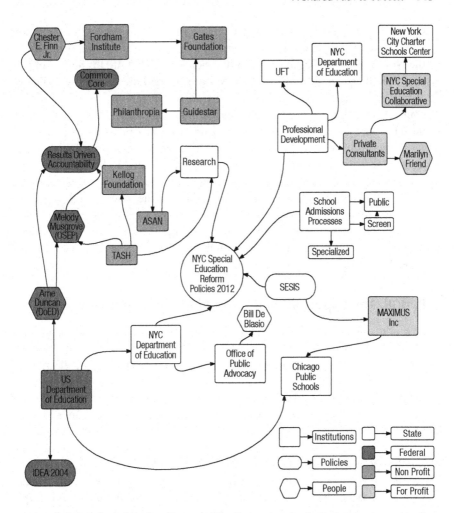

FIGURE 10.1 A Shared Path to Success: The Journey to Inclusion

which allows students to meet a lower and more flexible threshold on state exams and still receive a local high school diploma. This safety net, and the local diploma students receive, exist only for students with disabilities and are not offered to general education students.[23]

aSPtS was also influenced by the work of non-profits and advocacy groups, many of whom are cited as resources for reform on the DOE's website.[24] One of these groups, Autistic Self Advocacy Network (ASAN), was ranked number 6 in a 2013 national ranking of Disability Non-Profit Organizations. Philanthropia did this ranking. Philanthropia is a division of Guidestar, an organization that provides information on non-profit companies. Guidestar is funded in part by the

Gates Foundation, an organization that has a vested interest in the Common Core, accountability measures, and testing. A second non-profit that was cited by the New York City Department of Education is TASH. TASH is funded in part by the Kellogg Foundation. Melody Musgrove, the Director of the Office of Special Education Programs has served as a presenter and speaker at TASH conferences.[25] Both of these non-profits have provided research that confirms the need for the Special Education Reform, particularly around issues of inclusion.

These private and public interests are not perfect representations of the goals of reformers and advocates. There is certainly a relationship between ideology and practice, and alternative motives in funding special education reforms like aSPtS. However, the role of these organizations, and the power that they have to shape and influence policy, must be considered when attempting to understand the goals of this policy. While inclusion is an important goal for many of these stakeholders, after reviewing the way funding is allocated, it is clear that the focus on RDA and the testing that comes with it is the priority.

Part III: The Impact of Reform on Classrooms and Teachers

The implementation of aSPtS requires new sets of skills from teachers, from becoming familiar with the "Special Education Student Information System" (SESIS), to learning how to co-teach for the first time. These new skills require professional development, and schools under pressure to perform are constantly looking for meaningful workshops. Some of these are provided by the United Federation of Teachers (UFT), some by the Department of Education, and some by private consultants.

Since 2012, consultants who specialize in special education have found a niche and the opportunity to profit. On April 20, 2016, the Mayor's Panel for Education awarded 1-year contracts to 10 private vendors ranging from $100,000 to $2.3 million dollars. These vendors are contracted to provide physical therapy, occupational therapy, social work, and other services. Watchdog groups, like Class Size Matters, have criticized the DOE for not carefully reviewing these vendors prior to the awarding of these contracts. Class Size Matters has raised questions about these vendors for engaging in questionable practices. Some of these vendors had not received full background checks prior to the signing of the contracts and had previously engaged in fraudulent business practices.[26] These concerns were not enough to change the Panel's vote, and these contracts stand. It remains to be seen how effective these vendors will be.

An area of particular interest is the role of the Special Education Student Information System, or SESIS. SESIS was introduced in 2011 in an effort to systematize student information. The contract to develop SESIS was given to MAXIMUS Inc., a company that "provides software and consulting solutions for higher education institutions and PreK-12 School Districts."[27] MAXIMUS's work has been highly criticized in the press, by teachers and in a report by the

City Comptroller. The Comptroller's report concluded that SESIS did not meet its overall goal, that the DOE did not take adequate steps to protect SESIS data, and that users found SESIS inefficient and unsatisfactory.[28] The inadequacy of SESIS has cost the city millions of dollars in teacher overtime. Letitia James' 2016 lawsuit against the city centers around SESIS's flaws. This system and the role of MAXIMUS reveal the areas in which special education reforms have left the city open to profiteers who seek to find opportunity in the standardization of students who, by definition, do not fit the standard.

The clearest pedagogical change that has taken place as a consequence of aSPtS is the prevalence of the co-teaching model. The inclusion goals of aSPtS, the research on inclusion, and the Fair Student Funding model have all pushed New York City schools to quickly adopt the co-teaching model. This is a tremendous shift for many teaching professionals, and this shift has been met with limited support.

The United Federation of Teachers and the DOE's website feature information that highlights compliance to aSPtS rather than practical information on inclusion and co-teaching pedagogy. The UFT cites research from American Institutes for Research on "school practices," but, again, this research is rife with discussions of "accountability" rather than pedagogy and practice. The only practical information for teachers on the DOE's website comes from Marilyn Friend, the author of the *Co-Teaching Handbooks*. Friend's most recent handbook includes information on the definition of co-teaching, the "legislative basis" for co-teaching, co-teaching approaches, logistics, evaluation, and administrative roles.[29] Notably absent from Friend's work and many co-teaching resources on the DOE's and UFT's sites are information on curriculum and co-teaching.

Marilyn Friend is one of many former teachers, researchers, and educational professionals to put forth a co-teaching handbook. And while procedural information is available to New York City teachers, academic research around the success of the co-teaching model to support special education students is scarce. Researchers who have studied co-teaching argue that co-teaching requires a pedagogical shift for teachers and this model will "change the way one teaches."[30] However, the outcomes of this shift are inconclusive. Almost all of the available research on co-teaching laments the lack of data and research in this area.

The research that is available indicates a variety of results. One 2001 study indicates that co-teaching is as effective as previous special education models, like resource room or pull out instruction. Another study found a decline in student performance in a co-teaching setting, and yet another study found that co-teaching was a moderately effective strategy for productive student outcomes.[31] There is certainly more research that indicates co-teaching is moderately, or somewhat effective, rather than harmful to educational practices. However, given the lack of research and the speed at which the city implemented this practice it is disconcerting to consider the far-reaching effects of a shift to a co-teaching model on students, teachers, and schools.

The co-teaching model requires both a pedagogical shift for teachers and a practical shift for administrators and school organizers, particularly in small high schools. Sarah Butler Jessen, in her article "Special Education and School Choice," does a thorough job of unpacking some of the complex intersecting policies around small schools, school choice, and special education students. Jessen explains the unintended consequences that aSPtS and special education reforms have on small schools that have attempted to create community, and "limit their higher-need student populations in order to facilitate reaching performance goals."[32] In the framework of school choice, the option to limit high needs students was available for schools but, under aSPtS, schools now must embrace the special education students in their communities.

Under the current aSPtS framework, small schools now must provide ICT classrooms and an inclusive environment to their students but, financially, this can be challenging and, in some cases, almost impossible to manage. Under FSF each student that receives ICT instruction is allocated $7,142.20. Under aSPtS, ICT classrooms cannot exceed 12 students in a class, so if every seat is filled, FSF provides $85,706.40 of funding for services per ICT cohort. A first-year New York City teacher with the required Master's degree has a starting salary of $51,425. So, FSF provides the funds to hire 1.6 teachers. However, FSF also requires that in order for students to qualify for full funding, they need to be in ICT classes 60 percent of the day, or all their core classes. The FSF funding for one ICT cohort of 12 students does not cover the funding necessary to provide services for the amount of ICT teachers needed to fully program students with trained teachers. This is the exact predicament that many small schools find themselves in, and "creative" scheduling abounds and is encouraged. While small schools may have figured out ways to plug the holes in services, this begs the questions, what is the intention of aSPtS? And, is this the best way to service our students?

In order to effectively support special education students and the schools that serve these students, the Department of Education must support effective co-teaching partnerships and acknowledge that FSF means different things to differently sized schools. FSF allocations must take the size of the school into account and adjust accordingly. To ignore this factor is to have a hollow policy. Teachers need meaningful co-teaching professional development, and a restructuring of how co-teachers are trained and partnered. This should start in the teaching training programs, but that is not enough. Training and development for team teaching needs to have space in every level of teaching. Asking two professionals to share physical space, content responsibility, and ownership of a classroom is a tremendous task and requires thought and time to develop in every school environment.

Part IV: Is "A Shared Path to Success" Working?

A 2012 report from the Office for Public Advocacy studied the success of aSPtS and "found that the Education Department did well in preparing for the changes, including expanding its training for school personnel, developing a phone hot line for parents to call and setting up nine offices across the city devoted to providing information on special education."[33] However, the report also raised questions about the effectiveness of the funding that followed these policies, specifically expressing concern over the decision to fund schools based on the number of special education students rather than the number of special education classes. Ultimately, the report concluded that the city was implementing the policy well. At the time of the report, current Mayor Bill De Blasio led The Office of Public Advocacy.

In 2016, the New York City Department of Education released a special education report in compliance with Local Law 27. This report was the first of its kind and it was meant to reveal data about services and demographics around aSPtS for the 2014–2015 school year. The data revealed a number of areas of challenge around implementing aSPtS, particularly the fact that as many as 40 percent of special education students are not getting their required services.[34] National news outlets like the *New York Times* picked up this statistic and ran the headline that "Thousands of New York City Students Deprived of Special Education Services, Report Says."[35] The city however, pushed back, citing the ineffectiveness of SESIS as a barrier to accurate information.

The information on students not receiving services is by far the most startling and provocative, but the report is filled with important information for all stakeholders. Thirty percent of parents or teachers who requested evaluations for students did not get them within the mandated 60 days. Students with free and reduced lunch are disproportionately categorized as special education. Students with IEPs are disproportionately black. White students, more than any other group, experience being initially referred for evaluation but having the referral closed without an IEP meeting. More boys than girls are referred for IEP meetings. Referrals for IEPs peak in the first grade, and then get increasingly less, and seemingly almost impossible to secure in high school. And all of this, coupled with the overarching fact that not enough students are getting the services they need, reveals that the work of aSPtS has only just begun.

Part V: Recommendations and Conclusions

The implementation of "A Shared Path to Success" requires schools to navigate the complex balance of inclusion and accountability. Schools, teachers, and students must work to find ways to prioritize these two, often conflicting, goals, while fulfilling the letter of the law. The state asks schools to be "flexible" in scheduling, pedagogy, and funding, but this can lead to compromise, which leaves students, teachers, and schools open to private interests and opportunists. However, aSPtS also results in greater access for some students, who are now finding their way into elite schools that they would previously have been barred from. Whether or not these schools are capable of truly serving the interests of special education students is an open question, but at the very least there is more access, less restriction, and more interaction between students of differing abilities than before. Notably, the US Department of Education continues to list New York as a state that "needs assistance" in implementing IDEA.[36]

The federal trends and mandates that inform aSPtS highlight issues that are pervasive throughout the entire educational system, namely the importance of measurement and testing. This pattern is damaging to students who might not perform up to state and federal "standards." At the high school level, students, including special education students, who do not meet standards, can be made to repeat a grade, or a course. Schools that do not meet state testing standards are given improvement plans, and are monitored closely by higher offices. In extreme cases, schools that have repeatedly fallen below standards have been closed and deemed inefficient by the state. The focus on testing, and the very real consequences of failing tests, places schools and districts in the difficult position of reconciling individual student needs with sweeping mandates. States and districts, in an attempt to secure federal support and funding, often push schools to conform to the requirements of testing.

To teach special education students, and to do it well, requires flexibility on the part of the educational system. Flexibility is not an empty policy term; it means the capability and willingness of schools to meet the individualized needs of students via testing, curriculum, and pedagogical adjustments. However, the flexibility that schools have is severely limited by the testing requirements placed upon them. RDA and high stakes testing offer the exact opposite of flexibility. RDA and high stakes accountability measures fly in the face of the spirit of the Individualized Educational Plans that students are legally provided with. This creates a system in which special education students are experiencing an educational dichotomy of individualized education and simultaneous high stakes standardized testing. And, while some students are able to succeed in this climate, it is not due to the thoughtful and responsive nature of the reform policies of the New York City Department of Education.

A thoughtful and responsive policy is required when handling the diverse needs of special education students. However, for policy recommendations to be effective there must be a guiding framework behind the policy. The framework discussed here comes from researchers who have identified the categories that are used to conceptualize disability. *Incrementalists* see disability as a deficit that exists within the individual. This deficit requires a cure and, in the case of an educational disability, an educational cure is required. Standardized tests and RDA fit the instrumentalist model in that these exams serve to reveal deficits and serve as "data" to drive further instruction that will "cure" the student. *Reconceptualists* see disability as a social construct, and while they do not deny there are compromised functions that come with disability, they focus on changing environmental limitations rather than changing the student, or person.[37] The reconceptualist framing of disability would provide an opportunity for schools to adjust their environment, rather than "curing" the student. This would benefit the special education population tremendously, and allow schools to respond to the 2012 reforms in the spirit that they were intended.

Beyond the reconceptualist framing of disability, researchers Dr. Annamma, Dr. Connor, and Dr. Ferri have proposed a new theoretical framework, DisCrit, for thinking about disability that builds further on the understanding that disability is a social construct. These researchers argue that there is an intersection between the experience of dis/abled students, and students of color. There is overlap between the two groups, as black students are disproportionately represented in the special education population, and both are a part of oppressive systems that have historically allowed for segregation of students. These researchers demonstrate masterful use of history, legal precedent and educational policies to unpack their DisCrit theory.

DisCrit considers the relationship between race and disability, the construction of these labels, and how systems use these constructions to separate and underserve students who are labeled. While DisCrit provides many essential tools for better understanding the construction of disabilities, it must be noted that special education students, though all a part of a system of oppression, are not a monolithic group that can benefit from the same policy change. But, the entire Educational system could benefit from the understanding that "disability," like "race" is a construct and part of a system of oppression. High stakes testing is a highly oppressive tool and serves to doubly oppressed special education groups. The schools that serve special education students cannot effectively and consistently serve their student populations with punitive testing measures.

DisCrit, which is borne from a combination of Disability Studies and Critical Race Theory, relies on tenets from both camps. Critical Race Theory calls for "activism that links academic work to the community."[38] This concept is essential to the DisCrit theory and the rejection of RDA and high stakes testing. There is a need for activism to carve out space for non-oppressive special education policies. The DisCrit theorists acknowledge that there can be different kinds of activism, which is particularly important when empowering dis/abled communities, and "to suggest that activism cannot occur from behind a desk may be missing a larger point about what it means to resist forms of domination."[39]

Activism can occur from a desk, a classroom, a home, and from students themselves. aSPtS was informed by both a desire to improve the educational system for special education students, *and* by powerful players who seek to push accountability measures. However, stakeholders on the ground have a say in how this policy takes shape in their communities apart from the interests of those in power. This chapter notably did not include voices of families, because they are not yet a robust part of the academic conversation around aSPtS, but they should be. This chapter did not discuss the voices of teachers who are striving to learn how to best co-teach and serve their students, but those teachers exist. This chapter did not involve the experiences of school leaders who are finding flexibility even within the limitations of FSF to support teachers in creating inclusive spaces for students, but it is happening.

To allow a successful implementation of aSPtS, the Department of Education needs to look at places where meaningful educational growth is happening, and examine the context around that success. Where are partnerships between co-teachers thriving and why? Where are students meeting appropriate academic challenges and why? aSPtS has laid a framework for inclusion, but the particulars of what inclusion looks like needs to be determined on a school by school basis, *without* the fear of high stakes consequences around standardized accountability measures for both students and schools. When success is identified, it should be supported with further professional development that has grounding in researched practices, and partnerships between school communities that help to model and support each other. This is not to say that students and schools that serve special education students do not need to push their students to grow in the classroom and meet educational benchmarks, but these standards need to be appropriately aligned to student IEPs, and individual schools need the information, funding and space to make that a reality.

Activism by students, families, teachers, and school leaders in response to oppressive policies and systems is the appropriate response to the RDA policies of the state. aSPtS was meant to provide more opportunities to students, but these opportunities cannot be given with punitive standards attached. The community of parents, educators, administrators, and students has a responsibility to represent the interests of all students, and respond to the educational environment accordingly. Through a combination of academic understanding and community responsiveness, stakeholders need to demand that the reforms that were meant to provide increased access and education to special education students fulfill their intended purpose: true and meaningful inclusion.

Notes

1 Letitia James, "PA James Suit: DOE Failure Equals Lack of Services for Students with Disabilities, Loss of Funding for City," *Public Advocate for the City Of New York*, February 1, 2016.
2 Thomas P. DiNapoli, "Waiting for Special Education," Office of the State Comptroller, June 2008.
3 US Department of Education, "Building the Legacy: IDEA 2004" Sec. 601 Short Title; Table of Contents; Findings: Purpose, http://idea-b.ed.gov/explore/view/p/,root,statute,I,A,601,.html
4 "QC04full.pdf." Accessed April 28, 2017. https://www.edweek.org/media/ew/qc/archives/QC04full.pdf.
5 Garth Harries, Senior Coordinator for Special Education to Joel Klein, Chancellor, memorandum, July 2, 2009, New York City Department of Education.
6 "Rationale for and Research on Inclusive Education," National Center on Inclusive Education Institute on Disability at the University of New Hampshire (2011):

A Shared Path to Success **151**

http://schools.nyc.gov/NR/rdonlyres/0B3B6CCB-1B14-4228-8771-9400045B7E94/0/NCIE_Research_on_Inclusiive_Education.pdf
7. "System Wide Special Education Reform and SY 12–13 School Budget Allocation," New York City Department of Education, http://schools.nyc.gov/NR/rdonlyres/FB899312-2EC5-4F5E-B1D6-CC5E83B4D086/125775/FSFandSpEdReform_Panel_final.pdf
8. "Implementation for the Reform of Special Education," New City Department of Education, 2010, http://schools.nyc.gov/documents/d75/parent/ccse/FINAL%20-%20Implementation%20Plan%20for%20the%20Reform%20of%20Special%20Education.pdf
9. Geoff Decker, "At a Critical Moment, A New Special Education Chief Takes Over," *Chalkbeat*, July 20, 2012.
10. "Special Education Reform," New York City Department of Education, March 2012, http://schools.nyc.gov/Academics/SpecialEducation/tellmemore/spedReform.htm
11. "Special Education Reform Reference Guide," New York City Department of Education, 2012–2013, http://schools.nyc.gov/NR/rdonlyres/4C52B390-1162-4D9F-8ED0-0D96E21E4B55/0/SpecialEducationReformReferenceGuide060512.pdf
12. "A Question for Discussion—Can we hope to see the next Richard Branson, David Boies, Whoopi Goldberg, Charles Schwab, Steven Spielberg, and Wendy Wasserstein in New York City's Top Public High Schools?" David Rubel Consultant, September 2014, updated April 2016.
13. "A Question for Discussion" David Rubel Consultant.
14. New York City Department of Education, "Fair Student Funding and School Budget Resources Guide: FY 2016" Division of Finance, http://schools.nyc.gov/offices/d_chanc_oper/budget/dbor/allocationmemo/fy15_16/FY16_PDF/FSF_Guide.pdf, June 2016
15. "Fair Student Funding," New York City Department of Education.
16. Grace Tatter, "Pep Okays Special Ed Funding Plan, Despite Requests for Caution," *Chalkbeat*, May 24, 2012.
17. Philissa Cramer and Emma Sokoloff-Rubin, "City Might Take Special Education Funding Back from Schools MidYear," *Chalkbeat*, January 10, 2013.
18. "New Accountability Framework Raises the Bar for State Special Education Programs," US Department of Education, June 24, 2015, www.ed.gov/news/press-releases/new-accountability-framework-raises-bar-state-special-education-programs.
19. "Fair Student Funding," New York City Department of Education.
20. Chester E. Finn Jr, "Rethinking Special Education for A New Century," Thomas B. Fordham Foundation and the Progressive Policy Institute, 2001, www.specialed.us/Parents/ASMT%20Advocacy/wl/spedfinl.pdf
21. "Funding and Finances" Thomas B. Fordham Institute, accessed 2015, http://edexcellence.net/about-us/funding-and-finances.html.
22. "W.K. Kellogg Foundation Grant Promotes Digital Learning among Low-Income Communities," Kellogg Foundation, April 2012, www.wkkf.org/news-and-media/article/2012/04/grant-promotes-digital-learning-among-low-income-communities
23. "Compensatory Option Safety Net," New York City Department of Education, August 2015, www.p12.nysed.gov/specialed/publications/documents/safetynet-qa-dec12.pdf
24. "Rationale for and Research on Inclusive Education," New York City Department of Education.
25. "Melody Musgrove," TASH, 2014, http://conference.tash.org/speakers/melody-musgrove/

26 Leonie Haimson and Patrick Sullivan, April 19, 2016, "Comments on DOE Questionable Contracts and Fair Student Funding Formula," NYC Public School Parents, April 19, 2016, http://nycpublicschoolparents.blogspot.com/2016/04/comments-on-questionable-contracts-and.html?link_id=4&can_id=13a7febb9e1b6dd0b20ac9a44e48c919&source=email-save-the-dates-for-2-important-events-also-updates-on-contracts-attacks-on-schools
27 "Educational Consulting," Maximus, 2015, www.maximus.com/education
28 Tina Kim, "IT Audit and Research," Office of the Comptroller, 2013, https://comptroller.nyc.gov/wp-content/uploads/documents/7A12_114.pdf
29 "Integrated Co-Teaching, United Federation of Teachers, 2015, www.uft.org/teaching/integrated-co-teaching-ict
30 Lisa A. Dieker and Wendy W. Murawski, "Co-Teaching at the Secondary Level: Unique Issues, Current Trends, and Suggestions for Success," *The High School Journal*, 86.4 (2001) 1–13.
31 Hanover Research, "Three Tips for Effective Co-Teaching Implementation" *Hanover Blog*, November 18, 2014, www.hanoverresearch.com/2014/11/18/3-tips-for-effective-co-teaching-implementation/?i=k-12-education
32 Sarah Butler Jessen, "Special Education & School Choice: The Complex Effects of Small Schools, School Choice and Public High School Policy in New York City," *Educational Policy*, 27 (2012): 427–466.
33 Al Baker, "Mainstreaming Efforts Praised in School Study," *New York Times*, August 1, 2012, www.nytimes.com/2012/09/01/nyregion/schools-planned-well-for-special-education-changes-but-may-need-more-funds-study-finds.html
34 "Local Law 27 of 2015 Annual Report on Special Education: School Year 2014–2015," NYC Department of Education, February 29, 2016, http://schools.nyc.gov/NR/rdonlyres/6035782C-F95D-4224-8372-F2B1F7E9A226/0/LocalLaw27of20152292016FINAL.pdf
35 Kate Taylor, "Thousands of New York City Students Deprived of Special Education Services, Report Says," *New York Times*, March 1, 2016.
36 "Determination Letters on State Implementation of Idea," US Department of Education, June 2015, www2.ed.gov/fund/data/report/idea/2015-ideafactsheet-determinations.pdf
37 Susan Baglieri, Jan W. Valle, David J. Connor, and Deborah J. Gallagher, "Disability Studies in Education: The Need for a Plurality of Perspectives on Disability," Hammill Institute on Disabilities, November 28, 2015, http://rse.sagepub.com.ezproxy.gc.cuny.edu/content/32/4/267.full.pdf+html
38 Subini Ancy Annamma, David Connor, and Beth Ferri, "Dis/ability Critical Race Studies (DisCrit): Theorizing at the Intersections of Race and Dis/ability," Race Ethnicity and Education, October 30, 2012, p. 19.
39 Annamma, Connor, and Ferri, "Dis/ability Critical Race Studies," p. 19.

References

"Advocacy and Issues," *TASH*. 2015. https://tash.org/advocacy-issues/
Annamma, Subini Ancy, Connor, David, & Ferri, Beth, "Dis/ability Critical Race Studies (DisCrit): Theorizing at the Intersections of Race and Dis/ability," *Race Ethnicity and*

Education, October 30, 2012. www.academia.edu/2258717/Dis_ability_critical_race_studies_DisCrit_theorizing_at_the_intersections_of_race_and_dis_ability

Baglieri, Susan, Connor, David J., Gallagher, Deborah J., & Valle, Jan. "Disability Studies in Education: The Need for a Plurality of Perspectives on Disability," Hammill Institute on Disabilities. November 28, 2015. http://rse.sagepub.com.ezproxy.gc.cuny.edu/content/32/4/267.full.pdf+htm

Baker, Al. "Mainstreaming Efforts Praised in School Study," *New York Times*. August 1, 2012. www.nytimes.com/2012/09/01/nyregion/schools-planned-well-for-specialeducation-changes-but-may-need-more-funds-study-finds.html.

"Compensatory Option Safety Net," *New York City Department of Education*. August 2015. www.p12.nysed.gov/specialed/publications/documents/safetynet-qa-dec12.pdf.

Cramer, Philissa, & Sokoloff-Rubin, Emma. "City Might Take Special Education Funding Back from Schools MidYear," *Chalkbeat*, January 10, 2013.

Decker, Geoff. "At a Critical Moment, A New Special Education Chief Takes Over," *Chalkbeat*. July 20, 2012.

"Department Announces New Effort to Strengthen Accountability for Students with Disabilities," *US Department of Education*. March 2012. http://www.ed.gov/news/press-releases/department-announces-new-effort-strengthen-accountability-students-disabilities.

"Determination Letters on State Implementation of Idea," *US Department of Education*. June 2015. www2.ed.gov/fund/data/report/idea/2015-ideafactsheet-determinations.pdf

Dieker, Lisa A., & Murawski, Wendy W. "Co-Teaching at the Secondary Level: Unique Issues, Current Trends, and Suggestions for Success," *The High School Journal*, 86.4 (2001), 1–13.

DiNapoli, Thomas P. "Waiting for Special Education," *Office of the State Comptroller*. June 2008.

"Educational Consulting," *Maximus*. 2015. www.maximus.com/education.

Finn Jr., Chester E. "Rethinking Special Education for a New Century," *Thomas B. Fordham Foundation and the Progressive Policy Institute*. 2001. www.specialed.us/Parents/ASMT%20Advocacy/wl/spedfinl.pdf.

"Funding and Finances," *Thomas B. Fordham Institute*. Accessed 2015, http://edexcellence.net/about-us/funding-and-finances.html

NYC Public School Parents Blog. http://nycpublicschoolparents.blogspot.com/2016/04/comments-on-questionable-contracts-and.html?link_id=4&can_id=13a7febb9e1b6dd0b20ac9a44e48c919&source=email-save-the-dates-for-2-important-events-also-updates-on-contracts-attacks-on-schools

Hanover Blog, www.hanoverresearch.com/2014/11/18/3-tips-for-effective-co-teaching-implementation/?i=k-12-education

Harries, Garth. Senior Coordinator for Special Education to Joel Klein, Chancellor, memorandum, July 2, 2009, New York City Department of Education.

"Implementation for the Reform of Special Education," *New City Department of Education*. 2010. http://schools.nyc.gov/documents/d75/parent/ccse/FINAL%20-%20Implementation%20Plan%20for%20the%20Reform%20of%20Special%20Education.pdf

"Integrated Co-Teaching," *United Federation of Teachers*. 2015. www.uft.org/teaching/integrated-co-teaching-ict.

Jessen, Sarah Butler. "Special Education & School Choice: The Complex Effects of Small Schools, School Choice and Public High School Policy in New York City," *Educational Policy*, 27 (2012): 427–466.

James, Letitia. "PA James Suit: DOE Failure Equals Lack of Services for Students with Disabilities, Loss of Funding for City," *Public Advocate for the City Of New York*. February 1, 2016.

Jose P. v. Ambach, 3EHLR 551:245 (E.D.N.Y. 1979).

"Local Law 27 of 2015 Annual Report on Special Education: School Year 2014–2015," *NYC Department of Education*. February 29, 2016. http://schools.nyc.gov/NR/rdonlyres/6035782C-F95D-4224-8372-F2B1F7E9A226/0/LocalLaw27of20152292016FINAL.pdf

Kim, Tina. "IT Audit and Research," *Office of the Comptroller*. 2013. https://comptroller.nyc.gov/wp-content/uploads/documents/7A12_114.pdf

"Melody Musgrove," *TASH*. 2014. http://conference.tash.org/speakers/melody-musgrove/

"New Accountability Framework Raises the Bar for State Special Education Programs," *US Department of Education*. June 24, 24015, www.ed.gov/news/press-releases/new-accountability-framework-raises-bar-state-special-education-programs

NYC Department of Education. "A Shared Path to Success: A Parent's Guide to Special Education Services for School-Age Children," 2012. Updated version available at: http://schools.nyc.gov/NR/rdonlyres/DBD4EB3A-6D3B-496D-8CB2-C742F9B9AB5C/0/Parent_Guide_for_Students_with_Disabilites_Updated_Web.pdf

"Position Statements," *ASAN: Autistic Self Advocacy Network*. 2015. http://autisticadvocacy.org/policy-advocacy/position-statements/

"A Question for Discussion—Can We Hope to See the Next Richard Branson, David Boies, Whoopi Goldberg, Charles Schwab, Steven Spielberg, and Wendy Wasserstein in New York City's Top Public High Schools?" *David Rubel Consultant*. September 2014. www.davidrubelconsultant.com/publications/NYC_top_public_high_schools_and_students_discussion_paper.pdf

"Rationale for and Research on Inclusive Education Winter 2011," *New York City Department of Education*. 2011. http://schools.nyc.gov/NR/rdonlyres/0B3B6CCB-1B14-4228-87719400045B7E94/0/NCIE_Research_on_Inclusiive_Education.pdf

"Special Education Reform," *New York City Department of Education*. March 2012. http://schools.nyc.gov/Academics/SpecialEducation/tellmemore/spedReform.htm

"Special Education Reform Reference Guide," *New York City Department of Education*. 2012–2013. http://schools.nyc.gov/NR/rdonlyres/4C52B390-1162-4D9F-8ED0-0D96E21E4B55/0/SpecialEducationReformReferenceGuide060512.pdf

"System Wide Special Education Reform and SY 12–13 School Budget Allocation," *New York City Department of Education*. http://schools.nyc.gov/NR/rdonlyres/FB899312-2EC5-4F5E-B1D6-CC5E83B4D086/125775/FSFandSpEdReform_Panel_final.pdf

Tatter, Grace. "Pep Okays Special Ed Funding Plan, Despite Requests for Caution," *Chalkbeat*. May 24, 2012.

"UFT: Special Education Reform 'Pilot' Had Weak Results," *United Federation of Teachers*. November 2012. www.uft.org/news-stories/uft-special-ed-reform-pilot-had-weak-results.

US Department of Education, "Building the Legacy: IDEA 2004," Sec. 601 Short Title; Table of Contents; Findings: Purpose, http://idea.ed.gov/explore/view/p/,root,statute,I,A,601,

"US Department of Education Guidance on Issues Driving City's Special Education Reform," *United Federation of Teachers*. 2012. www.uft.org/teaching/federal-guidance-special-education-reform

"W.K. Kellogg Foundation Grant Promotes Digital Learning Among Low-Income Communities," *Kellogg Foundation*. April 2012. http://www.wkkf.org/news-and-media/article/2012/04/grant-promotes-digital-learning-among-low-income-communities

CONTRIBUTORS

Diane Price Banks is the Assistant Program Director to the Medical Laboratory Technician Program at Bronx Community College and student in the Ph.D. program in Urban Education at the Graduate Center of the City University of New York, USA.

Aminata Diop is a student in the Ph.D. program in Urban Education at the Graduate Center of the City University of New York, USA.

John Eric Frankson is a student in the Ph.D. program in Urban Education at the Graduate Center of the City University of New York, USA.

Amy Goods is a student in the Ph.D. program in Urban Education at the Graduate Center of the City University of New York, USA.

Sakina Laksimi-Morrow is a student in the Ph.D. program in Urban Education at the Graduate Center of the City University of New York, USA.

Corie A. McCallum is a student in the Ph.D. program in Urban Education at the Graduate Center of the City University of New York, USA.

Robert Randazzo is a student in the Ph.D. program in Urban Education at the Graduate Center of the City University of New York, USA.

Robert P. Robinson is a student in the Ph.D. program in Urban Education at the Graduate Center of the City University of New York, USA.

Joel Spring is Professor at Queens College and the Graduate Center of the City University of New York, USA.

Melanie Waller is a student in the Ph.D. program in Urban Education at the Graduate Center of the City University of New York, USA.

INDEX

Page numbers in bold denote tables. Page numbers in italics denote figures. Page numbers with "n" refer to notes.

academic achievement, and Turnaround Arts 60, 63
accountability: and excellence 20–21; neoliberal notions of 18–21; and SESIS 54; and special education 141–144, 147
accountability movement 7–8
achievement tests 8
activism, special education-related 149, 150
ACT (American College Test/Testing) Program, AVID's connection to 38, 40
Advancement Via Individual Determination (AVID) 32; board of directors 33–36; English Learner College Readiness initiatives 36; executive leadership of 36; flexians in 40; focus, implications for 38–41; funding structure of 32–33, 40; monitoring and reporting of data 40; structure of *37*; Summer Institute 33, 36, 39
Affordable Care Act (ACA) 52
American Association of Colleges for Teacher Education (AACTE) 98
American Council on Education (ACE) 110–111
American Dream 25, 115
American Enterprise Institute 23
American Institutes for Research 145
American Recovery and Reinvestment Act of 2009 110

Amnesty (1986) *see* Immigration Reform and Control Act (1986)
Annamma, Subini Ancy 149
Anthony, Marc 63
Anyon, Jean 115, 123
AOL Charitable Foundation 62
Apple, Michael W. 69
arrest, and Zero Tolerance policies 119–122
arts education 58, 59, 61, 63; *see also* Turnaround Arts
assessment, AVID 32, 38
Atlas 111
attendance, effect of Turnaround Arts on 60
Autistic Self Advocacy Network (ASAN) 143
Automate the Schools (ATS) 50
AVID *see* Advancement Via Individual Determination (AVID)
AVID Center 32, 34, 40
AVID Institute 33, 39
AVID Library 33, 39
AVID National Conference 39
AVID Weekly 39, 44n56

Ball, Stephen J. 2, 18, 40, 69, 115
Banks, Diane Price 83
Batalova, Jeanne 70

Berestein, Leslie Rojas 74
Berman, Mike 74
Bernstein, John 74
Bill & Melinda Gates Foundation 2, 5, 113, 142, 144
Black, Cathy 139
Black Codes 125
black culture 121
Bloomberg, Michael 52, 64, 78, 98
board of directors: of AVID 33–36; of UWD 75
Boehner, John 113
Boice, Robert 85
Bolt Threads, Inc. 36
Boyce, Freddie 45–46
Broad Foundation 5
Broadway Junior Collections 63–64
Brown, Jerry 33
Buher, Andrew 50, 56n13
Burch, Patricia 70
bureaucracy: and AVID 38, 41; government 4; in New York 123; political control of 9–10; school administration 3; and segregation 9; and special education 139, 141; Swiss-cheese 6–7
Bush, George W. 20, 23, 69, 79

California: Department of Education 33; funding of AVID 33; Turnaround Arts program in 62–64
California Applicants Attorneys Association (CAAA) 76
California Arts Council 62
California Commission on Teacher Credentialing 34
California Curriculum Development Commission 35
California Employment Lawyers Association (CELA) 76
California State University, Single Subject Credential Program 36
Center for Immigration Studies 79
certification 23; AVID 32, 33, 39, 40; Price Prep Policy 89, 91
Chan, Priscilla 111
charter schools 3, 6, 23
Chicago Public Schools 49
Children's First Networks 139
Children's Health Insurance Program (CHIP) 52
choice office 10
choice plan 10

Chubb, John E. 9–10
City Height Educational Collaborative 35
city schools 123–124, 130–131
City University of New York (CUNY) 23, 83, 89, 98, 101–102; Board of Trustees 98, **100**, 101; Dreamers 78; Graduate Center 84; operational cost of 97–98; structure of 99; University Faculty Senate 100–101; University Student Senate 99–100
Civil Rights Act (1964) 3
civil rights movement 3
classrooms: ICT 146; management skills, of faculty 84, 85, 88
Class Size Matters 144
Clinton, Hillary 80, 114
College Board, The 40, 142; AVID's relationship with 38, 40
college campuses, complaints on 22
College Readiness initiative 35
Colorado Mountain College 34
Colorado State University 35
Common Core State Standards 6, 38, 59, 113, 142, 144
community control of schools 7–8, 9
competition between schools 3; and student achievement 9–10
conflict resolution practices 131
Connor, David 149
Consumer Attorneys Association of Los Angeles (CAALA) 76
Consumer Attorneys of California (CAOC) 76
consumer-driven economy 23–24
content knowledge, of faculty 84, 86
continuing education (CE) credit 91
continuing education program 91
Cooc, North 80
Cornyn, John 72
cost: of AVID Institute 33; of Price Prep Policy 97
co-teaching model 140, 141, 145–146
Council for the Accreditation of Educator Preparation (CAEP), The 20
Crayola 62
Create CA 62
crime control paradigm 118, 119, 122–125
criminal justice system 119, 122, 124; prison-industrial complex 125–129
Critical Race Theory 149
culture of poverty 121

cumulative disadvantage of youth of color 121
CUNY Dreamers 78
Cuomo, Andrew 20, 98
curriculum: of AVID 39; narrowing of 25; for students with IEP 47–48; urban schools 124

De Blasio, Bill 53, 98, 147
decision making, about schools 7–8
DecisionPoint™ 52
deferred acceptance algorithm 138
Deferred Action for Childhood Arrivals (DACA) 72, 74, 77, 80
de-industrialization 122–125
democracy, and education 25
democratic control of schools 3–6, 7, 8; and free markets 9–10
deportation, of undocumented immigrants 74, 80
detention centers 119
Development, Relief, and Education for Alien Minors (DREAM) Act 71; lifespan in Congress 72, 74; opposition to 79; power of Dreamers 74; power of online networks, foundations, and philanthropies 74–80; structure of 73
deviance, labeling of 120
Diop, Aminata 69
Direct Loans 110
disability, conceptualization of 148–149
Disability Studies 149
disaster capitalism 22–23
disciplinary issues, effect of Turnaround Arts on 60
DisCrit 149
disenfranchisement, of felons 125, 126, 129–130
disinvestment, urban 122, 123
disruption in education: and incarceration 126; and Zero Tolerance policies 119–122
District of Columbia, Child and Family Services Agency 52, 54
DREAM Act *see* Development, Relief, and Education for Alien Minors (DREAM) Act
DreamActivist.org 74–75
Dreamers 72, 74, 76, 80
drug-related sentencing policies 127
D'Souza, Dinesh 4
Duncan, Arne 113, 141
Durbin, Richard 72

economization: of education 59–60, 66; of incarceration 122, 124
EdCyclopedia 111
EdTPA 98
Educational Defense Act (1958) 3
Educational Testing Service (ETS) 17
Education Central 111
Education for All Handicapped Children Act (EHA) 46, 48
elected representative governance 3
Elementary and Secondary Education Act (ESEA) of 1965 3, 44n49
11 essentials framework (AVID) 38, 39
Elia, Mary Ellen 20
Emiliani, Bob 88, 97
empathy 26
employment, and de-industrialization 122–124
endangered spaces 17–18
Equinox 77
Eric Frankson, John 16
Ermenegildo Zegna 77
Europe, performing and visual arts schools in 67
Every Student Succeeds Act (ESSA) 58, 61, 114; and accountability 8, 19; and charter schools 6, 10
excellence: and accountability 20–21; AVID's mission for 39
executive leadership of AVID 36, 39
Expected Family Contribution (EFC) 108–109
expert control of schools 8, 9

Facebook 74
Faculty Development and Preparation Policy for Higher Education *see* Price Prep Policy
faculty preparation 83; call for 87–88; networks of power 98–101; Price Prep Policy 88–98
Fair Isaac & Company 36
Fair Student Funding (FSF) 140–141, 146, 150
family control over education 3
Fariña, Carmon 52
Federal Family Education Loan (FFEL) 107, 110, 112, 113
federal financial aid networks: background 105–106; free college 114; funding 107–111; influential organizations and leaders 111–113; original insight and background 105–106

federal government: Common Core State Standards 6, 38, 59, 113, 142, 144; involvement of 3
Federal Housing Administration (FHA) 122
Federal Student Aid 109
Federal Supplemental Educational Opportunity Grant (FSEOG) 107, 108, 110
Federal Work-Study (FWS) 110
Ferri, Beth 149
Fields, Clarence 35–36
financial aid funding: origins 106–107; process 107–111
Finn, Chester E., Jr. 4, 142
flexibility, in special education system 148
Flickr 74
Ford Foundation 62, 75
Ford Freedom Fund 75
Fordham Institute 5
for-profit companies 1, 6; outsourcing to 6–7
foundations, and DREAM Act 74–80
Free Application for Federal Student Aid (FAFSA) 108, 109
free college 114
free markets 3, 4; and democratization of schools 9–10
Free or Reduced-Price Lunches (FRPL) 21–22
Friedman, Milton 3, 4, 9
Friend, Marilyn 145
Fuller, Matthew B. 106
Fund for Public Schools, The 49–50, 52–53, 64, 65–66; structure of *51*
funding: Fair Student Funding 140–142, 146; financial aid 107–111; for schools 10, 21–22; sources, for Price Prep Policy 97–98; structure, of AVID 32–33, 40; for Turnaround Arts 61, 62

Gaining Early Awareness and Readiness for Undergraduate Programs (GEAR UP) program 40, 76
Gates, Bill 111
Gates, Melinda 111
Gates Foundation *see* Bill & Melinda Gates Foundation
General Equivalency Diploma (GED) 126
George W. Bush Institute, Advancing Accountability program 35
Gianneschi, Matt 34, 39, 40
Gira, Robert 36

GIVE Steven & Alexandra Cohen Foundation 62, 63
Global Education Inc. 2
goals, Individualized Education Plans 47
Goods, Amy 45
Google 111, 114
Gordon, Dave 34–35, 38, 40
graduate-level teacher preparation programs 18, 20, 26
Graduate Record Examination (GRE) 16–17, 18, 22, 25–26
Graham, Lindsey 72
Grassroots Education Movement 113
Guggenheim 77
Guidestar 143–144
Gun-Free School Act (1994) 119, 120
Gutschow, Todd 36

Hagan, Kay 79
Hagel, Charles 72
Halstead, Ted 111
Harber, Jonathan D. 52
hard skills 80
Harries, Garth 139
Hatch, Orrin 79
Hayek, F. A. 4
Health Care and Education Reconciliation Act of 2010 110
Herb Alpert Foundation, The 62, 63
Heritage Foundation 5
higher education 16, 21; business of 83–88; *see also* Advancement Via Individual Determination (AVID); faculty preparation
Higher Education Act (HEA) of 1965 105, 106–107, 110; 1998 Amendments to 105; structure of *112*
Higher Education Opportunity Act (HEOA) 107
Highly Certified Site (AVID) 33
high stakes testing 142, 148, 149
Hirschfield, Paul 118, 124
HNC Software Incorporated 36
Hurlbut-Johnson Charitable Trusts 77
Hurricane Katrina 23
Husk, Sandy 33–34, 36
Hussein, Saddam 24
Hutchison, Kay Bailey 79
Hyatt 77

i3 40
IBM 129
"I have a Dream" Foundation 76

illegal immigrant, definition of 81n7
immigrants *see* Development, Relief, and Education for Alien Minors (DREAM) Act; undocumented immigrant youths
Immigrants Rights Legal Clinic 77
Immigration Act of 1924 79
Immigration Reform and Control Act (1986) 71
Improving Undergraduate STEM Education: Education and Human Resources (IUSE: EHR) 88
incarceration: economization of 122–124; post 129–131; *see also* prison-industrial complex
incentives, in Price Prep Policy 97
inclusion policies, in special education 139, 140, 142, *143*, 147, 150
incrementalists, framing of disability 148
Individualized Education Plans (IEPs) 46–48, 137–138, 147; criteria for 46; template 47; *see also* Special Education Student Information System (SESIS)
Individuals with Disabilities Education Improvement Act (IDEA) 46, 138, 141, 142, 148
information and communication technologies (ICT) 6; classrooms 146
Integrated Co-Teaching (ICT) 140, 141
Iraq and Afghanistan Service Grant 107–108
iTheatrics 62, 63, 64

James, Letitia 137, 145
JC Penney Cares 62
Jessen, Sarah Butler 146
JetBlue 77
Jimenez, Cristina 74
John Olin Foundation 4
Johnson, Lyndon B. 106
Jones, Dwight D. 19
Jose P. v. Ambach 137
J.P. Morgan 77
Juba, Nori 36
Junior State of America 76
Junior Statesmen Foundation 76
Junior Theater Celebration 64
Junior Theater Festival 64

K-12 education 21, 23, 59, 63, 90, 98
Kantrowitz, Mark 110
Kaplan 17
Keith Haring Foundation, The 62
Kellogg Foundation 142, 144

King, John 20
Kirk, David S. 119
Klein, Joel 52, 64, 139
Klein, Naomi 22
Kojima, Christopher 52–53
Korean Americans 77
Kyl, Jon 72

labeling, and Zero Tolerance policies 119–122
labeling theory, of school dropout 119
labor, prison 127, 129
LaGuardia, Fiorello 123
Laird Norton Family Foundation 62
Laksimi-Morrow, Sakina 118
leadership, AVID 36, 39
legal resident immigrant, definition of 81n7
Lessinger, Leon 8
Levin, Sue 36
LF Investments 36
liberals 4
Little Kids Rock 62
loans, student 112–113, 115
Local Law 27 (NYC) 147
Los Angeles Trial Lawyers' Charities (LATLC) 76
Lovett, Melendy 35, 40
Lugar, Richard 72
Lynford, Tondra 53

Ma, Yo-Yo 58
Maher, Frances 20
Major Food Group 77
Make a Musical 64
manufacturing industry, in cities 123
marginalization: and incarceration 125, 129–130; in school 119
Markee, Robert 36, 39–40
mathematics: scores, effect of Turnaround Arts on 60; skill levels of US students in 66–67
Maximus 49–50, 52, 144–145; special education systems, expansion of 53–54
McCain, John 72, 79
McCallum, Corie 105
media 5
Medicaid 52, 137
Medicare 52
Melody Robidoux Foundation 77
Meno, Lionel "Skip" 35
mentees, in Price Prep Policy 90–91, 97
mentors, in Price Prep Policy 89–90, 97
microblogging 74

Microsoft 78, 129
military recruitment, of undocumented immigrants 72
Minkwon Center for Community Action 77–78
Moe, Terry 9–10
monetization of prison inmates 127
money, AVID's role with 39–40
Montoni, Richard 52
Morgan Stanley 77
Moses, Monte 34, 38
Moses, Robert 123
Moynihan, Daniel Patrick 121
Mraz, Jason 63
Mullen, Michelle 36
Musgrove, Melody 141, 144
Music Unites 63
Music Theatre International (MTI) 62, 63, 64, 65

Napolitano, Janet 78
National Assessment Governing Board 35
National Assessment of Educational Progress 25
National Association for College Admissions Counseling 78
National Board Certification 36, 39
National Center of Education Statistics (NCES) 84
National Council of La Raza (NCLR) 74
National Council on Accreditation for Teacher Education (NCATE) 19–20; Blue Ribbon Panel 19
National Council on Teacher Quality (NCTQ) 98
National Endowment for the Arts 58, 61, 62
National Immigration Law Center (NILC) 74
National Science Foundation (NSF) 88
natural disasters, exploitation during 23
Navient 110, 113, 114
NelNet 110, 112
neoliberalism 26, 69, 115; disaster capitalism 22–23; notions of accountability 18–21
New America Foundation, Education Policy Program 111
New Jersey, manufacturing jobs in 123
new politics of education 1–2; accountability movement 7–8; democratic control of US schools 3–6; free markets and democratization of schools 9–10; shadow elite and Swiss-cheese government 6–7; Shelton, James 2
new privatization 70
NewSchools Venture Fund 2
news coverage of education 25
newspaper opinion pieces, written by scholars 5
New York City: foundations of special education reform in 138–141; manufacturing industry in 123; special education system in 137–138; *see also* "A Shared Path to Success" policy; Turnaround Arts in 64
New York City Department of Cultural Affairs 64
New York City Department of Education (NYC DOE) 47, 48–49, 64, 139, 144; SESIS contract to Maximus 49–50, 55, 144–145; Special Education report 147; *see also* Special Education Student Information System (SESIS)
New York State: Board of Regents 48; Division of Housing & Community Renewal 77–78; education issues in 23; GRE requirement of 16, 17, 26
No Child Left Behind Act (NCLB) 10, 25, 69, 114; and accountability 8, 19; and charter schools 6; complaint assessments 38; and hiring of for-profit corporations 7; and privatization 59
NumbersUSA 79
NY Education Reform Commission 20

Obama, Barack 5, 24, 72, 114; DACA program 78, 80; and Duncan, Arne 113; FASA process changes by 108; passage of ESSA 19, 61
Obama, Michelle 58
offender education programs 131
Office for Public Advocacy 146–147
Office of Insular Affairs 76
Office of Special Education Programs 141
Oh, Soojin S. 80
online networks, and DREAM Act 74–80
on-the-job training, for new faculty 84, 90, 101
Open Society Foundations 75
Opt-Out movement 19
Organization for Economic Cooperation and Development (OECD) 66
outsourcing: of arts education jobs 59, 60, 61, 62, 63; government functions to private firms 6; in Price Prep Policy 97

Panel for Education Policy 140
parent information center 10
parents, ability to choose between schools 10
Parker, Sarah Jessica 58
Parsons, Richard D. 20
Pearson 54, 98
pedagogical knowledge, of faculty 84, 85, 86–88; *see also* Price Prep Policy
Peer Assistant & Review (PAR) program *see* Toledo Plan
Pell Grant 107, 110, 113
people of color: de-industrialization and crime control paradigm 122–125; post-incarceration of 129–131; prison-industrial complex 125–129; *see also* youth of color
performance state 6
Permanent Resident Status 72
Petraeus, David 83–84
Philanthropia 143
philanthropies, and DREAM Act 74–80
Pierre Cardin 129
Plepler, Lisa 53
political control, of bureaucracies 9, 10
political participation, of felons 129
poverty guidelines, and financial aid funding 109
power: of Dreamers 74; in higher education 98; of online networks, foundations, and philanthropies 74–80
Powerschool 54
practical knowledge, of faculty 84, 86
Present Level of Performance (PLOP) 47
presidential election of 2016 24, 26
President's Committee on the Arts and the Humanities (PCAH) 58, 61, 62
Price Philanthropies 35, 40
Price Prep Policy 88–90, *91–97*, 101; continuing education credit 91; cost of 97; funding sources for 97–98; mentees 90–91; mentors 89–90
priority deadlines, financial aid funding 108
prison-industrial complex 125–129; federal and state prison population in private facilities **128**; total state and federal prison populations *126*
privatization: new privatization 70; of prisons 127, **128**, 129; in special education 144; Swiss-cheese government 6–7; and Turnaround Arts 59, 61–67
professional development departments 89, 90, 97

P.S. Arts 62, 63
PSC CUNY Welfare Fund 83
public control of schools 1; decline in 7–8
public opinion, mobilizing and controlling 5

race, and disability 149
Race to the Top (RTTT) 34, 38, 58, 59, 102, 114; and accountability 8; and charter schools 6; and CUNY 98
racism, school 9
Ralph Lauren Foundation 77
Ramden, Paul 87, 97
Ramos, Matias 74
Randazzo, Robert 58
rational choice theory, of school dropout 119
Ravitch, Diane 60
reading proficiency: effect of Turnaround Arts on 60; skill levels of US students in 66–67
Reagan, Ronald 69
recidivism, of felons 130
recommendation of dismissal 90
recommendation with continuation 90
recommendation without continuation 90
reconceptualists, framing of disability 148–149
rehabilitation, of felons 130
Reid, Harry 72
Rello-Anselmi, Corinne 139
Restorative Justice (RJ) 131–133
Results Driven Accountability (RDA) 141, 142, 144, 148, 150
Ricci, David 5
Riggio, Len 53
Robert Rauschenberg Foundation 62
Roberts, Paul 23
Robinson, Robert P. 33
Rockefeller Brothers Fund 78
Rodriguez, Laura 139
Rosenthal Family Foundation 62
Ross, Jerrold 53
Rubel, David 140
Ryan, Paul 78

"safety net" option 142–143
Sallie Mae 110, 112–113, 114
Sampson, Robert J. 119
Sanders, Bernie 114
San Diego State University 35
SAT score, and AVID 38
Schmidt, Eric 111

Schmidt, Wendy 111
scholarships 10; AVID 34; PSC CUNY 98
school boards 3, 9
school completion, effect of Zero Tolerance policies on 119–120
school dropout 119
school-to-prison pipeline 122
Schumacher-Matos, Edward 79
science, skill levels of US students in 66–67
Science, Technology, Engineering, and Mathematics (STEM) college students 84–85; federal grant for engaging 88
segregation, school 9, 122, 139, 149
self-motivation, of faculty 88
shadow elite 2, 6–7, 10–11
"A Shared Path to Success" (aSPtS) policy 138; accountability 141–144; foundations of special education reform in New York City 138–141; impact on classrooms and teachers 144–146; journey to inclusion 143; measurement and testing 148; outcomes of 146–147; recommendations 147–150
Shelton, James 2
Shenkman, Rick 24
Shorty, Trombone 58
ShowKit, The 64
Shubert Organization 64
SIG 40
Silberman, Steve 36, 39
Silicon Valley Community Foundation 77
Simon, William 4
Simpsom-Mazzoli Act *see* Immigration Reform and Control Act (1986)
Single Stop USA/Robin Hood Foundation 77
SLM Corporation 112, 113
Smith, Eric J. 35, 39
Smith, James 4
Smith, Lamar 79
social control theory, of school dropout 119
social isolation, of urban poor 122, 123
social media, and DREAM Act 74
soft skills 60
Sony & BMG Music Entertainment 77
special education: field, implications for 54–55; services 46, 48–49; *see also* "A Shared Path to Success" policy
Special Education Student Information System (SESIS) 48–49, 54–55, 144–145, 147; contract to Maximus 49–50; roll out, problems with 50; *see also* Individualized Education Plans (IEPs)
Specter, Arlen 79
Spring, Joel 1, 60, 115
standardization, in AVID 38–39
Starwood Hotels and Resorts 36, 39
state governments, involvement of 3
state scholarships 10
State University of New York 35
stereotypes of youth, and Zero Tolerance policies 120, 121
stigma: and incarceration 129; and labeling 119
Strongin, Steve 53
student achievement: and bureaucracies 9; and competition between schools 9–10
Student Information System (SIS) 54
subsidies, federal 122
suburbanization 122–123
SUNY Board of Regents 20
supplemental educational services 7
Swanson, Mary Catherine 32, 33, 34, 36
Swiss-cheese government 6–7

TASH 144
tax information, and financial aid funding 108
Teacher Accreditation Council (TEAC) 20
Teacher Education Assistance for College and Higher Education (TEACH) Grant 107–108, 110
teacher education programs 17–18
Teachers College, Columbia University 84
teacher training programs 19–20
Teaching Strategy courses 84
technology companies, schools as targets for 5–6
"test-and-punish" models 19
testing: accommodations, IEP 47; in AVID 38–39; standards, aSPtS 148
test scores, and accountability 8
Tetreault, Mary Kay Thompson 20
Texas Instruments 35, 40
Theatrical Education 64
theoretical knowledge, of faculty 84
Thomas B. Fordham Institute 142
Thompson, William C. 98–99
TIENET (software) 49, 53–54
TIENET 504 53
TIENET Instructional Management System 54

TIENET Response to Intervention (RtI) Management System 53–54
TIENET service capture 53
Title I funding 33, 44n49
Title IV funding 105, 107, 113
Toledo Plan 90, 98
Tommy Hilfiger 63
training: for mentors 89; on-the-job training, for new faculty 84, 90, 101; teacher training programs 19–20
trickle-down theory of ideas 4
Trinity Industries 35
Trio 40
Trump, Donald 80, 114
Turnaround Arts 58; corporate, philanthropic, and individual supporters 66; leading private organization supports 62; network 61–67, 65; talent show 59
Twitter 74
2U 2

Uber 77
Unbound Philanthropy Fund 75
undocumented immigrant youths 70–71; *see also* Development, Relief, and Education for Alien Minors (DREAM) Act
unemployment, and suburbanization 122, 123
United Federation of Teachers (UFT) 50, 67, 144, 145
United Kingdom (UK), Restorative Justice practice in 131
United We Dream (UWD) 74, 75
United We Dream Network (UWDN) 75
University of Bologna 106
urban ghetto, and school violence 121
urban schools *see* city schools
U.S. Conference of Catholic Bishops 78
U.S. Department of Defense (DOD) 72
U.S. Department of Education (DOE) 2, 5, 141; and federal financial aid 107, 108, 110, 113; and IEPs 48; Office of Federal Student Aid management 52; and Turnaround Arts 58, 61, 62
U.S. Department of the Interior 76

Vargas, Edward Lee 36
vendors, for special education services 144
venture philanthropy 4
veteran faculty 84, 85; as mentors 89–90
Veterans Affairs (VA) 122
Victim-Offender Dialogue (VOD) 131
Vimeo 74
vision, of AVID 38
Vista Equity Partners 54

Walcott, Dennis 139
Waller, Melanie 137
Walt Disney Company, The 63
War on Drugs 132
Washington, Kerry 58, 67
Washington University (St. Louis, Missouri) 84
Weber, Stephen 35, 40
Wedel, Janine R. 2, 6–7
well-rounded education 61
Wernikoff, Linda 49–50
Whitaker, Forest 63
white collar industry, in cities 123
white flight 122–123, 124
Whole-School Approach, Restorative Justice practices in 132
WibiData 111
Williams, Dennis 53
Wylde, Kathy 53

Xerox 35

YKASEC (Young Korean American Service and Education Center) 77
youth of color: incarceration of 126; subordination of 124; and Zero Tolerance policies 118, 119–122; *see also* people of color
YouTube 74

Zero Tolerance policies 118, 119–122, 131, 132
Zimpher, Nancy 19, 20, 21
zombie lies 24
Zong, Jie 70
Zuckerberg, Mark 2, 111

Taylor & Francis eBooks

Helping you to choose the right eBooks for your Library

Add Routledge titles to your library's digital collection today. Taylor and Francis ebooks contains over 50,000 titles in the Humanities, Social Sciences, Behavioural Sciences, Built Environment and Law.

Choose from a range of subject packages or create your own!

Benefits for you
- Free MARC records
- COUNTER-compliant usage statistics
- Flexible purchase and pricing options
- All titles DRM-free.

Benefits for your user
- Off-site, anytime access via Athens or referring URL
- Print or copy pages or chapters
- Full content search
- Bookmark, highlight and annotate text
- Access to thousands of pages of quality research at the click of a button.

REQUEST YOUR FREE INSTITUTIONAL TRIAL TODAY

Free Trials Available
We offer free trials to qualifying academic, corporate and government customers.

eCollections – Choose from over 30 subject eCollections, including:

Archaeology	Language Learning
Architecture	Law
Asian Studies	Literature
Business & Management	Media & Communication
Classical Studies	Middle East Studies
Construction	Music
Creative & Media Arts	Philosophy
Criminology & Criminal Justice	Planning
Economics	Politics
Education	Psychology & Mental Health
Energy	Religion
Engineering	Security
English Language & Linguistics	Social Work
Environment & Sustainability	Sociology
Geography	Sport
Health Studies	Theatre & Performance
History	Tourism, Hospitality & Events

For more information, pricing enquiries or to order a free trial, please contact your local sales team:
www.tandfebooks.com/page/sales

 Routledge
Taylor & Francis Group

The home of
Routledge books

www.tandfebooks.com